The Best Canadian Essays 2011

THE
BEST
CANADIAN
ESSAYS
2011

edited by IBI KASLIK
and CHRISTOPHER DODA

TIGHTROPE BOOKS www.tightropebooks.com

Tightrope Books
17 Greyton Crescent
Toronto, Ontario
Canada M6E 2G1
www.tightropebooks.com

Editor: Ibi Kaslik
Series Editor: Christopher Doda
Managing Editor: Heather Wood
Proofreaders: Emma Sowiak, Erin Sparkes-Brewer , Christine Tan
Cover Design: David Bigham
Typesetting: Christine Tan

Produced with the support of the Canada Council for the Arts and the Ontario Arts Council.

 Canada Council
for the Arts   Conseil des Arts
du Canada  ONTARIO ARTS COUNCIL
CONSEIL DES ARTS DE L'ONTARIO

Printed in Canada

Library and Archives Canada Cataloguing in Publication

The best Canadian essays 2011.

ISBN 978-1-926639-42-0

1. Canadian essays (English)--21st century.

PS8373.1.B48 2011   C814'.608   C2011-300995-X

contents

prologue

The essay gives testimony about this world through a personal story, inscribed just as the blows of a whip make marks on the skin.

—Jan Kott

I am an inveterate reader of essays. I love the essay format. Always have and always will. Anyone who has ever seen the office space in my home can attest to the presence of dozens of collections of essays on my bookshelves. From Virginia Woolf to Jorge Luis Borges to Sven Birkerts to Martin Amis to James Baldwin to Dubravka Ugresic to Octavio Paz to Friedrich Holderlin to Czeslaw Milosz to Nadine Gordimer to Salman Rushdie to Isaiah Berlin to Sigmund Freud to H.P. Lovecraft to Northrop Frye to George Steiner to J.M. Coetzee to T.S. Eliot to Orhan Pamuk to J.P. Stern and so on, I have taken enormous pleasure in the essay form. I've found that an essay is often the perfect length to pass the time on a daily commute, over breakfast, in a waiting room or, on a couple of occasions, during the intermission of a hockey game. Or as Daphne Merkin says, "the essay would seem to be precisely the form that our time, in all its channel-zapping, Net-surfing restlessness, should welcome."

Great essays, regardless of topic, evidence a clarity of thought, a sharpness of expression and hopefully a lasting impact on a reader, whether joy, enlightenment or anger. Or perhaps all three and more. Ever since I read Jacques Barzun's essays on literature and on writing twenty years ago, I've been convinced of the concentrated power of the essay format. As he puts it in "Rhetoric; What It Is; Why Needed": "The purpose [of writing] at large is always the same: it must be understood aright. Reader and writer have both wasted their time if mental darkness is the only result of their separate efforts." In other words, good writing should be clear and precise in order to communicate something to its readers. Nowhere is this truer than in the case of the essay. A great poem can convey meaning in an elusive manner (few people would describe *The Waste Land* as 'clear and precise') but an essay should not. An essay can be circumspect, can meander or elide but should never obfuscate or confuse.

So when I received the invitation from Tightrope Books to take over *Best Canadian Essays* as Series Editor, I could not have been more thrilled. I had read the first two volumes with great interest and thought it was a wonderful idea to produce an annual anthology of best Canadian essays. In fact, it was an idea that was long overdue.

This year we enlisted novelist and freelance journalist Ibi Kaslik as Guest Editor to pore over the numerous magazines and journals featuring non-fiction prose, and she has done a masterful job of arriving at the eighteen pieces presented here. A complete year's run of at least 25 journals were considered so I can't thank Ibi enough for her time and discriminating eye in this process. I sincerely hope that more magazines and journals will submit to increase the scope of future volumes. Her introduction covers both her belief that good writing should have a subversive element to it as well as the precarious financial straits of freelance writers in Canada. W.H. Auden once said that he wrote his poems out of love and his essays and literary criticism for money. Many of our writers are in the same boat and if they can't make a living here, it's likely they'll go elsewhere. Which is why applauding our talented essayists is crucial to the survival of the form at its best.

I hope you enjoy reading this volume as much as I've enjoyed having a hand in its construction: we've got everything from a pro-smoking diatribe to an appreciation of the great opera singer Maria Callas to pieces on Canada's ongoing war in Afghanistan and more. (If I had one disappointment, it was the lack of quality, George Plimpton-level sports writing in 2010, a year in which Canada hosted the Olympic Games.) If I've noticed one thing over the last year, it's that the variety of writing available in this country—from arts and culture to politics to economics to activism to personal journalism—is pretty staggering. Considering this, I would personally like to thank Alex Boyd for his work as Series Editor on the previous two volumes as well as Carmine Starnino and Kamal Al-Solaylee for their contributions as Guest Editors. Your time and labours are greatly appreciated. And, of course, I must thank Halli Villegas, Heather Wood, Shirarose Wilensky and everyone else at Tightrope for making this and future volumes possible.

When I sat down to write this prologue, I combed over the many collections of essays in my office looking for a suitable epigraph, including books from all those listed above, hoping to find something irreverent and concise like 'reading a good essay is like getting punched in the gut.' Sadly the abovementioned are too high-minded for such. I was discouraged until I recalled the quote affixed to the beginning of this piece. While it may seem hyperbolic and leave little room for humour (granted Kott was writing about a time and place far removed from our own, 20th Century Eastern Europe), the basic idea that an essay should leave an impression remains intact. I'm certain you'll take something away from this collection with you and sorry about the sore gut.

Christopher Doda

introduction

One afternoon, Ms. C, my tenth-grade Biology teacher, whipped chalk at my head and screeched, "Constipation of the mind, Kaslik!" What spurred this outburst was a casual remark I made during her lesson on 'How to Write an Essay.' As she drew brainstorming balloons all over the board and an endless series of arrows and lines leading to nowhere, I sighed, "Can't we just write the damn thing?"

In Ms. C's defense, I was a precocious teen often turfed out of class for eye-rolling and smart-ass comments. In my own defense, I was the only student listening in the first period after lunch, and Ms. C was not the paragon of pedagogical excellence. She behaved more like a cranky old prison guard, than a teacher with a penchant for bodily assaults, stapling late slips to students' shirts with an industrial stapler she always kept in her tool belt expressly for this purpose.

I am now grateful to Ms. C's terrible teaching skills, her non-lesson on essay writing and her warden mentality. That afternoon, I learned what Caroline Adderson realized when she was reprimanded as a child by a librarian for daring to write in a children's magazine: "for writing to be any good, it should be at least a little subversive."

Adderson's essay, "Highlights for Children"—one of the eighteen stand-outs featured in this 2010 collection—expresses what good essays do when they dare to speak on touchy subjects. Good essays, like all good writing, should contain "little moral bombs," as Adderson writes, beg "unanswerable questions," and take some risks. George Orwell wrote to "expose lies" and "to draw attention to some fact, to get a hearing." In some way, the same could be said of all of the essays in this collection.

Getting a hearing on a subject or sounding out to get a reaction can often have the same effect as telling your lover you use his toothbrush to clean the toilet or that you like to push old ladies down in the snow just for kicks. To write well is personally dangerous: people get upset when the ugly side of human nature is revealed, and whether it is yours or theirs doesn't matter. If someone calls you up and yells at you or posts an angry missive on their blog because of something you have written, chances are you have done a good job: you have challenged something held dear; you have threatened carefully constructed delusions and prejudices.

Many of the essayists here offer up something dark and damaged within themselves. In the essay, "Love is a Let-down," a painful detailing of the author's intense post-partum depression, Kerry Clare writes about new motherhood in such a way that feels exceptionally dangerous in this era of baby-deification and hyper-mothering. Clare's admission that the only reason she didn't immediately give up her baby for adoption was that the child's grandmothers would never forgive her is disturbing, disarming and, well, true.

Consider what is at risk for the ego and reputation, as well. Writer–editor Daniel Baird, a self-confessed alcoholic known for draining bottles of cognac by dumpsters and blacking out at literary and social events, uses his own addiction narrative merely to predicate his powerful and unflinching essay about the social, financial, and practical crisis the Canadian military is currently contending with as it deals with an unprecedented number of soldiers returning from overseas suffering from Post Traumatic Stress Disorder.

While flying high on the plant-based ayahuasca hallucinogenic, on the verge of what feels like his own imminent death,

Jeff Warren dares to become both Hunter S. Thompson gon-
zo and hippie-journo cliché in "Tourists of Consciousness."
Tripping heavily, Warren immediately recognizes the many
levels of his "situation's dark comedy" when he finds himself
tree-hugging in the South American jungle. Still the consum-
mate professional, even as he vomits, watches senior citizens
turn into snakes and caresses trees, Warren tries to access
the normal functions of his mind. He confesses that trying to
construct an essayistic narrative for his experience is "like
trying to assemble a nylon tent in a hurricane."

Besides getting drunk and high on occasion, good writing
requires going against common sense and sometimes being
downright offensive. For instance, good writing can mean
addressing a hate-letter to self-righteous non-smokers, as
Mark Mann does in his ode to cigarettes: "What nonsmokers
don't understand is that smoking is awesome." Smoking is
awesome but smoking, like writing, will not earn you many
friends (unless they are fellow smokers). Smokers share
something else with writers and that is being a loser: "Being
a loser is important because losers are more honest," closes
Mann in his short piece about his love affair with nicotine,
which could double as a mantra for writers.

The risks a writer takes are not only health hazardous but
also intellectually so. Take poet Chris Jennings' essay, "On
the Sonnet," which tackles the confounding poetic bugaboo
of the sacred form. Anyone who has ever struggled with composure of the fourteen-line enterprise—or tried to teach it to
a rowdy group of grade nines—has to agree with Jennings'
vitriolic assessment to "fuck the sonnet."

Poetry pops up again in Stephen Marche's essay, "The Patroclization of Pat Tillman," as the essayist makes the su-
perficially absurd yet rhetorically sound argument that "the
wars in Afghanistan and Iraq are much closer to *The Iliad*

than the great wars that followed." Paralleling the desperate and false attempt by American government and media to turn the handsome pro football star into a martyred warrior with the ancient Greek epic, *The Iliad*, Marche forces the reader to make intriguing leaps while facing hard truths. It is easy to make Tillman a hero, to fall into the "consonance of expectation" of the hero-warrior narrative rather than admit that golden-boy Tillman was (gasp) an atheist killed by friendly fire as opposed to felled in 'noble' combat in a war that has lost whatever little meaning it once had. As Marche points out, the battle between his family and the military over Tillman's memory shows that it is more difficult to comprehend that all wars, as in Homer's great poem, are stories about "a couple of corpses."

What these and other pieces in this collection reflect is the range of essay-writing in Canada over the last year. From those mentioned above to the plight of elephants in the Toronto Zoo to a journey into Paris' extensive system of catacombs to some amusing etiquette guides for the antiquarian bookshop to a woman inheriting her father's extensive collection of weaponry, the style and substance of Canadian journalism is in good hands. Certainly, it will continue to be so in the future.

STILL, GOOD WRITING OFTEN COSTS WRITERS in too many ways these days. To know that a good article, poem, story, or essay may cost us an argument or a relationship is an occupational hazard understood implicitly by writers. Ann Lamott said that one has to write as if one's parents are dead, and most writers I know write like their entire social network has been vaporized.

Every good writer, every real writer, has sacrificed something important, been sued, or nearly sued, ostracized, publicly mocked and humiliated, threatened—all because they were gripped by the urgency to tell a story and to tell it now: to uncover a truth. This is not a terrible aspect of writing, it is simply the reality; a writer's morality is suspended between the public and personal, and what makes a good story does not always make for good feelings. One must choose: if you consistently choose the story, the truth, you are a writer.

WHAT IS TERRIBLE is writers must generally contend with poverty with an added humiliating twist. In the digital age, writers have become "content providers," rather than paid professionals, who, like everyone else, have to pay bills and buy groceries. In no other profession I know, besides being a musician, must a professional beg to be paid. Case in point: in March 2011, Canadian novelist and freelancer Nino Ricci scandalized non-writers by posting a cheeky open letter to the *Globe & Mail* on his blog riffing on the fact that he hadn't been paid by the nation's newspaper for six months after submitting an invoice for an article. Ricci's colleagues shrugged their shoulders. His letter came as no surprise to legions of freelancers who spend most of their time begging, haggling, cajoling, maxing out credit cards, and pleading with everyone from payroll to editorial boards for payment. Ricci not only opened himself up to public scorn and ridicule, his letter uncovered the dirtiest little secret in the oh-so unglamorous world of Canadian journalism: freelancers do not get paid in a timely manner and, more often than not, in no manner at all. Considering the amount of time wasted chasing the often meagre payment for an article, freelance writing is often cost prohibitive. It is truly performed as a labour of love, driven by a need to tell a certain story. Canada is losing its best writers, journalist and essayists because of this *laissez-faire* attitude toward paying freelancers and low-ball rates.

Dear reader, as I share with you my memories of mad biology teachers and the current experiences of unpaid Cassandras while reading this year's carefully selected 2011 best Canadian essays, I would be remiss in my responsibility as guest editor of this collection if I did not point out the personal commitment and financial hardships of the intellectuals in our country. I say all this not to in any way lessen the tragic and beautiful moments while reading these essays, but so that you will understand the context and commitment of the writers who offer up their touching and profound work in this year's anthology.

Ibi Kaslik

The Best Canadian Essays 2011

HIGHLIGHTS FOR CHILDREN

Caroline Adderson
The New Quarterly

When I was six or seven my mother used to drive all the way to Edmonton so she could get in the decent sort of shopping that was not available in our town. Along with reading, shopping was one of two consistent pleasures for her and, even at the end of her life, stricken with lung disease and barely able to walk a block, she would perk right up if we were walking where there was decent shopping. Back in 1970, we went to the Bonnie Doon Mall, home to a fine store called Johnson Walker, located, conveniently, right next to a branch of the Edmonton Public Library. There she would leave me so that she could indulge herself without distraction. How guiltless those seventies mothers were! I would have left my six year-old unattended at the library as easily as I would have handed him over to slave-traders, but times were different then and I didn't mind. Far from it. I wanted to go. I wanted to look at *Highlights for Children*.

Highlights for Children was first published in 1946 and is going strong today as simply *Highlights*. The cover still promises "fun with a purpose," and many of the contents remain the same, though modernized. Back in 1970 the magazine looked quite different.

Highlights
THE MONTHLY BOOK for Children
INCLUDING Children's Activities
fun with a purpose
Hello!

It was displayed, along with other periodicals which have not survived in my memory, child-level, on low, angled shelves. The covers varied from month to month only in their two feature colours (in 1970 such combinations as turquoise and mint, lime and shamrock, butterscotch and crimson) and the small graphic in the corner. The best part of *Highlights for Children* was "Hidden Pictures" wherein small pictures were cleverly disguised in the lines of a larger one. "In this big picture find the bird, tepee, heads of two fiddlers, fish, pocket comb, two cups, letter S, bell, toothbrush..."

I took such exquisite pleasure in finding the pocket comb and the fish and the letter S, and I so clearly remember that pleasure, that it must have some larger meaning, a meaning quite obvious as soon as you see it, like the hidden picture itself. A story or a novel is a picture of something too. It satisfies as a rendering of whatever it represents, but if you look closer, you might find more in it. There are unexpected delights embedded there, surprising juxtapositions that give the picture a different, deeper meaning. You might find all the hidden pictures, or just a few, but each one gives that thrill of recognition, of a larger truth revealed. As a child I developed a strange sense of this activity being somehow daring, even risky. A frisson of near-shame still runs through me when I think of it, and this is why: something happened to me once while my mother left me at the Edmonton Public Library looking at *Highlights for Children*.

Though this theory is entirely anecdotal, I have noticed that childhood trauma is linked to a future in the arts. The least conducive upbringing you can have if you hope to be an artist is a happy one. Trauma is relative, of course. The more important factor is *sensitivity*, so lack of frequent beatings need not impede your gifts. Your reaction to the shame of a once-in-a-lifetime slap might do the trick, for example. Or some seemingly innocuous interaction at the library.

My mother dropped me off and, before she left, I asked, "Do you have a pencil?" She didn't ask what I wanted it for, just dug around in her purse and gave me one; in her mind she was already childless and shopping at Johnson Walker next door. I took the pencil, trotted eagerly over to the shelves and retrieved what I wanted, postponing the pleasure of "Hidden Pictures" with other favourite features like "Goofus and Gallant." In Goofus and Gallant, two young boys behave very differently in similar, pleasingly illustrated situations. "Goofus asks for things to eat at his playmate's house," contrasts with, "Gallant eats at his playmate's home only what is offered." I also enjoyed "The Bear Family" made up of Mother, Father, Woozy, Poozy and Piddy, Piddy being the littlest bear who always gets the witty last word. There was also "The Timbertoes," a comic strip featuring a family of stringless, wooden marionettes. In the "For Wee Folks" section, there were probing questions to ponder each month.

> What Makes You a More Interesting Person?
> e.g., Being able to play games well or being able to eat many pancakes?

Most of *Highlights for Children* I would have skipped over, like the stories. "Some People Like Pigs," "Jeremy Jamison's Birthday"—too many words! Also the science articles, like the one that showed how a water filtration plant works. Too difficult! Ditto "Science Letters" answered by Dr. Jack Myers Ph.D. (Dr. Myers, by the way, is still going strong at *Highlights*.)

> Question: In a past article (October 1969) you left me wondering about the chemical reactions that occur when electricity passes through a salt solution. What happens?

I would not have read the biography of that month's composer, nor the musical score that accompanied it. I was not interested in famous explorers or outstanding African Americans. Sadly, I probably skipped, "Try This! How to Make Quicksand" and the Haiku submitted by 6th grade readers.

> My dog is a mutt,
> But she is so beautiful!
> And she eats a lot.
> > Bruce Saar, Colonial Drive Elementary School, Miami, Florida

I would certainly have pored over the crafts: Paper Napkin Snowman, Spaghetti Pictures, Tissue Fun.

> From scraps of colored tissue paper cut designs that interest you. Paste them on waxed paper and tape the picture on your window. When the light shines through, it gives pleasing effect. Flowers are always pretty.

Highlights for Children was an astonishingly broad magazine. There was literally something for every child no matter his or her age or interest. Its worthy mandate declared:

> This book of wholesome fun
> is dedicated
> to helping children grow
> > in basic skills and knowledge
> > in creativeness
> > in ability to think and reason
> > in sensitivity to others
> > in high ideals
> > and worthy ways of living—
> for CHILDREN are the
> > world's most important people

MORAL DEVELOPMENT WAS STRESSED, but sometimes the lesson did not fully take. For example, I preferred lippy Piddy Bear. While I wanted to be like Gallant, Goofus with his steady scowl was funnier, so I liked him better. I did not so much as glance at the phonics lessons. I thought being able to eat a lot of pancakes would make a person fascinating. And this: when I finally turned to my favourite page, "Hidden Pictures," when I leaned over the page and felt the pulpy texture of the paper, I had something verboten in my hand. (Today I picture my ready tongue in the corner of my mouth and that, before I used the pencil, I licked its point... but this is embellishment.) I read the list of pictures I had to find then began digging, digging with my eyes. Sometimes something popped right out, other times it was elusive, in which case it was usually sideways or upside down. I concentrated fully, deaf to all distractions (like my mother next door riffling through the sale rack), and when I found the toothbrush or the letter S, I pounced. I pounced and, in triumph, I circled.

And then a hand came out of nowhere and seized me by the wrist. "We do not write in books! We do not! We do not!"

I cowered. Above me an eye-glassed, rage-contorted face. A clearly childless children's librarian who had never been a child herself, twisting the pencil out of my hand and taking it with her as she marched back to the desk so I could never, ever deface a book again. And then the long shameful wait for my mother. For every second that I sat, miserable, aching for her to come, the librarian likewise sat, one terrible all-seeing eye fixed on me lest I transgress again. I couldn't go to my mother—I probably had instructions not to—so for an eternity I sat, a child, one of the world's most important people, utterly still at the little round table, sucking in my sob. My shame attached itself to *Highlights for Children* and, in particular, "Hidden Pictures," and, blending with the pleasure I had taken in the task, became defiance. So that now, forty years later, I believe that for writing to be any good it should be at least a little bit subversive. Little moral bombs must be hidden in it, unanswerable questions asked. I'm never going to write about Gallant. Gallants don't interest me except when their own inner Goofuses get the better of them. If you're not pushing against the boundaries, if you're not making at least one librarian mad, what's the point?

THE ENEMY INSIDE

Daniel Baird
The Walrus

It was early morning at a rehabilitation centre for drug and alcohol addiction, and everyone was already standing outside their dorm rooms, decked out in sweatpants and T-shirts, their eyes bleary and their hair dishevelled. A short, stout, officious morning nurse with a clipboard marched down the hall, ticking off attendance. Then a recording of an old woman's voice crackled over the intercom and led us through our morning calisthenics. "Reach up to the sky," she called. "It's going to be a wonderful day!"

I was only a few days into a twenty-one-day residential treatment program for alcohol dependence, but I already knew a few of the characters standing in that lineup. There was a crack addict and compulsive shoplifter who ran a car wash in small-town Quebec; there was a raucous Montreal landlord who had gambled away half his buildings in a cocaine-fuelled fever. There were cracked-out lawyers and investment bankers, boozy police officers and firemen, and a surgeon obsessed with sex and OxyContin. And there I was, trying to touch my toes and reaching for the sky on this new, wonderful day, a writer and editor who had been chugging down whole bottles of Courvoisier beside Chinatown dumpsters, collapsing at public events, and waking up on park benches and in hospital emergency rooms.

I had heard rumours that there were rooms near the nursing station with signs hanging on their doors that read Do Not Knock, and that these were reserved for soldiers with post-traumatic stress disorder. Then, on a smoke break later that day, I met a man I'll call Dave. Thirty-something and wearing pressed khaki shorts and a tight purple sports shirt, Dave stood well over six feet tall and was built like an athlete, his shoulders broad, his stomach and chest rippled with muscle. He rocked side to side, clasping and unclasping his hands, the veins in his thighs, neck, and forehead swollen and throbbing. He spoke in a loud, incessant banter, riffing jokes and puns off the few words anyone else could get in edgewise, then laughing explosively. His electric blue eyes gazed out past us, toward some abstract point in the parking lot.

Eventually, his monologue began to darken, and I could see his regally poised body begin to implode. He launched into a frenzied diatribe, describing how he had seen friends get their faces blown off while he was sitting in a Jeep talking to them, and how when he got back from his last deployment he started going to bars, drinking, snorting cocaine, and seducing women while his wife stayed home with their infant daughter. "I would call my wife from the bar, screaming and crying," I remember him saying, "but I couldn't stop—not even my baby girl would make me stop."

The response was a dead, embarrassed silence, everyone hurrying to finish their cigarettes and head back inside. Lurid tales are the stock-in-trade of rehab smoke breaks; part of the bonding of treatment is the ability to reveal virtually anything without being judged. But Dave was different. He was a soldier, and with his pumped muscles and wild, sleepless, empty eyes and his almost squealing, propulsive, completely emotionless speech, with his trance-like inaccessibility, he was positively frightening.

Up to that point, my experience with troubled veterans was mostly limited to growing up in Los Angeles in the late '70s, a time when soldiers who had fought in the Vietnam War seemed to be everywhere and nowhere. They were the slightly sinister older brothers one never saw, holed up in converted garages in their parents' houses smoking pot and listening to Black Sabbath; the clutches of men in camouflage jackets hanging out in garbage-strewn city parks, their coolers stocked with Schlitz talls; the sources of empty bottles of Jack Daniel's, cigarette butts, and soggy piles of porn and gun mags in the bamboo grove beside a sludgy creek. They were treated with resentment and shame, and ultimately with the same embarrassed, uncomprehending silence that greeted Dave.

I gradually learned that Dave had been an infantry officer in the Canadian Forces, deployed in Somalia, Rwanda, Bosnia, Haiti, and Afghanistan. He rarely spoke of his experiences on his tours of duty, mostly maintaining his aggressive, alienating, and not very funny comic persona. But at least by his own account, he had conducted himself with a high level of professionalism and honour while at the centre of some of the most volatile places of the past twenty-five years. It was only when he returned from his tour in Afghanistan, in time to usher his first child into the world, that he found himself unable to cope. His was a textbook case of PTSD—"co-morbid," in psychiatric terminology, with addiction. I later heard of his struggles with treatment: stories about him freaking out in the middle of workshops, violently cursing the therapists, hurling chairs across the room and storming out.

One weekend afternoon, though, I noticed him sitting at a picnic table, engaged in what seemed to be a normal conversation with two other patients I knew had been in the military. It struck me that above all else Dave was incredibly isolated. He was among people who had no sense of the military culture that had shaped him, and no means for understanding the traumatic events he had been through. Even the counsellors and therapists were not in his league. They were benign, soft spoken, nurturing presences promoting sleep, nutrition, exercise, relaxation, and the spiritual wonders of the twelve steps to recovery.

Still, Dave was relatively lucky: at least he had found his way into treatment. When regular Canadian ground troops first arrived in Afghanistan in 2002, our military was ill prepared to deal with the mental health consequences of such a large deployment. Many traumatized soldiers who attempted to engage with the system found themselves on their own, stranded by a culture that regarded them as weak, or worse. With the mission in Afghanistan now standing as the biggest and deadliest deployment of Canadian forces since the Korean War, the need for change was enormous. And while the military has made dramatic inroads into the problem over the past eight years, PTSD is not an ordinary war wound. Its science and treatment are relatively young and experimental, and its long-term prognosis and consequences are still poorly understood.

IN 2002, ANDRÉ MARIN, ombudsman for the Department of National Defence and the Canadian Forces, issued a landmark report to the Minister of National Defence entitled Systematic Treatment of CF Members with PTSD. Based on hundreds of interviews with current and former members of the Canadian Forces, the report was a thoroughgoing study and critique of how the CF had handled PTSD in the past. Traumatized soldiers were often stigmatized, Marin discovered. Investigators "found overwhelming evidence that many within the CF are sceptical about whether PTSD is a legitimate illness. There was a distressingly common belief among both peers and leaders that those diagnosed with PTSD were 'fakers,' 'malingers' [sic] or simply 'poor soldiers'... We found that members with PTSD are often stigmatized, ostracized and shunned by their peers and chain of command."

The report described with uncanny accuracy the experience of a former Canadian soldier I met. John and I first spoke in earnest outside the entrance to a college on the edge of Toronto on a damp, bitter early-winter day, alongside groups of Indian students in baggy pants hanging out and rehearsing graphic rap songs. In his early forties, John had recently returned to school to get a certificate in paralegal studies, but things were not going all that well. His posture and expression were familiar: tense, self-conscious, gaze fixed elsewhere, in this case on the cigarette butts littering the cement. He wore a cheap parka and a heavy student backpack, a toque perched on his balding head. "You know," he said after a long silence, chuckling to himself, "it can be really, really hard to relate to people, to look them in the eye, when at any moment you might see someone totally evil staring back."

John grew up in a small town of 500 or so, north of Toronto, the adopted son of a United Church minister and a teacher. He had an ordinary, untroubled childhood, but when he graduated from high school he had no idea what to do with himself. So he made an appointment with the local Canadian Forces recruitment officer and signed up to be a sailor. When it became clear that he lacked the mathematical skills to be a naval weapons technician, he moved over to the army. By the time he was deployed to the unravelling former Yugoslavia, he was a fourth-year corporal in logistics with a specialty in mobile support equipment operation, which in his case meant driving trucks.

His first tour of duty went relatively smoothly, but certain incidents stand out in his mind. "We went into Bosnia and back, and usually on our drives we were getting shot at—we called it harassment fire," he told me. "Usually, there would be lots of chitter-chatter on the radio, but one day the convoy commander enforced radio silence. When we pulled into town, we could feel tank tracks on the pavement under our tires. The town was still on fire, people running around, and there was a one-armed guy carrying an infant who ran into my truck. He went down, blood spurting, but we kept going. It wasn't our mandate; our mission was to supply and nothing else. We were keeping the infantry alive."

During his second tour of the Balkans, things became even more intense. "I was going down the road, and our convoy got separated," he told me. "The first sign that things were bad is we heard sounds—crack, crack—and suddenly my windshield was full of bullet holes. I had my weapon, but the rules of engagement say no return fire. I put my head down, grabbed the wheel, and pushed down on the accelerator. I finally found out it was coming from an orange truck. There was a guy firing a machine gun—drunk, I later discovered." He continued: "The next day, we went with an interpreter to a burned-out area twice the size of a football field. It used to be a prisoner of war camp, where they lit the perimeter on fire to reduce the population of prisoners; there was a guard tower from which they would mow down people fleeing. When I went back years later, you could see the lumps below the green grass where bodies were buried."

Early on, John learned how other soldiers coped with what they were witnessing. "Some people want to call family; others overcompensate with jokes," he said. "But no one said shit about what went on. That's when I first saw people opening their boxes and sharing a stiff drink... One feeling a lot of people got was that it was a place where you could feel the hate. It made us feel dirty." By the end of his second tour, he knew something was seriously wrong. "I felt that something in me was gone. I didn't have a full-fledged personality anymore," he said. "Back in Canada, a seven-year relationship ended. I was numb, angry, and aggressive. I had this huge ego that said, 'I'm a soldier, you're a civilian,' but at the same time I was crying at nothing." He went on a third tour, as much to try to sort himself out as anything else. This time, it was a disaster. "On the third tour, I lost it, officially. I did six months—Bosnia, winter, mountains. I was tired of being shot at, tired of walking around with guns. I felt as though we hadn't done anything, and I was humiliated, angry, and sad."

Still a member of the Canadian Forces, he returned to Canada for good at the end of the 1990s, first to Edmonton, then Winnipeg, then Trenton. His mental condition swiftly deteriorated.

He would hole up in his apartment for days without seeing or speaking to anyone, going out only at night. Nightmares and flashbacks played out in his head. It was as though "in one eye, I was in a movie theatre; the other eye was projecting the movie, and all the atrocities, I couldn't stop them from playing." There were aborted suicide attempts, too—three of them. Though previously he had never been much of a drinker, he started boozing heavily, eventually putting away a bottle of rum a day.

In those days, he pointed out, there was little in the way of debriefing upon coming back from a mission, other than speaking with a padre. Though he wasn't specifically advised to see anyone, he sought and received sporadic counselling. In Edmonton, a psychologist at a University of Alberta Hospital group therapy program identified John's depression and alcoholism, and he was referred to the Edgewood alcohol and drug rehabilitation centre in Nanaimo, British Columbia. There, in 2003, he was finally cited as being at risk for PTSD. The following year, he was released from the Canadian Forces, after eighteen years of service. According to John, "They said I was not suitable—that due to my issues I was not deployable."

For a while, he floated along in a stupor, on multiple medications for depression and anxiety, relentlessly calling Veterans Affairs Canada. He applied to be classified as a PTSD sufferer, which would allow him to collect a disability pension, but he was rejected. He appealed and was reassessed, and then his appeal was rejected, too. In 2008, he arrived at the Carewest Operational Stress Injury clinic in Calgary, where he was given a preliminary diagnosis of chronic PTSD. Another year later, he appealed successfully to Veterans Affairs. To qualify for his pension, he had endured five assessments in eight years, despite having what seemed like a clear and obvious case. By then, the source of the original trauma was

at least ten years old. Why had it taken so long? John speculated to me that military physicians were reluctant to issue
a PTSD diagnosis because it would cost the military money.
But the answers reach deeper than that, into the history of
the disorder and the complications of diagnosis.

PSYCHOLOGISTS HAVE BEEN TRYING TO UNDERSTAND how trauma affects human beings at least since Sigmund Freud
and Joseph Breuer's work in the late nineteenth century, and to understand how war trauma in particular affects soldiers at least since the First World War.
Beginning almost immediately in 1914, soldiers were being sent back from the trenches with afflictions such
as amnesia, aphasia, blindness, and deafness. Some walked
with elaborate, unnatural gaits; some could not sleep, trem-
bled all over, gibbered incessantly, or cowered in the fetal
position. In film footage shot at the Netley Hospital near
Southampton, England, in 1917, researchers captured a very
thin man dressed only in his underwear strutting across the
room, stooped halfway over, his rear end thrust out, his arms
mechanically flapping, his whole body twitching and jerking.
For the British High Command, such exhibitions were symptoms of mass malingering and cowardice—signs, perhaps,
of the corruption of the British character brought on by the
years of relative affluence and leisure that preceded the war.
But the numbers were too great and the conditions too bizarre to completely ignore, so psychiatrists and neurologists
were hastily commandeered, hospitals were set up, and the
field of military psychiatry was born.

Spanning the twentieth century's two world wars, brilliant
and sometimes eccentric figures—Charles Myers, W.H.R.
Rivers, Thomas Salmon, John Rickman, Roy Grinker, and
Moses Kaufman, among others—made significant strides

in identifying, describing, and attempting to treat what was alternately called shell shock, war neurosis, battle fatigue, post–Vietnam syndrome, and finally, by the late 1970s, post-traumatic stress disorder. The early pioneers sought physiological causes for the disorder, but ultimately concluded that it was irreducibly psychological. By the end of the Second World War, they had identified its primary symptoms: intense anxiety, hyper-vigilance, flashbacks and nightmares, emotional numbness, volatility. They had also arrived at the rough outlines of appropriate and effective treatment: a period of rest, relaxation, and safety; therapy to bring the traumatic experience to consciousness and emotional acceptance; and, when possible, reintegration of patients with their units.

There remained, though, the sense among military people that most psychiatric casualties were malingerers and cowards, and a fear that the promise of pensions for psychically wounded veterans would create an incentive to mimic psychiatric problems. This perception began to change only after the Vietnam War. Early in the conflict, American psychiatric casualties were at a historic low, with most soldiers being swiftly returned to their units. But as the war unfolded, the incidence of psychiatric problems—or at least the perception of such incidence—among soldiers nine months or more after their tours of duty rose dramatically.

Amid an atmosphere of deepening hostility to the bloodshed abroad, organizations like Vietnam Veterans Against the War and sympathetic psychiatrists like Chaim Shatan and Robert Jay Lifton began pushing for recognition of post-Vietnam syndrome. In 1980, the American Psychiatric Association responded to the pressure, adding post-traumatic stress disorder to the third edition of its *Diagnostic and Statistical Manual of Mental Disorders*. This in turn placed pressure on militaries and governments to begin acknowledging and addressing PTSD as a legitimate, common illness.

The diagnostic criteria have evolved in the current manual, dsm-iv, to include an intense negative emotional reaction and persistent avoidance of the traumatic event, or any other association with it; flashbacks; nightmares; emotional numbing; hyper-arousal; and hyper-vigilance. These symptoms must last for at least a month; otherwise, one is diagnosed with acute stress disorder. And they are neutral as to the source of the trauma—that is, they do not speak to specifically military origins.

Harvard Medical School professor Judith L. Herman crafted an elegant description of the universal roots of PTSD in her 1992 book, *Trauma and Recovery.* "Psychological trauma is an affliction of the powerless," she wrote. "At the moment of trauma, the victim is rendered helpless by overwhelming force... Traumatic events overwhelm the ordinary systems of care that give people a sense of control, connection, and meaning." The presence of a discernible traumatic event should, in theory, make PTSD simple to diagnose. One psychiatrist I spoke with suggested that it should actually be one of the easiest conditions in the dsm to identify. But diagnosis can be complicated by other factors: a history of conditions like depression and addiction, or traumas unrelated to military service. (This may have been the case for John, for example.) Unlike most physical war injuries, PTSD is intimately intertwined with a person's psychological history.

Diagnosis might one day become easier, thanks to ongoing research into PTSD's neurological causes and indicators, and to advances in neuro-imaging. Dr. Ruth Lanius, a professor of psychiatry at the University of Western Ontario and one of the leading researchers in the field, says volume loss in the hippocampus, a region of the brain associated with the creation of new memories, may help explain why PTSD sufferers re-experience aspects of the trauma through flashbacks, dreams, and bodily sensations. The amygdala, the brain centre connected with emotions, appears to have been affected in people with PTSD as well. In healthy people, measurable fight-or-flight responses are triggered by threatening circumstances, and they dissipate at a predictable rate once the threat is gone. In those with PTSD, the fear switch is permanently on, or "disregulated," meaning they are in a continuous state of hyper-arousal. Sufferers also experience a general disconnection between the emotional function of the amygdala and the executive functions of the frontal cortex, the region of the brain responsible for rational planning and assessment of reality.

These neurological advances could eventually also lead to better, more focused treatments for PTSD, but that remains for the future. In the meantime, the Canadian military has been working to improve its prevention and treatment measures: the steps it has taken over the past few years to overhaul its mental health system look like a direct response to André Marin's original criticisms. In all likelihood, soldiers returning from recent tours in Afghanistan will not face the same challenges John and Dave did, and those who come home with signs of psychological trauma will be far less likely to go untreated. This has been a system-wide effort, but much of it has been driven by one particularly motivated soldier, Lieutenant-Colonel Stéphane Grenier.

I MET GRENIER ON A FEBRUARY MORNING at Le Moulin de Provence café in Byward Market in Ottawa. Now well into his forties, he is a wiry, animated man with a shaved head and wire-rimmed glasses. Grenier served under Roméo Dallaire in Rwanda, and since then has been deployed in Cambodia, Lebanon, Haiti, and most recently Afghanistan. He is an intense, focused, and driven man, and though he enjoys lengthy conversations ("I'm a Frenchy—I love to talk!"), he obviously had little patience for idleness. "I told our media people, 'I won't let him interview me if it's for less than an hour,'" he said a few moments after walking into the café. "I wanted to know that you are serious." The press officer assigned to sit in with us already looked exhausted.

"When we came back from Rwanda," Grenier said, "General Dallaire said, 'Let's record what happened to us.' So I made an internal video called *Witness the Evil*, where General Dallaire first came out about his struggles with PTSD." He recounted a bit of his own story for me. "When I first came back from Rwanda, I was a mess," he said. "From 1995 to 1998, I was a mess. I would smell dead bodies out of nowhere. I would wander around in a trance without any memory of it. I came into the hospital one day after contemplating suicide, and I wondered, 'What is wrong with me? I have a wife, children…'"

He was already frustrated by the military's mental health system, which was, he said, "too linear" and too disconnected from the experience of being a soldier. Previously, those who could bring themselves to acknowledge that they were having problems would be shifted from their units into a medical system with professionals who did not share their experiences, and whom they did not trust. The disconnect between soldiers and medical caregivers was an ongoing problem. Grenier became uncharacteristically sarcastic when speaking about the kinds of advice mental health educators used to give. "They would say, 'Make sure you relax, get enough sleep, eat properly, exercise every day, stay in touch with your friends.' But how are you supposed to do that when you're in a ditch outside the wire?"

His breakthrough moment came when his superior officer took him aside and told him, "Stéphane, you're not the guy I heard about." This, he told me, "gave me permission to seek help. The day I did that was the day I started to recover. And when I did that, I thought, 'Holy shit, what if this was general?'" Meaning, what if every struggling soldier had someone he trusted and respected take him aside and say, "Hey, you haven't been yourself. Maybe you need to go get some help"?

In 2001, Grenier launched the Operational Stress Injury Social Support (OSISS) program, which today includes some forty support counsellors—twenty Canadian Forces veterans who were once diagnosed with PTSD, and twenty family members of PTSD sufferers. "Operational stress injury" is a phrase Grenier coined to bypass the stigma associated with "post-traumatic stress disorder," a term most soldiers despise, because it implies that they have a disease rather than a kind of wound. One of the counsellors' most important roles, he told me, is to "pound the jungle drums and find people in the hurt locker"; another is to provide an easy segue into treatment—to give soldiers permission to get help.

"Early on, we didn't have expertise in deployment mental health issues," says Lieutenant-Colonel Rakesh Jetly. Dr. Jetly is a psychiatrist who, like Grenier, was deployed in Rwanda and has, in his current role as adviser to the Mental Health Directorate in Ottawa, twice spent time working at the base hospital in Kandahar. "In Rwanda, we didn't have people there, and then we didn't have any set program of how to help people post-deployment." Now, Jetly says, the Canadian Forces' approach to mental health is comprehensive. "It starts at the recruit level; they need to think of it in the same way as physical fitness," he told me. "Right off, we talk about coping and stress. The idea is that individuals have to take care of themselves, and also to start being responsible for others."

Among the military's new initiatives is the Joint Speakers Bureau, launched by Grenier after he returned from Afghanistan in 2007. The JSB teaches deploying soldiers, and especially leaders, how to detect and address operational stress injuries. These education programs began just last fall, and so will only impact the late stages of Canada's mission in Afghanistan, but they will be an important part of future deployments. In addition to the JSB sessions, soldiers received the *Road to Mental Readiness* manual, part of a program developed with input from the U.S. Navy seals. The guide contains tips on techniques for controlling stress, such as tactical breathing, and outlines the resources available to them in the field. Once in theatre, a full team is in place—not only peers and superior officers, but also chaplains, med-techs, medical officers, and a full mental health support team. If a soldier needs to be sent home, a psychiatrist can get on the phone and make the appropriate appointments in advance.

The Canadian Forces have also changed their reintegration practices. Notably, they have introduced a five-day decompression stay at a resort en route back to Canada, in keeping with the common belief that soldiers coming home from the Second World War reintegrated more quickly and successfully into civilian life than those who served in Vietnam, partly due to different methods of transport. The long journey by ship from Europe or the Pacific allowed for a slow period of readjustment, whereas the flight from Saigon was jarring. Jetly recalls for me how disorienting his return from Kigali was: "One day, I was sleeping in a stadium across from dead bodies; the next day, I was back in Ottawa."

Upon returning to Canada, soldiers are screened for PTSD, depression, and family problems. "I see everyone when the come back," says Lieutenant-Colonel Jim Kile, the regional surgeon for 4 Health Service Group in Toronto. "We do the pen and paper screening and a face-to-face interview. It's yet another opportunity to ask questions, and for red flags to be raised." According to Jetly, about 6.1 percent of Canadian soldiers screen positive for PTSD or depression and end up in treatment. The figure is the envy of his American counterparts, who see rates as high as 15 percent. The Canadian system isn't perfect—it may not account well enough for the fact that PTSD can take years to manifest after the initial trauma—but for those who are identified early on and need care, treatment is now rapidly and widely available. As Grenier told me, "We want to break down the barriers to care; we want there to be as many avenues to treatment as possible." And once the soldiers arrive, treatment is increasingly being influenced and assisted by their peers.

SITTING IN HIS CORNER OFFICE at the Operational Stress Injury Clinic at Parkwood Hospital in London, Ontario, Mike Newcombe looked nervous; a soldier's soldier, he was obviously uneasy speaking to a civilian about PTSD. In his late forties, compact, his hair brown and his face deeply lined, Newcombe was in the Canadian Forces for more than twenty years, mostly as an infantryman with the Royal Canadian Regiment. He deployed multiple times, including to the former Yugoslavia, and over the years became increasingly angry and anxious. Finally, he told me, one day "I was at a conference, and something went up on the screen and I completely blacked out. At that point, I realized this wasn't going away." By 2002, he knew he had to get out, and just a few years later he had a massive, near-fatal heart attack, which he attributes to a toxic accumulation of stress.

"When I first came into peer support,' Newcombe said, "I didn't want to be there, but then I thought, 'These guys are going through the same thing I am.' It's easier to talk to someone who has been in the military, and it gives you more confidence. Unless you've lived it, no one knows what it's like. When I got back from my missions, people would shake my hand, but they didn't know." He eventually became a peer support volunteer, and then was hired on as a coordinator.

Newcombe's office is down the hall from a full staff of nurses, psychologists, and psychiatrists, with whom he has a fluid relationship. Most patients come to him by word of mouth, and he talks to them individually and in structured group meetings. "About 75 percent of them are younger guys, but at least 25 percent come out of the woodwork," he said. "The oldest is eighty-seven or eighty-eight. And there is no difference between the young guys and the old ones."

Treatment at Parkwood, as elsewhere, tends to follow the program set forth by Herman's seminal *Trauma and Recovery*, moving patients slowly through the stages of safety, remembrance, and reconnection. "It's incredibly important to treat trauma," says Anne Pepper, supervisor of the PTSD and addiction program at Bellwood Health Services in Toronto, "partly because it doesn't just affect individuals; it affects all of society and future generations—look at the children of Holocaust survivors." The first priority for doctors is stabilization and grounding. "By far, getting sleep is the biggest problem," says Dr. Bill Jacyk, attending physician of the trauma and addiction program at the Homewood Health Centre in Guelph, Ontario. "We don't do any exposure therapy at first," in part because if a patient is not in a position to confront the trauma, it might make problem worse. "We first deal with ordinary life. Sometimes we have people who have been in the basement for a long time. We get people who say, 'Why can't we just talk about limbs being blown up?' But it's not spectacular things that entrap you; it's ordinary things."

Once a person has a sense of security, the next phase of treatment is trickier and subject to more disagreement among professionals. In an in-patient treatment context focused on both trauma and addiction—over fifty percent of PTSD sufferers also have addiction issues—therapy to address the trauma directly is often deferred until after the treatment program is completed, so as not to risk making the trauma worse. Once begun, though, the three principal therapies used in treating PTSD are exposure, cognitive behavioural, and emdr (eye movement desensitization and reprocessing). Exposure therapy involves working through the details of the trauma; cognitive therapy aims at developing better mental coping strategies; emdr focuses on specific traumatic memories and attempts to establish positive associations in their place. All three are, Pepper says, an effort to "change neural pathways, make it possible for them to interpret the world as safe." And all three approaches to PTSD speak to a deceptively simple aim: learning how to relax and to manage stress, typically through meditation and breathing, before it spirals out of control.

One of the most disabling features of PTSD (and addiction, for that matter) is how it tends to shatter a person's social support system. In fact, most psychiatrists in the field list strong social support as one of the indicators that a person who has suffered a traumatic experience will be less likely to develop PTSD. This concern can be especially acute for returning soldiers, who almost universally find it difficult to relate to people who have not been in a war zone. Newcombe tends to tear up when he speaks of his two children and his wife, from whom he is separated. (According to him, Grenier did the same when speaking about his family on a recent visit to the clinic.) "If I get back together with my wife," he said, "it will be because of OSISS." Both OSISS and the Joint

Speakers Bureau have programs for families, because a solid and understanding family substantially increases an individual's chances of recovery—though, according to Grenier, it remains difficult to get them fully involved.

Psychiatrists are fairly optimistic about the prospects for long-term treatment, especially given recent research advances. "As a rule, one-third recover, one-third remain symptomatic, and one-third don't respond well to treatment," says Dr. Don Richardson, a psychiatrist who works alongside Newcombe at Parkwood. "But if people follow treatment guidelines, you get 50 percent success rates."

Both Newcombe and Grenier are circumspect about the prospects for recovery, however: they believe they live with a condition that can be managed but not cured, and that relapses into old triggers and symptoms and habits are inevitable. The condition also presents new challenges with every new mission. Steve Lively, who became a peer support coordinator some time after being deployed with Joint Task Force Two in Africa in the 1990s and now works with the JSB, told me they are already seeing people from the relief effort in Haiti. "I was talking to navy guys who said that in collapsed houses in Port-au-Prince, exposed body parts were being devoured by animals," he said. "And family members were [the ones] cutting them off."

For soldiers like Lively, or like John and Dave, these missions abroad are typically the culmination of years of education and training. They are, as a young reservist and student at the University of Toronto told me, soldiers' best opportunity to employ the elaborate skills they have acquired. No one expects to come home from their adventure entirely changed. But as Ruth Lanius says, PTSD affects the whole person, and it remains hard for the afflicted and their peers not to believe that something in them is flawed or weak.

Lanius also points out that one of the characteristics of the disorder is a lessening of one's capacity to identify the emotions that drive one's behaviour—something that is also true of addiction. I could never explain to myself or anyone else why, when going to a polite, bookish cocktail party intending to have a glass of wine and casually socialize, I would end up being found splayed unconscious on the sidewalk outside. As a result, I felt more at home in dives among alcoholics, drug addicts, ex-cons, and, yes, a few veterans. Soldiers with PTSD often report that they have "no idea what is happening to them," and they similarly isolate themselves from friends, family, and colleagues out of shame at what they have become. One decorated veteran Grenier told me about went so far as to change his name, out of fear of being discovered by someone he knew.

Treatment helps instill a sense of control, but in a way it never really ends; one has to remain vigilant, wary of triggers and relapses into old habits and patterns of behaviour. Like Grenier and Newcombe, I'm not optimistic that the sense of self-doubt and brokenness, the sense of one's very self as shaky, that comes with the experience of both PTSD and addiction ever completely goes away. If elderly veterans are still finding their way into Mike Newcombe's OSISS groups, then despite all the current neurological research and soldier education, it seems likely that the veterans of Afghanistan will still be seeking help thirty, forty, fifty, even sixty years from now. That alone should give us pause when our politicians decide to send courageous young men and women off into harm's way.

LOVE IS A LET-DOWN: SOME LESSONS FROM THE STORM OF NEW MOTHERHOOD

Kerry Clare
The New Quarterly

for Alyssa Polinksy

I don't think I just imagined her, the woman I was left alone with in the last few minutes before I was taken into surgery. I don't know if she was a nurse, or some kind of technician, but she seemed terribly official, sitting at a table with paperwork while I contemplated the IV needle stuck in my hand.

"Section?" she asked me, and I told her yes.

"What for?"

I said, "The baby's transverse." Lying across my womb, its little bum wedged in at the top and refusing to budge no matter how much I stood on my head, played soothing music into my pelvis, or shone a flashlight into my vagina.

"Well," said the woman at the table, sorting through her papers. "Kids will screw you somehow. If it wasn't that, it would be labour, then they'd grow up to be teenagers. They always find a way."

"But it's all worth it, right?" I asked her.

"No." She put down her papers. "I don't think it is." Then she got up, left through a different door, and I never saw her again.

THAT NIGHT, MY NEWBORN DAUGHTER sucked colostrum from my nipples until five o'clock in the morning, spending about twenty minutes on one side and then screaming until we placed her on the other. Because my abdomen had been sliced in two just hours before, I had to lie down to feed her, which required my husband, Stuart, to rise from his bed on a vinyl chair in the corner (a jacket for his blanket), hold the baby while I went through the painful process of turning over, and then he'd place her on my other side, and start the twenty-minute cycle again.

I spent that night imagining various scenarios in which we gave the baby up for adoption. Which has become an amusing-sounding anecdote I pull out now and again, but that night I'd never been so serious, or desperate. If nothing else, I thought, we might sneak out of the hospital without anyone noticing, and go home to resume life as normal. Surely this was a possibility My daughter was perfect, and beautiful, and I was extraordinarily blessed, but the last point was something I had to keep telling myself. I was exhausted, it hurt to breathe, the baby kept crying, a swaddled bundle of discontent, and her tiny button face was a stranger's.

There were people out there who would have given everything they owned for our good fortune, for this wonderful baby, for the opportunity to be parents. Which was, I thought, all the more reason for us to offer our daughter to them, never mind the nine months we'd spent preparing and waiting, how thrilling it had been to finally meet her. *I'd just never thought it would be like this.* That first night, lying there in my mechanical bed with a baby whose needs I was incapable of meeting, I could only think of one good reason to keep her, no way around it. The only reason we couldn't give the baby up for adoption was that her grandmothers would never forgive us.

I'D JUST NEVER THOUGHT IT WOULD BE LIKE THIS: what a spectacular failure of imagination. Though the failure wasn't mine alone— a baby's birth in movies is a cue for credits to roll; the TV newborn grows into a wisecracking toddler in the space between episodes; tiny babies in literature are especially rare, or maybe I just hadn't been paying attention to them. Some women have written about new motherhood, in memoirs in particular, and I'd even read these, but their words hadn't registered, I hadn't conceived the weight of it all. The days without sleeping, how time slows down, the world shrinks, the unceasing cries, that unceasing *need*, and being the one person in the world equipped to meet it. All those things you really have to experience to understand, which is another way of saying things you'll have a spectacular failure to imagine.

Such a failure, however, is reasonable, because who would want to imagine it? The enormity of the experience would hardly be lessened by this preparation. People don't make movies about this stuff because nobody would want to watch them. A novel about three days in the life of a new mother would be the longest book in the world. It's no coincidence that it's visual artists who have cornered the market on newborns, their babies being inanimate, quiet, and usually sporting a halo.

I was more miserable than I'd ever been during my first days of motherhood, and by "first days" I really mean about six weeks, and three months, and maybe more than that. And I'm not even talking about postpartum depression. Though no doubt, PPD is a very real affliction, it's also a label that undermines the very simple fact that living with a newborn is, as writer Ariel Gore describes it, "like suddenly getting the world's worst roommate, like having Janis Joplin with a bad hangover and PMS come to stay with you."

WHEN WE FINALLY LEFT THE HOSPITAL, after three days, it was with a great deal of fanfare. The nurses were gathered, waving good-bye. I heard one of them telling another, "Harriet's going home now," the first time I'd ever heard the baby referred to as an autonomous someone. Stuart was laden with everything we'd brought with us, and all the extra we'd acquired since—cards, teddy bears and flowers, a tangle of ribbons attached to a helium bouquet. He was pushing me in a wheelchair, and I held our daughter in my arms. She was wearing a white cap with yellow ducks on it, a sleeper with gender-neutral stripes. The temperature outside was over thirty degrees, but she was wrapped in the thick blanket I'd knit while I was pregnant.

I was crying. For four days the hospital had cradled us, with its climate control and fluorescent lights, fourteen stories up in the sky. And now we were being released into the outside world, into the sunshine glare, the traffic and smog, the towering staircase up to our front door, and no saviour to appear at the press of an alarm bell. We were taking the baby away from the only home she'd ever known.

The elevator was crowded but stopped partway down to let on another passenger. She looked down at me (admiringly, I imagined), at the tiny baby sleeping in my arms, but then she hinged at her hips, yanked the knitted blanket over my knees. I was wearing a sundress, the first time I'd worn clothing indays. She spoke to me in that tone reserved only for small children or people in wheelchairs. "Oh, honey," she said. "You've gotyour legs wide open. You don't want to go showing that to everybody, do you?"

Downstairs, I waited in the lobby while my husband went to get the car. I can't remember now if the baby was sleeping or awake, but I remember her solid shape tucked in my arms, the still-strangeness of her funny little face. The outside doors kept sliding open, and I could feel a thick layer of heat in the air.

The crowd was big-city typical—someone brought in by the police after a fight, homeless people bunkered down in vinyl chairs for the afternoon, various people chatting to themselves, a crying teenage girl with make-up running down her face, and someone else who kept laughing at nothing.

I whispered to the baby, "Don't worry. Not everybody is schizophrenic." I thought it was kind of funny.

A woman sitting across from me was staring. "You've got a beautiful baby," she said. "Boy or girl?" and I answered her friendly inquiries until my husband arrived.

She didn't notice when I said good-bye though, too busy talking to the empty chair beside her. "It's a girl," she was saying. "Her name is Harriet. She was born on Tuesday. On Tuesday, I said. It was a cesarean. She's going home now. Her name's Harriet."

Motherhood is a storm, a seizure: It is like weather.
Nights of high wind followed by calm mornings of

*dense fog or brilliant sunshine that gives way to
tropical rain or blinding snow. Jane Louise and Edie
found themselves swept away, cast ashore, washed
overboard. It was hard to keep anything straight. The
days seemed to congeal like rubber cement, although
moments stood out in clearest, starkest brilliance. You
might string those together on the charm bracelet of
your memory if you could keep your eyes open long
enough to remember anything.*

> —Laurie Colwin, from *A Big Storm Knocked It
> Over*

IN HER WONDERFUL MEMOIR *A Life's Work: On Becoming a
Mother*, Rachel Cusk writes about how reading is different
after her daughter is born: "Like someone visiting old haunts
after an absence I read books that I have read before, books
that I love, and when I do I find them changed: they give
the impression of having contained all along everything that
I have gone away to learn." Of course, I didn't understand
this until I experienced it myself, the first time when I reread
Laurie Colwin's novel in the days after Harriet's birth and
discovered the one paragraph that finally articulated to me
the truth about new motherhood.

The paragraph doesn't say it all, however. Laurie Colwin
was a writer whose touch was agonizingly light, and she
shied away from the eye of the storm, or maybe my point is
that everybody skirts the issue. Although motherhood is a
storm that passes, fleetingness is little consolation before the
passing is done. When it's still not clear whether it's a storm
or whether your life has just descended into an all-enveloping
hell. When it seems as though your entire universe has ex-
ploded, probably because it has.

I want to write it down though, how it was, because most people don't ever talk about this. They don't talk about it because
it passes, and because of what you get to show for it, and because if everybody told the truth, pregnant women would start
jumping in front of buses in droves. And also because this
truth is not everybody's—writer Katie Roiphe published an
article called "My Newborn Is Like a Narcotic." But for those
of us whose personalities are less addictive, the narrative of
new motherhood is remarkably different from the standard.

STANDING OUT MOMENT, IN CLEAREST STARKEST BRILLIANCE #1:
That walk we took in the hospital, halfway down the corridor
to the "Hey Diddle-Diddle" mural—it was the farthest we'd
ever been. And then we had to stop because I was exhausted,
my incision ached. "Hey Diddle-Diddle, the cat and the fiddle,
the cow jumped over the moon. The little dog laughed to see
such sport, and the dish ran away with the spoon." It was
Harriet's first nursery rhyme. "And the thing about Harriet,"
I said to my husband, "is that she's so little that she doesn't
even realize that fleeing cutlery is something unusual."

I was crying.

The understatement to end all understatements, during
this time in which everything had been an understatement,
was that I would find myself "a little weepy" when my milk
came in. I'd had the impression that weeping would be purely physical, that tears would simply roll down my face and
I'd look on, somehow removed from the experience. I hadn't
counted on full body-racking sobs, and that with each one,
I'd feel the emotion so intensely. That all these feelings would
be brutally real, and somehow worse for having no point of
origin, for their aimless churning. It was impossible to articulate what exactly was wrong, partly because everything was

wrong, but also because it was nothing, and the feelings were pummeling me over and over again.

I cried the day after we left the hospital, when Stuart and I went for a walk and we only made it to the end of the driveway. I cried because our daughter was so wonderful, it was unfathomable, and because I loved Stuart so terribly, and now I'd gone and destroyed our life. I was dreadfully sorry about that. Then I cried because I couldn't help it, and the sky was so blue, the trees were so green, and the entire universe was such a miracle—what a gift to be here. And also because I kind of wished I was dead.

I cried at the space the new baby had made in my life, how she'd managed to overwhelm everything else, and how I hadn't ever realized what I was lacking before. Maybe because I hadn't been lacking anything. And I also cried because now I knew that if anything ever happened to her, it would destroy me, a new vulnerability that was terrifying to consider, and then when I was finished crying about that, I cried at "anything ever happening to her" in the most benign way, that life was hard and I wouldn't always be able to protect her.

I wasn't the only one who cried. Harriet cried too, a lot, though later we discovered this was mostly because of gas. Stuart cried a couple of times, during those rare instances in which he had neither hysterical wife nor hysterical child to comfort, when it would suddenly dawn on him that he couldn't take it anymore.

Once Stuart went back to work, the baby and I spent much of our time crying together. I cried because the breastfeeding consultant told me to spend my days on the couch watching Oprah and Doctor Phil. I cried because I wanted to walk out of the house and never come back, and I cried because I knew I never could. I cried because the baby had been up all night, and was still going come the morning, and it seemed that administering to pure, insatiable need (for what, though?) was going to be the rest of my life.

I thought that if I wailed with the windows wide open, somebody might come along and take her away from me. One day when I was crying and thought things couldn't get any worse, the baby threw up in my mouth and I had it confirmed that whenever you think you've come to know the baby, she will always turn around and surprise you.

STANDING OUT MOMENT, IN CLEAREST, STARKEST BRILLIANCE #2: Setting the alarm clock all night long, to get the baby fed every three hours. CBC radio when the world is asleep featuring programs by international public broadcasters. Listening to Sweden, Australia, The Netherlands, and Britain. I don't remember the content of any of these shows, but I remember the company of their voices, the accents which confirmed that there was life out there while we three were cloistered in our bedroom whose four walls were the whole world, which seemed room enough but how amazing were those messages from the farthest reaches of outer-space.

I was crying, but this wasn't unusual. And though it was sort of unusual that the baby was nursing properly, she was only doing it because somebody was watching. When she breastfed unobserved, she'd either fall asleep or start screaming, but with someone looking on (and particularly someone who was trying to determine why exactly our daughter had lost 11 percent of her body weight), the baby latched on and sucked away like a champion.

Here's something I'd spectacularly failed to imagine: when eight pounds is your entire mass, every bit of every ounce is extremely important. It can be a matter of life and death, though we were fortunate to get only so desperate that ours was a matter of life or lethargy. Harriet had lost so much weight that she was too tired to feed, a vicious cycle we had to counter by stripping her down to her diaper and shocking her with dripping, cold washcloths, by supplementing her breast milk with formula, by feeding her through a narrow tube attached to a syringe so as not to put her off the breast altogether with "nipple confusion."

My milk had come in, in the way that I'd thought that the weeping would, pure physiology. Except that it wasn't entirely, because it was the milk that had me weeping, but the connections between all things weren't yet apparent. During my pregnancy, I'd feared that I'd have no milk at all; how could my body know how to do it? But it did, amazingly, without even consulting with my mind, the great micro-manager. My milk was even plentiful—people kept squeezing my breasts and telling me so.

The baby was feeding now, displaying that fantastic latch that had tricked everybody in the hospital into thinking we were doing just fine. I was sitting in my living room, the window shutting out the fine spring day because there was a breeze and we were concerned about the baby getting a chill. The midwife was crouching before me, slightly adjusting our position—my hand on the back of her neck, the angle of her mouth on my nipple. I could feel the sucking, a gentle tug-tug that pulled deep inside of me, and from the way her jaw moved I could see she was swallowing.

The problem, however, was that she would stop. Her mouth remaining at the same angle, me still holding her head as taught, but the movement of her jaw was different, smaller. I could feel the tug-tug still, which was the tricky thing, but this was her sucking for sucking's sake, for pure comfort, rather than for the sustenance that was so important now.

"So, you've got to wake her up," said the midwife. "Start again, and keep going. Breastfeeding takes patience."

Harriet gained her first half-ounce when she was four days-old, this confirmed by that midwife weighing her in a sling scale. And when she peed through the sling's fabric and onto our bed, it was a further sign of an upswing: confirmation of hydration! I duly recorded the incident in the log I was keeping of all the baby's outputs, a log I would keep for nearly three weeks. These were the details that consumed me, the difference between green shit and yellow shit, or whether a wet diaper could be classified as "heavy." The daily tallies I kept of wet and dirty diapers, which got confusing when one day leaked right into another, but the days were like that then, borderless, giving the impression that time had ceased to exist. And then the clock would tick over.

The sun came up and the sun went down, not that it made any difference to us.

STANDING OUT MOMENT, IN CLEAREST, STARKEST BRILLIANCE #3: When Harriet spits up onto her burp pad, and the stain has a reddish tinge. We could almost ignore it, because it was easier, and then she spit up again, undeniably blood. The rush to the emergency room, waiting in an enormous queue behind a man whose daughter has apparently been barking like a seal since November (and, do note, now it's June). I'm crying, clutching my five-day old daughter. I imagine that she's dying, that this is what you get when you wish you'd never had a baby in the first place. I know that she's singularly beautiful, that I'm undeserving of her, and the sadness I feel at her deprivation of true maternal love makes me cry even harder.

We get to bypass the queue, walk through corridors of visibly ill children and infants stretched out on gurneys, their anguished parents. Because Harriet is so small and the hospital is rife with disease, we are quickly ushered into a room with a door, a doctor comes to us quickly.

The doctor diagnoses a cracked nipple: Harriet has been drinking my blood. I didn't even know it was cracked, but these things can happen deep under the surface. But the doctor wants to be sure, to get a second opinion. Two more doctors come in to examine her that night, pressing carefully on her tiny belly, working around her tender umbilical stump. Our case is easy; we're a brief holiday from awful. The doctors tell us our baby is beautiful.

We leave the hospital at three in the morning, the corridors still lined with the children we'd passed on our way in. We've just been given a glimpse into the darkest places life can take us, and then we are lucky enough to turn around and come back out again.

IT WAS THE CARDS THAT KILLED ME, they really did, though I'm grateful that people were thinking of us, that we were connected to so many who cared. We had the cards lined up all along the windowsill, three or four deep. The messages inside them were heartfelt and so comforting, scrawled in all manner of hands, from friends and family, from people we hardly knew. But it was their outsides I had a problem with, their candy-floss tones and insipid greetings. *The softest little cuddles / and the sweetest / dreams-come-true, / The warmest hugs / and love to share— / your baby girl / and you!*

I began to think that sympathy cards might have been more appropriate—"We are thinking of you at this difficult time." In fact, that very sentiment delivered me a great deal of comfort. The friend who said, "You know, it's natural to grieve for the life you had before." Another who told me, "I remember how hard it was, and the worst part is that *I'd thought I would be good at it.*" Someone else said, "They're dark days, the early ones," and I wondered why the cards were so incongruous. Why they kept mocking me with lines like, *A baby girl! You must be over the moon.*

When the baby was about two weeks old, I ran into a woman who'd been in my prenatal yoga class. Her due date had been close to mine, our daughters born a week apart. I was out buying baby wipes, wearing jeans and a warm fleecy jacket, even though the temperature was in the high-twenties. I kept doing that, forgetting it was nearly summer, forgetting the world until I went outside and it surprised me. My attire was the least remarkable feature of my appearance, however. My pallor was ghostly, my eyes ringed with blue.

"So, you did it," she said to me, and we wished one another congratulations. It felt strange to be there, on the other side, like we shared a few secrets we didn't want to talk about now.

But I did want to talk about it. "It's so hard," I answered when she asked me how I was doing. "We're still trying to figure out the difference between day and night, and I'm so tired. I never thought it would be like this, but I guess you know how it is."

"Well, not really," said the woman, who was dressed for the weather. "We're doing pretty well, having fun together. It's pretty great, actually. I don't know if I've ever been so in love in my life."

STANDING OUT MOMENT, IN CLEAREST, STARKEST BRILLIANCE #3: When we start walking in the evening, which is the time when Harriet cries. We usually walk in the direction of ice cream, which delivers me enormous comfort during this time of need. As does the setting sun, the summer evening, the mild temperature, the fresh air as I breathe it deep, and the comfort of my husband's hand in mine. He's wearing the baby on his chest, and she's asleep, tucked in so snugly against him. We walk the neighbourhood in circles, part of a parade of families in similar arrangement. I used to see them before I had a baby, looking on admiringly at their quiet containment, and it is ironic now to think that they'd been my inspiration. I'd missed the point of them so entirely.

But there was a great sense of comradeship between us. One night, we walked past one couple whose desperate expressions were like looking into a mirror.

"Good luck, tonight," I told them.

"Thanks. How old's yours?"

"Four weeks. You?"

"Six."

"I've heard it gets easy at six."

"Hmm, no."

"Oh."

"We passed a couple back there though, two weeks. They were totally shell-shocked."

"Two weeks."

"I know."

"I could never go back there."

But we wouldn't have to, and right now the babies are sleeping. A moment of reprieve, as we soldier on our separate ways. We had the summer breeze, and the ice cream cones, and the sidewalks before us stretched on until sunset.

I NEVER FELT MY LET-DOWN, when the baby latches onto the breast and the milk begins to flow. In some ways, I am lucky because for many women let-down can be inordinately painful. (And this is one of the many ways in which I'm lucky, I realize. Having struggled so much without any problems, I wonder how badly I might have fallen apart had something actually gone wrong). I worried about it though, that it might mean the milk wasn't coming. When your child has lost 11 percent of its body weight, that kind of anxiety lingers.

A quick internet search would reveal my experience as normal, however—the physical symptoms of pregnancy and motherhood are all remarkable in their failure to conform to generalizations. Harriet was getting enough to eat, as attested by my daily tallies (since abandoned) and the weight she was now gaining at a steady pace. I'd even become savvy at detecting when she was eating or simply soothing, and therefore I could get feedings down to twenty minutes at a time. I figured out how to hold a book so I could read during those twenty minutes. The pacifier had become my friend, helping Harriet sleep, and I'd learned that she slept best beside me, her fist wrapped around my little finger.

Things never got easy, but they became eas*ier*. Some time between three and six weeks, I stopped crying every day. There began to be mornings again, though I was usually still exhausted when they found me. Moments standing out in clearest, starkest brilliance started to be strung closer together.

That I was thinking this was the denouement, however, demonstrates precisely what was wrong with my approach to everything—neither pregnancy nor motherhood was an end in itself, and the story would have no conclusion, not for a long, long time.

There remained the question of love. *I mean, of course I love the baby, but.* Which was a phrase I'd kept saying though the reservation made me uneasy. Wasn't I supposed to be "over the moon"? I wondered if my c-section had been the problem—if I'd given birth to her naturally, would I have never been so in love in my life? Would I have been writing articles entitled, "My newborn is like a narcotic." Or was I simply cold and heartless, *Mommie Dearest*, Susan Smith. And how much had I compromised my child's development by failing to give her the love she was entitled to by virtue of existing?

But love is a let-down, I realized, as the weeks went on, and we started measuring the baby's life in months. Love, though I couldn't even feel it, had been there beneath the surface all along, doing its job. Love was me not walking out of the house and never coming back. It was throwing out the bathwater but not the baby. And it was persevering through two hour nursing sessions twelve times a day. It was holding her when she cried, even if I was crying too; it was keeping her clean and warm, having her sleep on my chest and learning ingenious ways to provide her with comfort, desperation being the true mother of invention.

In those terrible early congealing days, love was *doing*, instead of feeling. And sometimes it wasn't worth it, but sometimes it was, and then (though this is far from the point) one day I noticed that the storm had been over for a while.

BALANCING ACT: THE STATE, THE MARKETS, THE FUTURE

David Crane
Literary Review of Canada

I n the wake of the financial and economic crisis, the worst since the Great Depression of the 1930s, a major debate is now underway on the future role of the state and the version of capitalism that is best suited to a modern economy. At issue is the free market philosophy that had dominated thinking—and policy—in the G7 world since the Thatcher-Reagan revolutions.

This crisis does not mark the end of capitalism. But as we know, there are many different varieties of capitalism, from the more laissez-faire versions of the United States and Great Britain, through the middle-of-the-road versions found in Germany, France, Canada and Australia, to the social democratic versions of Scandinavia and on to the state-led capitalism that accounted for the rise of Japan, Korea and Taiwan and that, in various forms, is now being followed by China, Russia and Brazil, as well as the resource-rich economies of the Gulf Cooperation Council.

This debate, of course, is not new. In 1997, John Kenneth Galbraith delivered the first annual Keith Davey Lecture at Victoria College in Toronto, in which he examined both the strengths and weaknesses of capitalism. Despite its flaws, capitalism, Galbraith said, had clearly delivered a productive and innovative economy capable of creating goods and services in abundance. In the world that exists, he continued, "there is clearly no plausible alternative. The age of presumed choice between alternative economic systems is over." But that did not mean turning the world over to free market zealots. Indeed, it is through the efforts of what he called "the socially concerned" that capitalism has survived.

"Capitalism in its original form was an insufferably cruel thing," said Galbraith. "Only with trade unions, the protection of workers and workers' rights, pensions for the old, compensation for the unemployed, public health care, lower-cost housing, a safety net, however imperfect, for the unfortunate and the deprived, and public action to mitigate capitalism's commitment to boom and slump did the market become socially acceptable." Yet since the Thatcher-Reagan revolutions and the ascendancy of free market zealotry, there had been an incessant effort to undo these reforms in the name of returning everything to the market.

Richard Posner, a highly respected Court of Appeals judge in Chicago, has been closely associated with the free market school that represents the core of the University of Chicago's faculty of economics. In his latest book—*The Crisis of Capitalist Democracy*—he reveals himself to be a strong Keynesian, observing that Keynes is constantly attacked by free market, small government conservatives in the United States (this is true in Canada as well). Posner dismisses the theories of rational expectations and efficient markets, each of which is used to justify light regulation and free market capitalism.

Keynes gave us the theory that explains the business cycle and how government can ameliorate its excesses. He taught, Posner says, "that there is more that government can do to arrest a downward economic spiral than just pushing down interest rates. It can offset the decline in private consumption in a recession or a depression by increasing public investment. When we say that the government builds highways, we mean it buys highways from private contractors." The more it buys, the more investment, income, output, and employment are enhanced. The stimulus packages in the recent crisis are Keynes grandchildren, as Posner remarks.

Posner makes it clear that he, like Galbraith, believes in capitalism. "But capitalism is not a synonym for free markets," Posner says. "It is the name given to a complex economic system with many moving parts." It includes not just buying and selling and investing and borrowing but also "a system of laws for protecting property and facilitating transactions, institutions for enforcing those laws, and regulations designed to align private incentives with the goal of achieving widespread prosperity." But, he insists, "if the regulatory framework is defective, it must be changed, because competition will not permit businessmen to subordinate profit maximization to concern for the welfare of society as a whole, and ethics can't take the place of regulation."

Although Posner does not use these words, this is the role of the state—to address the flaws of capitalism and ensure that the wider goals of society are being achieved. Business, as we have seen repeatedly in Canada, will fight policies that are clearly in the public interest but that force business to change practices or products. Current examples include the urgent need to deal with climate change and, in public health, to seriously reduce the use of salt and sugar in processed foods and fast food restaurant meals. Leaded gasoline, CFCs and tobacco have all led to pitched battles in the past. Laissez-faire or free market capitalism will not address these issues.

The private banking system, a key part of the capitalist world, is inherently unstable, Posner argues, and if it fails it can bring down much of the rest of the economy with disastrous consequences. "That is one reason a capitalist system cannot consist of just free markets." In Canada, for example, we need the Bank of Canada and the Office of the Superintendent of Financial Institutions, with effective regulatory powers and oversight, to keep the banking system working, as they showed they could in the recent crisis.

In the U.S., Posner argues, the root of the financial collapse in September 2008 was "a failure of regulation, compounded of unsound monetary policy and deregulation, non-regulation, and lax—excessively permissive—regulation of financial intermediation." Financial markets, it turned out, were not self-regulating but this view had become orthodoxy as a result of policy capture by free market ideologues. Yet as Posner argues, "if the consequences of a firm's bankruptcy for the economy are catastrophic, it is government's responsibility to force the firm to take fewer risks than are in the firm's self-interest to take. It is no different from forcing a polluting enterprise to reduce its polluting at the cost of sacrificing some profits."

Posner believes that major changes are necessary in the way the capitalist system functions. But, if the U.S. is also to address its growing burden of debt, the necessary changes "may be especially painful and difficult because of features of the American political scene that suggest that the country may be becoming in important respects ungovernable. The perfection of interest-group politics seems to have brought about a situation in which, to exaggerate just a bit, taxes can't be increased, spending programs can't be cut, and new spending is irresistible." One reason for this is that "campaign contributions—insulated in the name of the Constitution by a conservative Supreme Court from effective limitation—make the legislative system one of quasi-bribery."

Joseph Stiglitz, a Nobel Prize–winning economist, offers his own sharp critique of free market thinking in his latest book, *Freefall: America, Free Markets and the Sinking of the World Economy*. He underlines the importance of government in the economy, including the importance of having a vision. Stiglitz reminds us that "the big question in the twenty-first-century global economy is, what should be the role of the state?" For him, the answer is fairly clear: the state should combine social justice, opportunity and equity or fairness with the market's power for innovation. The question is how to strike the balance—a heavy-handed state will squash innovation and investment while a light-handed state will fail to constrain the excesses of the free market economy or ensure that prosperity reaches all. The role of the state should include maintaining full employment and a stable economy, promoting innovation, providing social protection and insurance, and preventing exploitation, Stiglitz argues.

In other words, we need to create what Stiglitz calls "a New Capitalism" based on new levels of trust between the financial community and the rest of society, and on a new level of trust in the workings of democratic institutions and government. But this comes back to restoring political institutions and political life. The political influence of special interest groups makes "rational policy making all but impossible," Stiglitz contends. In the U.S., campaign finance and powerful lobbying have ended serious political debate on the public interest in favour of advocacy for the private interests of the powerful and wealthy. Fortunately, in one of his final pieces of legislation, Jean Chrétien brought in political financing rules that sharply curbed the use of big money in Canadian politics.

For Tony Judt, the late British-born historian who lived in New York, the seeds of the economic crisis were planted well before it hit; he argues in *Ill Fares the Land* that "for thirty years we have made a virtue out of the pursuit of material self-interest." Since the 1980s, he argues, western society has been obsessed with wealth creation, "the cult of privatization and the private sector," ignoring growing inequality. Above all, he contends, we have been obsessed by "the rhetoric which accompanies these: uncritical admiration for unfettered markets, disdain for the public sector, the delusion of endless growth."

But, Judt says, "we cannot go on living like this." The crash of 2008 "was a reminder that unregulated capitalism is its own worst enemy: sooner or later it must fall prey to its own excesses and turn again to the state for rescue. But if we do no more than pick up the pieces and carry on as before, we can look forward to greater upheavals in years to come." The problem, though, is that "we seem unable to conceive of alternatives." For much of this short book, Judt traces how the Left lost its way and why the great role of social democracy in the 20th century has largely dissipated in the face of the battle for minds waged by neoconservatives in championing the role of free market capitalism and the notion of government as the problem.

He blames the breakdown in support for collective goals and community on both the Left and the Right. In the 1960s, he argues, baby boomers entering university had only known a world of improving living standards, access to medical services and education, a sense of upward mobility and, above all, a sense of security. "The goals of an earlier generation of reformers were no longer of interest to their successors. On the contrary, they were increasingly perceived as constraints upon the self-expression and freedom of the individual." The transition from a society with shared goals and interests to a world of individualism was well underway.

The tragedy today is that the new generation appears to be taking the next step—distancing itself from political life altogether, so that democratic institutions and attention to broad social problems, such as the growth in inequality and problems of poverty, the need for public goods such as education and a clean environment, and a more acceptable form of globalization are neglected until an even bigger crisis emerges. Yet, as Judt stresses, elections are "our only means for converting public opinion into collective action under law." The challenge is to restore faith in our political institutions.

In some important respects, as Judt shows in a series of graphs, Canada has produced a better society than either of those centres of free market capitalism, the United States and Great Britain. We have a better rate of social mobility—the ability of people to move out of poverty—than the U.S. or Britain. We have a fairer society in that income inequality is not as great. And we have longer life expectancy, which is probably the best marker of a country's overall performance. In addition, Canadian schoolchildren perform better than their American counterparts. Americans have a higher per capita gross domestic product but that tells us nothing about how its wealth is distributed. To be sure, the Scandinavian countries, and especially Sweden, do better than we do. We do pay more in taxes than Americans, but we also get value. Knowing that all Canadians have access to public health care and other social measures is better than building a society of gated communities. More importantly, a strong social framework will make it easier to deal with the huge changes we face in the years ahead. It represents a form of social solidarity that underlines community at a time when the U.S. and Great Britain in particular have embraced an excessive individualism. We are not immune to that same pressure and conservatives would move us much further in that direction.

Canada has evolved with a different capitalism from the United States for a number of reasons. One may be that the origins of our political institutions are different. Parliamentary government evolved from the Crown, whose mandate was to act on behalf of the people. The American congressional system was founded on the fear of government, so, through intricate checks and balances, it was more difficult for government to act. Our history is also different. Canada has been engaged in a nation-building exercise from its inception—a nation of vast distances and a thinly spread population. When Canada was established in 1867 we had a population of only 3.5 million people, and even in 1945 we had just 12.1 million people. This has meant a different role for government, one where government was much more engaged in economic development, from transcontinental railways and electric power utilities to a national airline, a protected national banking system and support for the resource industries. Crown corporations—state capitalism—are a significant part of that story.

The notion of sharing was an important part of Canadian development, given our small population. That has helped Canada remain a united country despite its vast space and distances and the temptation of the United States, and despite linguistic differences and the more recent mix of cultures. All of this has shaped our own form of capitalism and our own ideas on the role of the state. Although the differences should not be exaggerated, there is a Canadian approach that, I would argue, has served us well.

But there is no doubt that the emerging powerhouses among the BRICs—Brazil, Russia, India and China—are changing the global dynamic. This is why we have moved from the G7 to the G20, and this global shift of power is something we will have to get used to—even more so in the years ahead. Moreover, assuming the world is able to work its way out of the crisis (and this includes the U.S. dealing with its huge fiscal, political, social and environmental challenges) and we avoid the traps of protectionism and competing regional trade and currency blocs, then it will not be surprising if the role of Chinese state capitalism also diminishes.

The biggest test for market capitalism moving forward is outlined in *Losing Control: The Emerging Threats to Western Prosperity*, by HSBC chief economist Stephen King. Not only are some of the major western economies facing an extended period of fiscal austerity and stagnant incomes. But as the population and economies of the BRICs grow, these countries will put strong upward pressure on the price of food, energy and minerals so that workers on stagnant incomes and seniors and others in the West on flat incomes may actually experience a decline in living standards.

It is not a happy prospect. Workers in the West will face a world of smaller income gains, pensioners will find life increasingly difficult, and western societies will be forced to sell assets to the BRICs and will lose control of many key industries, King argues. As for today's children, they will be forced to compete for the best jobs against graduates from emerging world universities and to pay high taxes to repay the debts of the current generation. Moreover, governments will have to pay more attention to redistribution; otherwise, popular support for open markets and trade—and other aspects of globalization—will wane, leading to a much uglier world.

Any move to protectionism and other barriers in an effort to defend western interest "might be a vote winner, but it would ultimately be a job-loser," King warns. The experience of the 1930s Great Depression makes that clear. We need the wisdom to recognize that the West will lose in a relative sense, but that is better than the entire world losing in an absolute sense, King concludes. But that means we really need to think through the role of the state and how to make capitalism work for all.

Increasing the risk of protectionism and a slower economic recovery is the emerging threat of a sovereign debt crisis in the western world. In the early 1980s a debt crisis in the developing world sprung forth. In 1997 the Asian financial crisis hit the world, spilling over into Russia and South America and leading to the establishment of the G20 in 1999. Now, we see signs of a rich-world sovereign debt crisis, as a succession of governments face huge fiscal deficits. These have been triggered by the need to respond to the recent financial crisis with rich stimulus packages that led to massive deficits, but this only accelerated a fiscal crisis that would have emerged in the not-too-distant future. The unravelling began in Ireland, spread to Greece and now threatens Spain and Portugal. Greece had to be rescued by its Eurozone partners since it could not raise new funds in financial markets. At the same time, Britain's new coalition government has been forced to embark on what may be the harshest dose of austerity ever experienced by the British in peacetime, with the risk of civil disorder, while Japan's latest government has been forced to recognize that its huge public debt and rapidly aging society will require truly tough measures to correct.

This leaves the United States, where a large budget deficit is sending the debt level soaring while rising costs of social security and health care mean the deficits and accumulating debt could increase through much of the next decade. The U.S. Congressional Budget Office estimates the fiscal deficit in 2010 will equal 9.2 percent of GDP (compared to 3.1 percent in Canada), and this follows a deficit equivalent to 9.6 percent of GDP last year. Moreover, the U.S. has depended on foreign government and other foreign entities to finance 48 percent of its US$8.8 trillion of debt, and this dependence will continue.

The uncertainty arising from the risks of a sovereign debt crisis will make financial markets more skittish, put upward pressure on interest rates, slow the recovery, generate more speculation on the future of the U.S. dollar, risk increased protectionism and make it harder for poorer countries to raise the capital they need. As the U.S. increases its foreign borrowing, it must also increase its payments to foreign creditors. If the U.S. fails to deal with its economic challenges, the fallout would be especially hard on Canada, with new barriers to trade, slower U.S. growth and a collapsing U.S. dollar.

Even without a U.S. fiscal and currency crisis, for Canadians the question is where our country will fit in this difficult new world. What we can say is that it will not be easy. The nature of international competition will become more intense, and Canadians will have to fight much harder for jobs and investment. There will be a continued role, although evolving, for the state in enhancing the knowledge-based economy—research and development, infrastructure, risk sharing in advancing new technologies, education and skills development, and finance. This will not be laissez-faire capitalism or state capitalism but something in between. Social policy will present new challenges. The losers in economic transformation need assurances they will have a place in the future world. Income inequality will be a major challenge, as will dealing with an aging society. We will face both costs and opportunities in dealing with climate change and transforming our energy systems.

The most difficult and crucial decisions will be political. It is in Parliament where we will make the spending choices, design the incentives to ensure that market decisions deliver broader social benefits, pass the laws through which we govern ourselves and determine the nature of the country. Today, too many Canadians look upon Parliament and politicians with disdain. Bright people who are needed in our political life are not participating. Politics has been hijacked by its ugly side of negative advertising and opportunistic actions. At a time when we must grapple with a scale of world change never experienced before and must redefine the future role of the state, our politicians are missing in action. But reinvigorating our political life is our most urgent challenge as we navigate a very different but nonetheless capitalistic world.

DEATH FROM ABOVE: CANADIAN MILITARY QUIETLY PREPS FOR LONGER AFGHAN MISSION

John Duncan
This Magazine

On Monday, November 3, 2008, while on patrol in Afghanistan, near the village of Wech Baghtu in the district of Shah Wali Kot in Kandahar province, international and Afghan pro-government troops came under fire from insurgents. The ground troops called in "close air support," military aircraft that bombard enemy positions—in this particular case, as in most in Afghanistan, U.S. Air Force and Navy jets armed with GPS and laser-guided munitions.

The following day, the U.S. *Air Force Print News* reported that they dropped several 300-kilogram bombs "onto a building where anti-Afghan forces were hunkered down and firing at coalition forces near Kandahar. The mission was confirmed a success."

Approximately 24 hours after the bombing, while most of the world was focussed on election day in the U.S., bombing victims began arriving at the radically under-resourced Mirwais hospital roughly 100 kilometres away in Kandahar City. That was when the story was picked up by Jessica Leeder and Alex Strick van Linschoten for *The Globe & Mail*. Villagers claimed the assault hit a wedding party—which according to local tradition separates women and men for most of the day. Later the United Nations Assistance Mission in Afghanistan (UNAMA) reported that although pro-government sources "claimed that insurgents used villagers' houses to attack the patrol and had infiltrated the wedding-party compound that was bombed.... eyewitnesses and victims interviewed by UNAMA ... strongly denied the presence of any insurgents at the wedding party."

After the attacks, victims reported, international troops took pictures of the carnage, which intimidated and delayed them. Days later, reporting from the hospital for Al Jazeera English, David Chater interviewed Khowrea Horay, a hospitalized 16-year-old, who said: "We ran into the garden when the bombing started, but they bombed us there as well. I suddenly realized my foot was in small pieces. I saw my cousin lying dead next to me, the bodies of my relatives all around me. The Americans ... saw us. They realized we were women. They even shone lights on us, but they kept bombing and their soldiers were firing on us."

Disturbingly, Shah Wali Kot was the second wedding bombing of 2008. Early on July 6, a wedding in Nangarhar province was beginning according to custom with the entire family of the groom escorting the bride from her home to meet the groom at his. While crossing a mountain pass, at least three bombs were dropped on the procession. Despite initial claims to the contrary by U.S. forces, no insurgents and approximately 35 children, nine women, and three men—all civilians—were killed in the attack. On August 22 a bombing strike hit a memorial service in the province of Herat. U.S. forces initially claimed that between five and seven civilians died in that incident, but later video footage seemed to verify local claims that some 90 villagers were killed. Six weeks after the memorial bombing, the U.S. concluded that 33 civilians had died; UNAMA put the toll at 92 civilians, including 62 children.

Soon after Herat, the then commander of international forces in Afghanistan, U.S. General David McKiernan, issued a "tactical directive" to his troops, which amounted to repeating existing orders—notably the requirement to avoid killing civilians whenever possible. Two months later the Kandahar wedding was bombed.

Maimed and left in the blast rubble to mourn at least 37 killed (locals put the death toll at 90), most of them women and children, we may guess what the people of Shah Wali Kot feel about our war in their country, but it is clear that alleging insurgent responsibility, delaying acknowledgment, and understating the number of people killed by airstrikes are tactics aimed at winning our hearts and minds, not theirs.

SUCH DEATH FROM ABOVE, as alarming as it is, involves all pro-government forces, including Canadian forces. The tactic shows every sign of being a fixture of NATO's Afghanistan strategy for years to come, and whatever role they play there after 2011—the withdrawal date our government has pledged to keep—Canadian forces will continue to be involved in it.

Virtually nobody believes that the surge in U.S. troops in Afghanistan begun by President George W. Bush, and twice super-sized by President Barack Obama, will lead to a military victory. The insurgents will continue to use "asymmetrical tactics," or what we used to call guerrilla warfare back when the West was encouraging insurgents to use them—successfully—against Soviet troops in the 1980s.

Because NATO troops must be spread thinly, they often face ambush, and so depend on air superiority—thus far unchallenged—for combat support. Even doubling the number of troops on the ground would do little more than double the number of targets for insurgents. Virtually everyone was in agreement with the commander of NATO forces in southern Afghanistan, Dutch General Mart de Kruif, early in spring 2009, when he warned that "a significant spike" in violence would follow the first part of the surge. However, the General's prediction that it would be "planting the seeds" for "a significant increase in the security situation across southern Afghanistan next year" is not panning out. On average, NATO airstrikes killed a civilian every day during 2009, admittedly an improvement over 2008 when the average was more than 10 per week, but civilian deaths rose 14 percent overall in 2009, and pro-government forces were responsible for a full quarter of them. During the Iraq surge and counter-insurgency reorientation in 2007—the model currently being implemented in Afghanistan—both civilian deaths caused by pro-government forces overall and those caused specifically by airstrikes spiked radically, so it is unlikely that civilian deaths will decrease in Afghanistan anytime soon.

The problem is that while commanders know airstrikes kill Afghan civilians, the mission is impossible without close air support. A declassified Pentagon report on a May 4, 2009, bombing in Farah province that killed 86 civilians (according to the Afghan Independent Human Rights Commission) determined the strikes happened despite the fact commanders could not "confirm the presence or absence of civilians" in the targeted village buildings, and this "inability" was "inconsistent with the U.S. Government's objective of providing security and safety for the Afghan people."

The implication is that in cases of such an inability, bombs ought not to be dropped. In fact, on July 2, 2009, the new commander of international forces in Afghanistan, U.S. General Stanley McChrystal, issued yet another tactical directive to international troops in Afghanistan, calling for a "cultural shift": "Commanders must weigh the gain of using ... [close air support] against the cost of civilian casualties.... The use of air-to-ground munitions ... against residential compounds is only authorized under very limited and prescribed conditions." This is but one element in the massive reorientation McChrystal is calling for. Charged with turning the mission around, he is attempting to change it from an anti-insurgency to a counterinsurgency operation, which requires winning the support of the population as much as killing Taliban. The stakes are high. In his August 2009 report, written eight years into the war, McChrystal wrote: "Failure to gain the initiative and reverse insurgent momentum in the ... next 12 months ... risks an outcome where defeating the insurgency is no longer possible." However, in the case of the Farah bombing (again, according to the declassified report), the ground force commander concluded that a particular group of individuals "presented an imminent threat to his force." It is inconceivable in such a case, where an "imminent threat" to pro-government troops is perceived, that the possibility of harming civilians would override the decision to call in an airstrike. Whenever troops are in perceived danger, close air support will continue to be used whether or not the presence of civilians can be confirmed, resulting inevitably in civilian deaths.

ON DECEMBER 5, 2001, while President Bush was signing into effect a law to make every December 7 a day to honour the fallen of Pearl Harbor, Hamid Karzai, now Afghanistan's president, "and a few dozen Afghan fighters, along with U.S. Special Forces advisers, were in a village called Shah Wali Kot"—the capital of the district by the same name. According to a sympathetic book on Karzai, written by Nick B. Mills, who was granted extensive interviews with the new Afghan President during the fall of 2005, Karzai was almost killed by a 900-kilogram satellite-guided bomb that morning, dropped by U.S. forces. Among the many casualties, five of Karzai's most experienced men and three U.S. servicemen were killed—the first U.S. soldiers to be killed in combat during the war. Initial coverage of this friendly-fire incident that almost killed Karzai himself was severely censored to manage perceptions at home. While Karzai, sitting blood-spattered amongst the rubble, received phone calls confirming the Taliban's surrender and naming him Afghanistan's interim president, the Pentagon and U.S. military officials near Kandahar prevented journalists from reporting the incident. According to the Committee to Protect Journalists: "Journalists from 11 U.S. news organizations," including CBS News, CNN, *Newsweek*, and *The New York Times*, "were confined to a warehouse while injured soldiers were transferred to the base for treatment. That night, the journalists were pulled out of Afghanistan altogether." From the beginning, close air support, its seemingly unavoidable and murderous consequences, and the urge to manage its public perception, have been essential features of this war.

SHAH WALI KOT ITSELF, with a population estimated at less than 40,000, is one of the districts with which the Canadian mission has struggled. The district, under Canadian jurisdiction for more than four years, is a microcosm of Afghanistan as a whole, with which the entire international mission has struggled for more than eight years. In late 2006, when the focus on Iraq still eclipsed Afghanistan, Sam Kiley, a correspondent for PBS *Frontline World*, travelled to NATO's forward operating base (FOB) Martello, a formidable outpost built by Canadians earlier that year, to make a documentary called *Afghanistan: The Other War*. FOB Martello is located near the main road that connects Kandahar City to Tarin Kot in the province of Uruzgan to the north. Travelling from Kandahar City to FOB Martello—a distance of not much more than 200 kilometres—the road runs near the district capital of Shah Wali Kot, past the Arghandab River reservoir behind the Dahla Dam (the restoration of which is one of Canada's major development projects in the area), by the village of Wech Baghtu, to the tiny village of El Bak (where FOB Martello is located), and then out of both Shah Wali Kot district and Kandahar province toward Tarin Kot in Uruzgan. Kiley's reporting provides a rare candid look at the 120 Canadian troops stationed at FOB Martello. Their attempts to fight the insurgency, and especially to win the hearts and minds of the 30 families of El Bak, continually come up short, and usually because of very minor obstacles—for example, the inability to come up with what would be a few tens of dollars worth of sparkplugs in Canada. Along with soldiers' blogs, Kevin Patterson and Jane Warren's *Outside the Wire*, a collection of first-hand accounts by Canadians on the ground in Afghanistan, illustrates the same frustrating difficulty over and over again: asymmetrical war in an impoverished region makes mountains of molehills.

On April 22, 2006, four Canadian soldiers were killed near the Gumbad Platoon House, a Canadian outpost on another road running north from Kandahar City through Shah Wali Kot. That day General Rick Hillier talked with reporters about Canadian efforts to establish footholds in the area: "Shah Wali Kot is the area for a significant period of time, without question. The locals are absolutely ecstatic … that we are there," he said. "Things are actually changing on the ground."

Changeability became the dominant characteristic of the Canadian presence there: Within months, the new Gumbad outpost had been abandoned because Canadian troops were needed nearer to Kandahar City. While Kiley was still filming at FOB Martello, the troops were ordered to pull out there, too, in order to move closer to Kandahar City, abandoning the people of El Bak to the insurgents who very likely would punish them for working with the Canadians in the first place. Almost as quickly as they began, Canadian efforts to secure Shah Wali Kot, as well as other regions of Kandahar province, were largely abandoned in order to deal with formidable insurgent offensives closer to Kandahar City. According to the *Globe & Mail*'s Graeme Smith, a detailed U.S. security assessment made available to the newspaper in July 2008 concluded that Shah Wali Kot had fallen back under Taliban control.

In early 2008, Canadian forces began moving up the road in the direction of El Bak again to put together the hundreds of massive squat cement slabs called Texas Barriers for a new FOB about 70 kilometres north of Kandahar City. FOB Frontenac, nicknamed "FOB Fabulous," apparently for its scenery and food, is located near the Dahla dam in order to provide security for the $50-million Canadian signature development project: repairing the massive, decaying dam

facility. Recommended by the January 2008 report of the Independent Panel on Canada's Future Role in Afghanistan,
chaired by former Liberal cabinet minister John Manley,
"signature" projects are supposed to be genuine development
projects that double as great symbols that ramp up the message that Canada really is in Afghanistan to help— the hope
being this will win hearts and minds in a war zone. The three-
year Dahla project was announced in June 2008 just as FOB
Frontenac was completed. The main prize at Dahla is not
electricity, but rather an extensive irrigation system with the
potential to quench fertile but thirsty land in the Shah Wali
Kot, Daman, Arghandab, and Panjwaii districts, as well as
Kandahar City itself, serving 80 percent of the population
of Kandahar province. Ongoing silting in the reservoir has
reduced its capacity by perhaps 30 percent, the valves and
gates that manage water-flow are no longer working, much of
the canal system downstream requires restoration work, and
there have been years of drought. The quantity of water in the
reservoir and the control and delivery of its outflow have been
so reduced the reservoir now irrigates well under half the territory it could reach. The goal seems to be to have the system
back up and running by the 2011 end-date for the Canadian
military mission in Afghanistan.

Another dam being restored by NATO about 100 kilometres
west of Dahla is the Kajaki dam on the Helmand river—a project
which has faced serious insurgency attacks. Back in June 2008,
when the Dahla project was announced, reported predictions
were mixed about whether or not it would attract insurgent
activity. During the first few months of 2009, before the prime
minister's surprise visit, five Canadians were killed and 14
injured in the area, presumably working on or near the dam
or travelling to and from the FOB: on January 7, Trooper
Brian Richard Good was killed (with three other soldiers

wounded); on March 8, Trooper Marc Diab was killed (four wounded); on March 20, Troopers Corey Joseph Hayes and Jack Bouthillier were killed (three wounded); and on April 13, Trooper Karine Blais was killed (four wounded).

In each of these cases, as well as the incident that killed the four soldiers near Gumbad in 2006, improvised explosive devices (IEDs) did the killing. Because IEDs may be both concealed in the road when no troops are around, and remotely detonated, insurgents can use them to inflict significant losses without risking direct combat with technologically superior pro-government forces. To grasp the essential role of IEDs in Afghanistan it helps to look at the asymmetrical situation abstractly: (a) the insurgency meets superior progovernment forces on the ground, and is outmatched; (b) the insurgency adapts by avoiding direct combat and by adopting hit-and-run, ambush tactics; (c) pro-government forces respond with close air support, making guerrilla tactics much more dangerous, and so less effective; (d) the insurgency adapts by devoting resources to IED attacks. In the U.S. Marine Corps' September 2005 manual *Improvised Explosive Device Defeat*, it is acknowledged that IEDs are a weapon of choice for insurgents in asymmetrical warfare. The intervention of "technologically superior forces" in a region is likely to be met with "adaptive approaches," such as IED use, which "in selected niche areas" may "achieve equality or even overmatch" superior forces. Manufacturing, planting, targeting and detonating scores of IEDs, and evading technologically advanced counter-IED measures, is no easy matter, but increasingly it is the tactic of choice for insurgents in Afghanistan for whom combat against technologically superior forces and the death they hurl down from above is uselessly suicidal. Death from below the road surface, according to Canada's counter-IED task force established in June 2007, is now "the single largest threat to [Canadian Forces] personnel in Afghanistan."

Canadian troops have almost every technological advantage over Afghan insurgents, from portable high-trajectory smart-artillery cannons that can hit precise targets 40 kilometres away to the ability to call in U.S. airstrikes. U.S. Defence Secretary Robert Gates has told journalists that "between 40 and 45 percent of the close-air-support missions ... are flown in support of our allies and partners," so while it is a U.S. plane dropping the bomb, it is often Canadian troops selecting the targets. Virtually all pro-government forces in the country have been using, and will continue to use, the close air support largely provided by the U.S. military; without it, they would be sitting ducks. Despite the fact that Canadian Defence Ministry officials call IED attacks "cowardly," the insurgent response to advanced weapons systems and close air support will not be to "stand and fight"—which would be absurd. The response will be, and is, the IED.

One of the reasons that motivated Pentagon insider Daniel Ellsberg to leak in 1971 the massive secret documentary record of U.S. policies in Vietnam, was that although the senior administration knew an indefinite commitment of U.S. air support was required in Vietnam, President Richard Nixon talked publicly about winning and ending the conflict. These days, Ellsberg points out, the official spin on the war in "Vietnamistan" is similarly troubling.

The pattern of hit-and-run guerrilla attacks met by overwhelming aerial bombardment, leading to improvised roadside bombs, is bound to repeat indefinitely. While Canada's Afghan mission is currently slated to end in 2011, virtually every analyst expects some kind of Canadian military presence long after. One possible scenario is that Canada reduces its ground troop commitment and takes to the skies, turning from a force that calls in airstrikes to one that flies them—as it did in the 1999 NATO bombing campaign in the former Yugoslavia. For example, in a March 26, 2009, *National Post* story, Matthew Fisher and Mike Blanchfield wrote: "Canada's combat forces are slated to leave Afghanistan sometime in 2011. It is widely expected that they will be replaced by a smaller force that may include helicopters, police and army trainers, a provincial reconstruction team and, Canada's fighter pilot community hopes, CF18 Hornet attack aircraft." Indeed, according to the director of the international air campaign in Afghanistan, who happens to be the Canadian Gen. Duff Sullivan, who has a long and distinguished career as a fighter pilot and commander (including the Yugoslavia campaign), and who was called the "air czar" by the former commander of international forces in Afghanistan, there are requests from mission headquarters in Afghanistan to bring in Canada's Hornets before 2011. There is also lobbying at home to "send in the Hornets," as former chief of defense staff and retired general Paul Mason urged in an *Ottawa Citizen* op-ed in January.

This year, the Canadian Air Force is due to complete a C$2.1 billion, two-stage, mega-upgrade program for the fleet of Hornets, and a short Department of National Defence video on the Canadian Army website, entitled "Close Air Support: A service to ground troops," has Maj. Scott Greenough explain: "Certainly ... the Canadian fighter force ... has turned its training emphasis onto close air support in the event that we would deploy to Kandahar, let's say, in Afghanistan to support the troops on the ground with close air support ... It's become a huge part of the fighter force training element ... Close air support is basically our training emphasis right now." Is Canada preparing to replace its ground troop contingent in Afghanistan with CF-18 Hornets? It is still too soon to tell, but preparations have been made. Whether or not Canada plays a role in Afghanistan after 2011, security will remain a mission priority. Because security in Afghanistan will depend on close air support for the foreseeable future, Canada would therefore continue to be involved in the murder of Afghan civilians after 2011.

IN A FAMOUS INTERVIEW FROM JANUARY 1998, Zbigniew Brzezinski, national security adviser to U.S. President Jimmy Carter, said "we knowingly increased the probability" that the U.S.S.R. would invade Afghanistan, which "had the effect of drawing the Russians into the Afghan trap.

"The day that the Soviets officially crossed the border, I wrote to President Carter. We now have the opportunity of giving to the U.S.S.R. its Vietnam War. Indeed, for almost 10 years, Moscow had to carry on a war unsupportable by the government, a conflict that brought about the demoralization and finally the breakup of the Soviet empire."

For the foreseeable future, Canada is going to be in Afghanistan trying to evade IEDs and either calling in close air support missions or flying them. Whether the threat is airstrikes from above, or improvised explosive devices from below, the "Afghan trap" has lured in a new set of victims.

THE YEAR CHRISTMAS CAME TO THE ARCTIC

Randy Freeman
Up Here

When Santa Claus appeared in the doorway of the trading post, the Inuit children screamed in terror. They covered their faces and huddled behind their parents, horrified by the fat, bizarrely-dressed *qallunaaq* in the overgrown beard. Even the adults backed away. For the Kogluktogmiut, this was their first encounter with Father Christmas, and it wasn't going well.

Introducing Santa to the Inuit of the Central Arctic had been the idea of a young Scottish physician named Ian McKay, who was one of just a handful of *qallunaat* who spent Christmas of 1929 at Fort Hearne. The tiny outpost—later renamed Coppermine, and now the bustling community of Kugluktuk—is in the Barrenlands of western Nunavut, where the winters are long, dark and lonely. McKay wasn't thrilled about being stuck there for the holidays, but he'd decided to make the most of it.

A newcomer to Fort Hearne, McKay had come up that summer to run the hospital—a facility that, along with the Hudson Bay post, wireless radio station and Anglican and Catholic missions, formed a beachhead of civilization in the polar wilderness. McKay knew the holidays would be bleak for his fellow white men (there were no *qallunaat* women at Fort Hearne). He also knew that during Christmas, the churches would summon the nomadic Inuit from hundreds of mile around, seeking to convert them. McKay hoped he could also share with them the more secular joys of the Yuletide, and have fun with the *qallunaat* as well.

To do this, he'd planned ahead. For his trip north, McKay had packed not only trunkloads of medical gear, but also small toys, candy, Christmas decorations and even the ingredients for plum pudding. He looked forward to decorating a spruce tree, exchanging gifts and introducing the Inuit to Kris Kringle—that most famous of Northerners, who flew through the air in a sleigh pulled by magic caribou.

As December set in, though, finding a spruce tree was a challenge. Fort Hearne was above the treeline, and the closest spruce was dozens of kilometres south, along the banks of the Coppermine River. Being unfamiliar with Arctic travel, McKay needed an Inuk who, for a few dollars, would take a dog team and go hunting—not for a caribou, but for a spruce the perfect size and shape to be a Christmas tree.

There should be a bronze plaque dedicated to that intrepid Inuk, but no one bothered to record his name. However, he apparently succeeded, returning after several days with the ideal tree. It didn't take long for McKay to put it up in his house and decorate it. Then he called all the white men of Fort Hearne to gather around. Gazing at that festive tree, their gloom seemed to dissolve. The Christmas spirit overtook them.

Suddenly, plans were hatched to make this the best holiday season the settlement had seen. The radio operators not only started to organize a special Christmas dinner, but also baked batch after batch of cookies for the incoming Inuit. With these, they said, they'd lure the Inuit to the colourfully decorated radio shack and surprise them with the latest *qallunaat* inventions. To that end, they hooked up a string of electric lights—cutting-edge technology at the time. Better yet, they ran a secret wire to the nearby generator shed, hid a microphone inside, and plotted a special announcement.

By Christmas Eve, the sea ice in front of Fort Hearne was dotted with igloos. The Inuit began making their rounds to the various homes and buildings, where they were given hardtack and tea. As they approached the radio shack for the cookies they'd been told about, the signal was given. A switch was thrown and Fort Hearne's first electric lights pierced the Arctic night.

The glowing bulbs attracted a crowd of Inuit onlookers, who whispered about what they saw. Then a spokesperson emerged from the crowd and, through the Hudson's Bay Company interpreter, proclaimed that the lights were no big deal. The Kogluktogmiut, he said, had shamans who could fly to the moon. By comparison, putting a spark in a glass bulb was a simple stunt.

So the radio operators tried another trick. They ushered the Inuit into the radio shack and turned the radio on, tuning it to a New York station. Festive dance tunes filled the room. The Inuit smiled, yet they declared they were still not impressed. This, they felt, was just a different kind of gramophone—a device with which they were familiar.

But then the music stopped, replaced by a human voice. It spoke in Inuktitut, greeting every Inuk by name. At this, finally, the Inuit were impressed. Still, they weren't dumb. The voice sounded familiar and, after a brief discussion, a young man went to the receiver and followed its wires out the door. He traced it to the nearby generator shed, where the Hudson's Bay interpreter sat speaking into the microphone. The jig was up.

Amused by this strange *qallunaat* holiday, and by the clever *qallunaat* devices, the Inuit walked back to their igloos talking excitedly about what wonders Christmas morning would bring. They were not disappointed.

The next day, when the sky brightened to a faint glow, everyone at Fort Hearne gathered for Christmas services. Then all of them—white and Inuit, Anglican and Catholic—headed to McKay's house for the big party.

The centrepiece of the house, of course, was the elaborately decorated Christmas tree. There was candy for the children and tea and platters of cookies for the adults. Every room was filled with laughter. Then the door swung open, in burst Santa Claus, and all the holiday cheer came screeching to a halt.

As the children screamed and ran, the adults reached for the knives they kept tucked in their caribou clothing. The situation remained tense until the interpreter stepped forward to explain. This, he said, was Santa Claus: a benevolent white man who lived at the North Pole, flew through the sky in a *qamutiq* pulled by *tuktu*, and was making a special visit to give them gifts.

After a brief silence the Inuit began to laugh. Flying caribou! The idea was hilarious—and clearly, the way Santa was dressed, he could never survive at the North Pole! This was just another *qallunaat* joke. A child pulled off Santa's fake beard and everyone had another laugh. Undaunted, the barefaced Santa doled out gifts, the radio was dialed to more dance tunes, and, in McKay's festive little house in the middle of the Arctic, everyone kicked up their heels.

NOTES TOWARDS AN ESSAY ABOUT MARIA CALLAS

———————

C.E. Gatchalian
Ricepaper

My journal entry, dated April 5, 1994:
"Homosexuality = shamanism = the cho*sen* = *an-tennae of the world.*" Further down: "*Art points skyward, defies nature, transcends the muck. It is, without question, the highest human faculty.*" Anthropology and Camille Paglia nudging a Filipino gay boy towards self-acceptance. The ego consolidation of a newly out sophomore. But despite a new-found Buddhist emphasis on ego-devaluation, those ideas are still with me, still motor my daily existence.

I want to write an essay about Maria Callas, the greatest operatic soprano of the twentieth century. Most modern classical music stars dwell in rarefied peaks, free from the glare of the masses, subjects of esoteric study. Maria Callas was an exception. She was a pre-Stonewall icon, the gay cultural intelligentsia's Judy Garland. To adore Callas in the twenty-first century is to retreat. Regress. Which is why I want to write this essay: to remember a fabled, war-torn time.

The essay I want to write is about adoration and inertia.

LA BOHEME WAS MY FAVOURITE OPERA once upon a time but I eventually tired of it, coming to see it as "opera lite." But surfing Youtube two years ago I happened across an audio recording of Mimi's Act One aria, rendered by Maria Callas, a singer I'd never particularly cared for. Her voice emerges from my laptop—that hard-to-describe, naked sound that has always divided opinion. Two and a half minutes in, the aria swells towards its high point: *Ma quando vien lo sgelo, il primo sole mio.* The simple, virginal Mimi singing of how spring's first kiss is hers. Callas and orchestra in perfect synchronicity as the world, for a moment, lifts the veils from sensuality and a stodgy, effete art form becomes a container for living truth. I've listened to more renowned Mimis—Tebaldi, Scotto, Stratas—but none achieve the miracle that Callas pulls off. I'm not hyperbolizing when I call my Callas moment one of existential clarity, when my east met my west, when all came to librium.

So began my personal study—one undertaken, so it seems, by many other gay men—of the life and art of Maria Callas: ugly duckling, musical genius. The narrative of her life, informed by egomania, willpower, metamorphosis, sexual frustration and fulfillment, and finally tragedy, is undeniably queer: the lonely outsider who pays the price for professional and personal acceptance. But the most efficient manifestation of her queerness is her art, a masterpiece drawn from imperfection, insecurity, and a bit of hate.

Callas' voice takes me inside myself and out again—the exact opposite of what happens when I listen to a more conventionally beautiful voice. The latter is escapism—a fireworks display from which I return unchanged. The Callas voice is too flawed, too human for escape: the dark, eerie timbre; the ferocious, almost manly chest tones; the bottled middle register; the forced and wobbly high notes (especially later in her career) were the musical equivalents of her personal flaws and, in turn, mine. Tito Gobbi christened her "La grande vociaccia"—the Great Ugly Voice; but it was ugliness contained in the most refined and exquisite musicianship. The impeccable diction; the flawless weighing of every note; the silken fioriture; the perfectly placed *portamenti*—what was great was not the voice but rather what she did with it.

It was, in short, a voice from the closet.

You know the story—he's bullied and ostracized. So the young gay boy retreats to be the best at whatever he's good at. Not the best he can be, but the best, period. Just as society invokes "objective standards" in condemning his burgeoning sexuality, so the young gay boy invokes them in his quest for perfection. Callas attracts a lot of gay men because she's the best, period. And she became the very best despite a bevy of disadvantages: a broken home, a difficult mother, an ungainly figure, and a seemingly untameable voice. In *The Queen's Throat*, his brilliant and now-legendary paean to opera, Wayne Koestenbaum writes, "The listener's body is illuminated, opened up: a singer doesn't expose her own throat, she exposes the listener's interior." When I listen to Callas, every trill, every cadenza becomes a journey out of the dregs, a manifestation of her personal triumphs and by extension, mine. In her unflinching artistry I see my own obsessive-compulsive perfectionism; in her astonishing mid-career weight loss, my metamorphosis from willowy geek to muscle-bound quasi-Adonis.

As a young gay boy I was shy and artsy, and while I managed to escape physical bullying, back-talk and exclusion were inevitable. Scholastic excellence was my weapon, as was success as a classical pianist (which lessened the trauma of my teenage years by significantly abridging my school schedule, including exemption from P.E.). Egos that are mutilated eventually balloon, and for most of my life it's been egomania that's gotten me up in the morning, a narcissistic search for vengeance against a world that I was convinced was against me. (Therapy and meditation are doing their job, I'm happy to report.)

I adore Callas because she avenges on my behalf. The Greek-American fat girl-become-svelte prima donna of La Scala. Each diamond-pointed gruppeto, every sweeping arpeggio, is an act of revenge against gay bashers, against all who ever crossed me. Indeed, Callas' own words—"We [artists] must whip ourselves into shape like a soldier," and "I would not kill my enemies, but I will make them get down on their knees," suggest a militaristic, score-settling approach to her craft.

Her 1949 career-breakthrough was one of the queerest events in twentieth century opera. While performing Brunnhilde in Wagner's *Die Walkure* she was asked, on a few days' notice, to fill in for a sick colleague who was to sing Elvira in Bellini's *I puritani*—a part Callas had never before performed. She opened as Elvira to an incredulous audience. To perform, back-to-back, the heavy verticality of a Wagner opera and the florid horizontalness of a bel canto one was an unheard of feat—akin, almost, to a skater speed-skating one week and figure-skating the next. This was Callas at her

queerest—doing the unthinkable, defying categories. Breaking the seemingly impenetrable wall between the dramatic
repertoire and the coloratura one, Callas—despite her self-
declared aesthetic conservatism—was a bona fide postmodern opera star: a convention-busting, boundary-blurring
sui generis.

There is, also, the curious quality of Callas' sexual persona. There was an affected, contrived quality to her famously
genteel way of moving and speaking, a quality undercut by
the unaffectedly fierce, "masculine" manner in which she approached her work. Unlike her alleged archrival, the musi-
cally demure and unthreatening Renata Tebaldi, Callas attacked the music with a decisiveness normally associated
with male singers. The end result was a compellingly solip-
sistic persona, hermaphroditic, self-completing, narcissistic.

And there is the story of Maria the woman, whose nun-like
devotion to her calling ended, for all intents and purposes,
when she met shady Greek shipping magnate Aristotle Onassis. The virginal high priestess of opera had lived most of her
life in her throat; the extraordinarily sexual Onassis opened
her up to the rest of her body, a body she'd hated, even when
she lost weight; a body that, for most of her life, nobody had
ever wanted.

My journal entry, dated August 7, 2000:

> "*Went the full nine yards, finally. Pure, total
> blandishment. That a man like D, with his manliness,
> his Greekness, his swagger, would want me, with my
> awkwardness, my Filipino-ness, my inexperience.
> He's a collector, yes; I was willing to be collected. My
> first real man; he left me a bit more of one.*"

OPERA IS PREMODERN, steeped in the past, home to myth, old-style melodrama and stereotypical notions of sex and gender. When I embrace opera I am embracing a world that shunned me, thereby accepting the beast and consequently disembowelling it. If opera remains popular, even outside gaydom, it has little to do with the inner (i.e. plotlines) and almost everything to do with the outer (i.e. the music, the staging).

When gay men love Callas, they are embracing premodernism while queering it up royally. For she drags hidden human truths out of sexist, archaic stories—out of the effete, rococo, centuries-old closet that is opera. Absolute honesty is queer; notions of normalcy are always relative. Callas simultaneously embraced the norms of bel canto singing and broke through them to illuminate the only reality that ultimately counts: human emotion. She was the most profoundly gifted vocal artist of her century, one whose polychromatic voice could encapsulate every nuance and sub-nuance of feeling. There is no irony in Callas-philia, as there is with Garland-philia or Monroe-philia; when gays align themselves with Callas, they align themselves with greatness. But it is greatness haunted by the omnipresence of the abyss, by intimations of what can and, in Callas' case, did go wrong. The great Callas scholar John Ardoin likens the experience of listening to Callas to watching a trapeze act. Usually there is a net below; but on those rare instances where there is not, a completely different atmosphere is created. "The very being of each spectator seems to be bound up in each step taken on high," says Ardoin, "for there is no longer any semblance of pretence."

Callas vocal fall was legendary, ugly. Her hard-won artistic victories were Pyrrhic—unequalled greatness for a too-brief time. Pushing her voice beyond its natural Fach, tackling the most technically intimidating repertoire, giving every ounce of herself to each and every performance, she seemed constitutionally incapable of performing with a net. And while this cost Callas her voice (her career was essentially over by age forty-two) it is what gave her singing its abyss-defying, life-and-death intensity. "Singing for me is not an act of pride, but an effort to elevate toward those heavens where everything is harmony," she once said. But she could never escape the abyss—indeed, she seemed always to be staring it down. Her singing, even at its most technically brilliant, never sounded easy, the way the vocalizing of her great bel canto rivals Sutherland and Caballé did. It always carried with it a knowledge of the fragility of greatness—and of the unspeakable horrors that lurk beneath it.

"DEATH—THE OPPOSITE... IS DESIRE," says Blanche in Tennessee Williams' 1947 masterwork *A Streetcar Named Desire*—a startlingly prophetic précis of the late twentieth century gay male experience, defined as it was by the polarities of erotic fulfillment and deadly disease. Physical love—in the face of sordid, mythopoeically ladenfatality, became even more intense, more transcendent—an act of ecstatic defiance against the ever-present threat of death.

Indeed, early death is the final italicization of gay-icon status. Callas died at age fifty-three in her Paris apartment, *sola, perduta, abbandonata*. Onassis, the love of her life, had left her for Jackie Kennedy; and her final world tour betrayed a voice in irrevocable ruins. From *la dolce vita* and unprecedented heights of operatic artistry she had come to this—a recluse wasting away on Quaaludes and memories of a once-glorious voice. Apparently on her deathbed she had never looked lovelier or more immaculate: undimmed beauty even in her darkest moment. As it was will that allowed her to achieve artistic greatness and physical beauty, it was will that propelled her to her early, quiet death—if not technically a suicide, then a perfectly paced winding down. To die beautiful and young is in concord with gaydom's cult of youth, with that familiar refrain of the vain club bunny, "Who wants to die an old queen?"

La grande vocaccia. The ugly voice become the instrument of the century's sublimest operatic expression. To mould beauty out of ugliness is the queerest of acts. From the channelling of deviancy into the creation of polychrome frescoes to the transmuting of HIV-positive statuses into marks of desirability, gay men are often expert alchemists, reliant on magic to survive. In the magic of Callas' music we see the sanctioned version of our own all-too-private narratives, our own tortuous, ferociously willed ascents to greatness. Whether these ascents are actualized or merely dreamt of is moot; Callas reminds us that, no matter how brilliant we make ourselves or how accessible become the corridors of power, disaster is always just a stone throw away.

ALAS, THESE ARE ONLY NOTES TOWARDS AN ESSAY. To actually write one would be to regress completely to an age of masks, when passion was sublimated, when brilliance was borne of suffering. When we revered the likes of Callas because there was no out and proud icon to revere. When we fed off hetero-normativity and built a parasitic culture out of parody and pastiche.

To align with Callas is to align with pre-Stonewall gays, the closet-dwelling, aesthetic types gays my age were supposed to have left behind. But I am attracted to the closet, cannot and will not leave it completely. For in it survive narratives whose universality not even postmodernism, with its rejection of the universal, can wish away. Narratives that will remain relevant as long as gays are a numerical anomaly. A space of shared experiences from which emerges the beautiful.

These love-notes to Callas, then, are love-notes to the closet, a place that inhibited action but that ignited imagination. Where unassuaged pain and suffering were catalysts for great art. Where a voice as queer as Maria Callas' could be called beautiful.

WHAT THE ELEPHANTS KNOW

Nicholas Hune-Brown
Toronto Life

On the morning of November 30, at around 7:45, three keepers entered the elephant enclosure at the Toronto Zoo to begin their daily routine. The elephants live on a dusty one-hectare tract of land with huge umbrellas for shade and three simulated termite mounds. During winter, they spend their nights in a concrete building with a corrugated roof, a poured rubber floor and metal bars as thick as tree trunks. That morning, the keepers were greeted with an alarming sight. Tara, the 41-year-old matriarch of the group, was on her side, unable to get up.

Most elephants can't lie on their sides for extended pe-
riods of time—their sheer mass puts too much pressure on
their internal organs—so zoo staff immediately began trying
to raise her. Getting into the pen with an elephant is dangerous work—one elephant gored a keeper in 1993. But there
wasn't much time, and the team was desperate.

The eight staff who tend to the elephants had agreed that
they wanted to be called in if one of their charges ever went
down, and soon off-duty keepers were rushing down to the
enclosure to help out or, more likely, to say goodbye. The
African animal supervisor, Eric Cole, a 30-year zoo veteran
with short-cropped hair and the remnants of an Irish brogue,
had had some success coaxing fallen elephants back to their
feet in the past. At first, Tara swiped angrily at the keepers
with her trunk. She eventually calmed down, allowing Cole
and his team to get straps underneath her. Using a winch,
they raised the 3,800-kilogram animal to her sternum. Tara
struggled. She managed to lift her hind legs but wasn't able
to pull her front legs under her. Keepers tried a few more
times to raise her, but she wouldn't budge. At around 11
that morning, Tara died. "She didn't appear to have the will,"
recalled Maria Franke, curator of mammals. "It's like she decided to let go."

The keepers were devastated. "It was pretty shattering,"
Cole told me. "Everyone was just drained; the staff was all
crying." They brought Tara's body out to the paddock so that
the other elephants, Thika, Toka and Iringa, could mourn
her. Elephants are highly social animals, and females live in
tight-knit groups their entire lives. When an elephant, particularly the matriarch, dies in the wild, the loss can reverber-
ate for months or even years. There are stories of elephants
returning to the bones of a family member years after the

death, rubbing their trunks along the teeth of the skull's lower jaw in the same way they greet one another in life.

Tara had to be autopsied, so mourning could last only a few hours. The zoo's remaining elephants—animals who lived with Tara for decades—straddled her and stroked her skin. They used their trunks to throw dirt on her. At the end of the day, keepers transported Tara and brought the rest of the elephants back inside for the night. Because the elephants don't always get along, they are often kept in separate pens and spend the night apart. When keepers arrived the next morning, however, they found all the elephant dung piled close to the connecting corners of their respective pens. The three elephants—the final members of a haphazardly formed family group that had once been eight—had spent that night huddled together, as close to one another as possible.

Two days later, the Toronto Zoo was quiet, empty save for a few groups of teenagers playing hooky and a handful of daycare kids who toddled past the simulated Serengeti bush camp toward the empty Africa Restaurant (a Harvey's and a Pizza Pizza outlet in a jungle-themed pavilion). It was a bright, unseasonably warm day, and most of the animals were in their outdoor display areas: tigers stretching out in the sunny section of their Indo-Malaya enclosure, muddy-looking polar bears in the new Tundra Trek area, a group of impalas and kudu blinking in a broad pasture, indifferent to the intruding raccoon and flock of Canada geese that compromised the verisimilitude of their savannah habitat.

At the African elephant exhibit, the mood was sombre. A young zookeeper in gumboots and khakis told me that she'd had an emotional few days. "We look after these animals eight hours a day," she said. "We become close." Since Tara's death, the elephants had been unusually subdued, keeping near to one another, acting tentative. Thika, a 30-year-old female, stood motionless under one of the large wooden umbrellas, one foot cocked at the ankle. In the stillness, you could hear the swish of her trunk as she rubbed it over her rough body, over her head, over her ears, over her eyes.

That day, in a quiet spot in the Rouge Valley on the other side of the 290-hectare zoo, staff were burying Tara. The autopsy had proven inconclusive—no one would ever know the exact cause of death. Still, the incident presented an unpleasant public relations problem. Tara's death was the fourth elephant fatality in four years at the zoo, and it set off a storm of criticism. Zoocheck Canada, an organization dedicated to monitoring wild animals in captivity, demanded that Toronto shut down its elephant exhibit. The advocacy group In Defense of Animals rated Toronto the second worst zoo for elephants in North America (a ranking based mainly on newspaper reports). Joyce Poole, a noted elephant expert who has studied the animals in the wild for more than 30 years, wrote a letter to city councillors arguing that the zoo is unable to provide the warm climate, opportunities for social interaction with other elephants, and space to roam that the huge land animals require. The four elephants that died were all around 40 years old; in the wild, elephants can live 15 to 20 years longer. "Toronto," Poole wrote, "is no place for elephants." Tara's death leaves the Toronto Zoo with just three elephants, the minimum recommended by the Association of Zoos and Aquariums, and puts it in a tough position: either press forward with the elephant enclosure despite the negative attention, or close one of its most popular exhibits.

The controversy couldn't have come at a worse time. The zoo's CEO, Cal White, after 23 years in charge, retired four months before Tara died. Before White left, he declared the zoo's fundraising capabilities inadequate and cut ties to the volunteer foundation that had been attached to the zoo for 34 years. The zoo is owned by the City of Toronto, which doles out about a quarter of the institution's $45-million budget each year. White planned an ambitious 10-year, $250-million fundraising initiative—a haul that's required to improve various animal habitats, build a new animal health centre and create new exhibits—but didn't believe the zoo's foundation was capable of handling the challenge. Two of the board's members—city councillors Mike del Grande and Michael Thompson—quit in protest of White's scheme. Since that time, the fundraising has been done in house, and John Tracogna, the former head of Ontario Place, has replaced White as CEO.

At this moment of transition, the death of Tara—the last surviving member of the original trio of elephants brought to Toronto in 1974—marked the end of an era. The zoo is no longer the forwardlooking institution it was when Tara arrived. The monorail is gone, closed after a serious accident in 1994, and though there are some impressive new exhibits, including the new tundra area, many of the other enclosures are beginning to show their age. Something else has changed, too. In the years since the Toronto Zoo opened, the way we think about our relationship to the natural world has undergone a serious transformation. As scientists learn more about the intelligence of certain animals, the complexities of their socialization, and the depths of their emotion (a word that would have been dismissed as flagrant anthropomorphism a few decades ago), the business of keeping wild animals in captivity has come under scrutiny. The modern zoo is in many ways an anachronistic creation, a Victorian institution that has been awkwardly remodelled to fit the contemporary age, with ideas about conservation and education grafted onto the zoo's core business: entertaining people with exciting creatures. Balancing entertainment and conservation, commerce and education, local politics and animal rights is a difficult trick, and zoos seem to embody all the complicated, contradictory attitudes humans have toward animals.

As head of the zoo, Tracogna will be expected to do more than revitalize a tired civic institution and kick-start a fundraising campaign. In the broader context, the death of a single elephant is a small thing, but it's representative of some of the bigger questions that zoos will face in the coming years, questions Tracogna will be forced to answer: How does an elephant like Tara fit into a modern zoo? Should she be there at all? What can we learn from her life and death? And, most pressingly, what should a zoo be in 2010?

WHEN TARA WAS BORN IN 1969 IN THE WILDS OF MOZAMBIQUE, she was 250 pounds, nearly blind, and as close to helpless as the world's largest land animal can be. Elephants aren't born with sophisticated abilities but instead develop them over their first years of life. Like human beings and other intelligent mammals, they stick close to their mothers, often literally walking beneath them. Young elephants also grow up within a network of allomothers—the aunts, siblings and cousins that, in effect, teach a calf how to be an adult.

For Tara, this formative period was cut short. From the '60s until the early '90s, tens of thousands of elephants were killed across southern Africa in government-approved culls designed to prevent the animals from overwhelming local ecosystems. Armed with semi-automatic weapons, teams would descend on a family group in light airplanes or helicopters, followed by trucks loaded with labourers who would perform the skinning and butchering that would follow. The organized cull is a nightmarish scene. Frightened calves scramble to find safety between the legs of adults; panicked, trumpeting elephants are mowed down by the dozen, their still-warm bodies stripped of their hides and valuable tusks. Cullers, aware of the deep emotional bonds that form between family members, had a perversely humane aim: to kill every single elephant, leaving no grieving survivors.

Calves were the exception. Small enough to transport and valuable enough to make the effort worthwhile, young elephants were often spared. For Tara, Tessa and Tantor, the first group of elephants adopted by the Toronto Zoo, this meant that their introduction to humans was traumatic: probable witnesses to the massacre of their entire family, they were put into crates and shipped overseas. The young elephants were bought by a German animal dealer and sent to facilities in Europe, where a curator from the newly formed Toronto Zoo selected them as the first animals in what was to be an ambitious new exhibit. In the summer of 1974, they were shipped to Hamburg, where Toby Styles, the senior elephant keeper at the brand new Toronto Zoo, was preparing to escort them across the Atlantic.

When I met him in his Ajax home, just down the highway from the zoo that employed him for 26 years, Styles was getting ready for a road trip. Since retiring in 1999, he and his wife,

Suzanne, have travelled a lot. The two spent five years in Africa following elephants in a beat-up Land Rover, driving down unmarked paths in the savannah, observing the animals to which Styles had devoted his life. He is a zoo man from a different era— a gruff, bull-necked lifer who came up through the system at a time when trainers were called "wranglers" and were more likely to have worked their way in through the cir-

cus or the farm than through a masters program in zool-
ogy. He was raised in Banff and has worked with animals his entire life, from a boyhood gig wrangling weasels
for Walt Disney's "True-Life Adventures"—a series of
notoriously not-true-to-life animal documentaries—to
a job with a California company that trained animals for
films, to years as a keeper at the Calgary Zoo. In Toronto,
he rose from elephant keeper to executive director of mar-
keting and communications, becoming the public face of the
institution, the man known as Mr. Zoo in his dozens of TV
and radio appearances.

Above all, though, Styles has always been an elephant
lover. "In my opinion, there are two kinds of animals," Styles
told me. "Elephants, and everything else." Styles named Tara
after his daughter, who was herself named after an older elephant. In his Ajax home, he keeps two photo albums devoted
to elephants. He showed me pictures of Tara, Tessa and Tantor from their first meeting. In the carefully mounted photographs, the young calves are up to Styles shoulder, their
broad foreheads traced with a light fuzz of brown hair, their
dark, wide-set eyes peering out from between the bars of the
reinforced wooden crates that were their homes for two weeks
during their crossing.

Styles took the three elephants, along with a black rhinoceros, from Hamburg to Toronto on the Polish ocean liner Zabrze,
one of the few boats that would take deck cargo at the time. The
elephants were still wild, not yet used to humans, and Styles
remembers the trio using their trunks to knock down overly
curious Polish sailors. Rounding the coast of Scotland, the
water got choppy. Against the advice of the captain, Styles
strapped on a life jacket and harness and staggered across
the deck to feed and water the elephants. He remembers the
crossing as a stressful time spent shovelling elephant dung

in gale force winds and constantly worrying that the increasingly aggressive rhinoceros would burst out of its crate. Tessa, the smallest of the three, became sick on the journey.
She developed sores on her trunk that were tended to by a
retired German doctor onboard. When they finally pulled into
Montreal 14 days after setting sail, the elephants were loaded
onto a flatbed truck and driven to Toronto, where they arrived at their new home on a warm evening in July. Just
weeks before the grand opening, the new zoo was teeming
with last-minute activity. That same evening, a shipment of
fur seals from South Africa had arrived. Tessa had grown
weak, and Styles was eager to get her out of her cramped
crate, but workers were still putting the finishing touches on
both the elephant and seal enclosures. The keepers improvised, and the young elephant spent her first night in Toronto
sharing the hippo exhibit with a group of barking seals. Two
days later, Tara, Tessa and Tantor moved to the zoo's new
African elephant exhibit, where they would spend the rest of
their lives.

THE FIRST MODERN ZOO WAS BUILT IN LONDON IN 1828, born out of
a public fascination with the exotic creatures found in Britain's growing empire. The animals were arranged taxonomically: all the cats in one building, the odd-toed hoofed mammals in another, the birds of prey in another. The aim was to
create a moving, breathing catalogue of living things, a kind
of stamp collection of nature's creations.

For the next 125 years, despite numerous changes and
innovations, the basic structure and purpose of zoos remained the same. Animals in barred cages were presented
for the edification and amusement of the public. In the late
1960s, that began to change. The birth of the environmental movement prompted new concern about our treatment

of animals, which filtered its way into the world of zoos, where a few leading institutions recognized that in order to justify holding wild creatures in captivity, zoos needed to be more than just theme parks. Conservation became the industry buzzword. Zoos began to think of themselves as stationary arks, safe havens in which to breed and rehabilitate endangered species while their wild populations recovered.

The Metropolitan Toronto Zoo (as it was originally called) was built in the midst of this change in philosophy. The old Riverdale Zoo, a traditional monkeys-behind-bars institution, had been around since the turn of the century, but in 1966, a group of 11 citizens formed the Metropolitan Toronto Zoological Society with the aim of creating something better. Like professional sports teams or opera houses, zoos are civic status symbols, and Toronto, a growing city with growing aspirations, would need a top-notch zoo.

The man chosen to direct the operation was Gunter Voss, a passionate, uncompromising German zoologist who was, by both profession and inclination, most definitely not a people person. A prickly micromanager, Voss knew what he wanted and fought hard to get it. Instead of arranging animals taxonomically, Voss made Toronto the first zoo divided entirely by "zoogeographical" regions, displaying groups of animals based on their natural habitat and range. He also emphasized the role conservation would have. "Four words can describe the zoo," he told a reporter from Toronto Life in 1974. "Recreation, education, research and conservation, the last being the most vital point. We're living on a limited planet, living with limited resources. Nature is being wiped out. Zoos must begin to match game reserves and natural sanctuaries to propagate and maintain the gene pool."

Voss ambition extended to the elephant enclosure. Elephants have always been at the centre of the modern zoo. Along with lions, gorillas and other large, lovable mammals, they are what zoologists call "charismatic megafauna" and what show business people call "a big draw." At the Toronto Zoo, Tara, Tessa and Tantor were soon joined by Patsy, Tequila, Iringa, Jo and Toka (young elephants also captured in Mozambique), creating a much larger group than most North American zoos could accommodate. Unlike the majority of zoos, which kept elephants chained up overnight, Toby Styles decided his elephants would be allowed free movement within their enclosures. The zoo's decision to adopt Tantor, a young male, was also ambitious. Male elephants are easy to care for up to a point, but as adolescence hits and they become violent and unpredictable, they require their own enclosure and extra staff. Owning a male elephant is expensive, but the zoo was eager to begin the breeding work that Voss had said was so important.

Soon Tara and the others settled into their new home. Patsy, the largest of the group, quickly asserted her dominance, and a crude hierarchy was born. One of the ironies of zoos, which in theory are supposed to allow visitors a glimpse of a wild animal, is that in order to survive in a zoo an animal must be at least partially tamed. In Toronto, the keepers and elephants developed a routine. When the staff arrived each morning, they fed the elephants breakfast before putting them through a set of "behaviours"—training routines designed to stimulate the elephants and to make their life at the Toronto Zoo more manageable. Tara and the others learned to present their feet to be inspected for wounds and sores. They learned to touch assigned targets. They learned to come when called, move when told, and stand still while keepers took blood samples, for which they were rewarded with jellybeans. During the summer, the elephants graze in their outdoor exhibit, where they are on view to the public until closing. During the winter, they are shifted around their indoor cement enclosure, moved between different 400-square-foot pens while mechanical metal gates bang and buzz like prison doors.

In 1980, Thika was born to Tantor and Tequila, the first African elephant bred in Canada. She was followed by Tumpe (who was shipped to Vancouver and eventually died at Disney's Animal Kingdom in 2009), Toronto (who died of salmonella poisoning at the age of 10), and T. W. (who died just two days after birth). In 1989, Tantor collapsed hours after surgery to remove an abscessed tusk, leaving the zoo without a bull. For a time, keepers hoped to use new advances in artificial insemination to try to increase the group, even beginning the long process of preparing Thika for the procedure. In the end, however, they decided it was too risky, effectively ending the Toronto Zoo's elephant breeding program.

YOU CAN'T KNOW WHAT GOES ON INSIDE AN ELEPHANT. They seem somehow inscrutable, possessing a mind that is profoundly different from primate brains. As Eric Cole says, "Their intelligence seems to come from a different direction." Over the past few decades, however, while Tara and her companions continued their circumscribed routine in Toronto, scientists have been making some impressive discoveries about the elephant mind. Fieldwork by experts like Joyce Poole has revealed their intricate social networks. Using MRIs, researchers have discovered that there's some basis for the cliché about elephants never forgetting: they have a huge hippocampus, one of the structures in the limbic system that is important in memory.

Elephants have passed what is known as the "mirror test." Put in front of a mirror, most animals are unable to recognize themselves (dogs, for example, bark at their reflection and peer behind the mirror in search of the other animal). In 2006 at the Bronx Zoo, a female elephant called Happy stepped in front of a mirror and looked directly at her reflection. Using her trunk, she then reached up and touched a white X that had been painted on her forehead. According to researchers, the test showed that elephants are self-aware, able to recognize themselves as individuals separate from their environment, joining a "cognitive elite" group that consists of primates and cetaceans. In other words, elephants seem to have consciousness, the ability to gaze at themselves and think: I am elephant.

The picture that emerges from all this research is of a creature that is socially complex and empathetic. Scientists now recognize that animals like elephants are capable of intricate decision-making and feelings. In small ways, the rigid barrier we have put between human beings and all other living creatures has come to seem slightly more permeable. With that, the moral questions about keeping these animals in captivity have grown more urgent.

Captive elephants commonly suffer from a range of physical maladies: herpes, tuberculosis, arthritis, and especially foot disease, caused by decades of walking on hard floors. Now scientists have begun to discover serious mental issues. Large groups of unrelated females never form in the wild, yet Tara and the others were thrust together with the expectation that they would form a family unit. Gay Bradshaw, a psychologist and academic, argues in her 2009 book Elephants on the Edge that African elephants orphaned by the cull display signs of post-traumatic stress disorder. They startle easily and exhibit asocial tendencies, inattentive mothering and other characteristics typical of humans who have undergone a profound trauma. Tara and the other elephants who may well have witnessed the death of their families had been deprived of the intricate social support network most young elephants are given during their early neural development. Like troubled kids pushed into a foster home, the elephants didn't always get along, and carefully managing the shifting alliances, bullying and moments of aggression that flared up between roommates became a big part of the keepers' job. The keeper gored in 1993 was injured while trying to break up a fight between Iringa and Thika. Last summer, Tessa, the elephant who got sick on the boat and became a weak, somewhat odd adult, was jostled by Thika during feeding, causing her to topple over and eventually die. "These orphaned elephants are misfits; they always have been," says Eric Cole. "Considering their backgrounds, I'm surprised we've never had any psychotic elephants."

In the wild, elephants can range for miles in a single day, encountering other elephant groups, new foods, new threats and mental challenges. Toronto's herd has lived on the same one-hectare patch of land for 36 years. The staff tries to stimulate their minds as best they can—giving them tree trunks to strip, teaching them new behaviours, giving them balls that contain a hidden treat—but it's difficult to create a healthy mental environment in a cement box. One of the ways the elephants have reacted is by engaging in what scientists call "stereotypic behaviour," a mindless repetitive motion that is never exhibited in the wild. In circuses and zoos, elephants neurotically sway back and forth or bob up and down, a behaviour displayed by people with autism. According to Poole, this is an elephant's coping mechanism to handle the stress of captivity.

This new information has led zoos to rethink their position on elephants. Most are trying to rebuild their facilities, creating larger enclosures that can better meet elephants' needs, but some institutions have decided that humanely keeping elephants in a cold urban environment just isn't possible. In May 2004, the Detroit Zoo announced that it would be closing its elephant exhibit after 76 years. In a memo explaining the decision, the director, Ron Kagan, stated, "Now we understand how much more is needed to be able to meet all the physical and psychological needs of elephants in captivity, especially in a cold climate." In 2006, the Bronx Zoo—perhaps the most famous zoo in the world—announced that Happy and her two companions will be the final elephants in its collection.

At the heart of these decisions is a tacit admission that the conservation agenda of zoos, at least when it comes to elephants, has failed. When the Toronto Zoo opened, Gunter Voss said that zoos needed to "propagate and maintain a viable gene pool." The zoo has had some success with this. It participates in a number of valuable conservation programs around the world and has created breeding programs for such creatures as the black-footed ferret, the Vancouver Island marmot and the Puerto Rican crested toad. Overall, though, and with elephants in particular, the dream of the zoo as a centre of conservation hasn't come to fruition. Across North America, zoos aren't able to breed enough elephants to maintain their own collections, relying on wild-captured animals to stock their exhibits. When the cull was banned in South Africa in 1995, the supply of orphan elephants shrank to almost none, leaving zoos like Toronto with aging elephants and little chance of getting new ones.

Zoos have begun to recognize that an argument based purely on conservation doesn't stand up to scrutiny. After all, is a theme park in a northern city really the best place to preserve an African species? The new industry buzzword has become education. Zoos are places that teach children about the natural world; captive animals are charismatic ambassadors for their wild cousins, creatures that inspire people to make meaningful conservation choices. Peter Evans, the long-time board member who acted as interim CEO before Tracogna was hired, says that the aim is to "create an awareness of life." Elephants and other charismatic animals that immediately draw people in are essential.

Giorgio Mammoliti, the outspoken city councillor running for mayor who has a prominent role on the zoo board, believes that elephants are a vital part of the zoo, but his argument is financial. "Right now, if we got rid of those elephants, you can take that 1.5 million people that are coming through the gate and probably cut it in a third," he told me. "People want to see elephants. There's no question about that." Mammoliti has big plans for the zoo. The junket he took to China to lobby to bring pandas to Toronto drew headlines last year. The ambitious councillor dreams of making the zoo a classy destination, with black-tie fundraisers that attract the Bay Street crowd and private partnerships with companies that can bring innovative ideas. Why not a zoo château, for people who want to explore the grounds over multiple days? What about a chairlift? The councillor won't contemplate a radical rethinking of the zoo's approach to animals. "We're hearing criticism primarily from groups that want to shut down zoos completely," Mammoliti told me. "Credibility comes into play."

The elephant issue is just the beginning of a radical animal welfare agenda. Rob Laidlaw, the executive director of Zoocheck and one of the most prominent critics of the Toronto Zoo's elephant exhibit, does indeed advocate for big changes. The argument over elephants, he says, is "the leading edge of a debate about what zoos should be." Holding elephants in captivity is especially problematic, but what about gorillas? What about tigers? What about impalas? David Hancocks is the former director of Woodland Park Zoo in Seattle and one of the most forward-thinking authorities on zoos. In the 1970s, he recommended closing Seattle's elephant exhibit and was quickly told by a city councillor that he would be leaving town before the elephants would. He says the recent outcry over the treatment of elephants is a sign that zoos aren't keeping up with the times. "I think 20 years from now, people will be saying, 'How did zoos get away with all of this?'" He sees the zoos of the future as places that legitimately try to live up to the promises about conservation they have been making for 35 years. Places that may have smaller collections, fewer exotic animals, and a real focus on animal welfare. Places that most assuredly will not have elephants.

When I asked Toby Styles about the future of Toronto's elephants, there was a long, considered pause. Styles has been as integral to the Toronto Zoo's elephant exhibit as anyone, so he wanted to make himself clear. "Those elephants, living all that time in Toronto, they've made a difference," he said emphatically. "They've made an elephant real to a whole lot of people. We've learned things from them." He stopped for a moment. "But, with all that, I'll say that it's time to let them go. All of those good things don't make up for the winter weather." The things he's learned about elephants in the past 35 years have convinced him that they have no place in Toronto.

THE NEXT TIME I VISITED THE ZOO, on a morning in March three months after Tara's death, things had settled down at the elephant enclosure. The living arrangements in the elephants' house had been reorganized, with the three surviving animals sharing a space designed for eight. Thika, despite being more than a decade younger than the other two, had taken over as matriarch, and she was using her new-found power to antagonize Toka. The keepers, like concerned primary school teachers, were trying to teach the two to get along, forcing them to spend time with one another in short "compatibility sessions."

That day, Iringa and Toka faced away from Thika, a sign of submission, while the new matriarch paced back and forth by the entrance to the pen, snaking a searching trunk through the bars. Eric Cole rubbed it affectionately. Like everyone who works with the elephants, Cole is in love with them. During a particularly bad heat wave a few years ago, he decided to try keeping the elephants outside all night rather than in their steamy indoor pen. For the first week, Cole and his staff worked 24-hour shifts, staying with the animals through the night to make sure they were adapting to their new circumstances.

Standing outside the enclosure, watching the three creatures, Cole told me he's hopeful that the zoo can figure out a way to continue with the exhibit. He's fighting hard for a new multimillion-dollar facility that could make them more comfortable in the winter, and hopes that they can bring in more elephants one day soon. Right now, it isn't possible, but in South Africa (where the elephant population has more than doubled since the cull ended 15 years ago), officials have announced they will begin the controversial cull again. Soon orphan elephants could be available. Soon the zoo's breeding program could begin again.

"If we had a baby elephant, that would be a top draw," he said hopefully. He warmed to the topic, enthusiastically spinning out his dreams for the exhibit to which he's devoted so many years. "If we build a facility and we draw the public in, we have the potential to raise a lot of money for conservation in the field. We could fund a whole lot of programs that could immediately affect elephants' long-term survival."

As he talked, the elephants continued to shift and pace in the enclosure behind him. Moving away from the others, Iringa stood silently in the muddy paddock. She's an intelligent elephant, the fastest to learn a new behaviour, and, though he was reluctant to admit it, Cole's favourite. Up close, she is awe-inspiring—enormous and beautiful, projecting a grave, alien intelligence that suddenly makes you understand why humans have long attributed unlikely magical powers to elephants. From here, I can see the thick, wiry eyelashes that shade her eyes. I can see the soft padding on the bottom of her enormous feet, a touch of pinkness at the base of a craggy mountain of grey. She is smelly and huge and more real than any National Geographic video, which, of course, is the reason so many zoo people think that the public needs to see her.

While we watched, Iringa began to sway. With her feet stock-still, her right hind leg cocked at an angle, she rolled her head back and forth, her trunk swinging from left to right, left to right.

I asked Cole if she was showing stereotypic behaviour. "Yes," he said slowly. "That developed after Patsy died. Of all the elephants we've had, Iringa's probably the one who's been most affected by the loss of her cohorts. It's funny, she didn't even like Tara. She probably just misses having all those other elephants around."

He suddenly caught himself. Cole is an unsentimental man. He doesn't buy into the mysticism around elephants. They are intelligent creatures, but they aren't people, and he is constantly vigilant against the kind of sloppy thinking that tries to give them human emotions. "Who really knows what she's thinking?" he said, correcting himself. "I could say, 'She's swaying because she's thinking about her own mortality' or something like that. The truth is, you can't know what goes on inside their heads."

We silently watched her. Without moving from her spot, Iringa swayed from left to right, her trunk swinging like a pendulum. It was a joyless, mechanical movement, detached from emotion or instinct, and in that moment—bobbing back and forth—she was not a wild creature. She was something else, something in between, something that exists only in the places where humans keep animals captive.

ON THE SONNET

Chris Jennings
Arc Poetry

There's no more-popular poetic form than the sonnet.[1] I'm not going to lay claim to any statistical insight here; I haven't leafed through all of my anthologies or the last five years of every Canadian poetry journal or run a search of *Representative Poetry On-Line*.[2] I haven't dedicated many musty hours to counting rather than reading poems. I'm willing to bet, though, that no one can readily dispute the fact that more poets attempt sonnets, create variants of sonnets, publish sonnets, anthologize sonnets, dive headlong into sequences of sonnets, or come to have their reputation rest on sonnets than any other set form in the English language. This used to intrigue me, then it began to puzzle me, and now it annoys me so much that the right stimulus sends me into a rage. Frankly, I am *done* with sonnets. That almost-instant recognition that yes, this is yet another self-congratulatingly correct sonnet makes me wince. I grow increasingly narcoleptic with every re-imagining of the sonnet that I see, and my jaw aches after every book or review lauding yet another poet for their fine achievements in the sonnet. These last are the worst. They proselytize; they lead to ever-more sonnets. Well, fuck that. And for that matter, fuck the sonnet.

Look, this is not a crank's knee-jerk reaction. I've done my time with sonnets, so I know what there is to like about them and how hard they can be to resist (so are chicken wings, but they rarely appear on fine dining menus). I still love Donne's sonnets, Hopkins, and Geoffrey Hill's "An Apology For the Revival of Christian Architecture in England" whenever I can forget that they're sonnets long enough to re-read them. You could say that, like a reformed smoker, the militancy of my response is in inverse proportion to the strength of my old sonnet habit. Like your parents, I'm telling you to learn from my mistakes. Unlike your parents, I'll give you an explanation for my paternalism other than "because I said so." My complaint can be divided into the following four parts: the sonnet has no inherent advantage over other forms that would explain its popularity; its pre-eminence depends on habitual collusion rather than merit; we confuse its pedagogical value with its purely aesthetic value; and in combination, we've made the sonnet a glass ceiling for innovation with the tools of traditional poetics. If that isn't grounds for a profane response, sue me.

Let me be precise in this and call the sonnet a *"Tradition-al Poem of Set Length."*[3] Seems like an odd place to put the emphasis, but in practice, it really is the idea that the sonnet is a 14-line endeavour that distinguishes it from many other fully-defined forms. Stanzaic forms like the ode or terza rima, or stichic forms like blank verse or alliterative verse, can continue indefinitely in the sonnet's rhythm and approximations of its rhymes. Iambic pentameter is the base rhythm of everything from five act plays to extended essays in heroic couplets to two line maxims. The rhyme scheme of the sonnet octave consists of two quatrains in most variations, with either the same or different rhymes between the two (*abba abba* or *abab cdcd*, for example). It's a stanza form that lends itself to any number of repetitions and it crops up ubiquitously. The sestet is also a well-defined, six-line stanza pattern that can be strung together ad infinitum. Combining four (or eight) and six line stanzas is irregular but not unique. The sonnet's basic rhetorical patterns (point/counterpoint/solution, or situation/complication/resolution etc.) aren't proprietary; blank verse and heroic couplets argue just as well, and the ode offers an even stronger dialectical structure with its strophe, antistrophe, and epode. What does that leave in terms of basic components other than the number of lines? And if the number 14 is the key to the sonnet then… so what?

Is there some numerological significance to 14? Even if there were, not every 14-line poem is a sonnet, and some poets don't feel constrained by that 14-line dictum. Seamus Heaney has written double sonnets, and many poets have extended the sonnet to 16 lines while still claiming an essential sonnetty-ness. Some of the variations have their own names: the Curtal Sonnets of Hopkins have a truncated final line; Caudate Sonnets extend to 20 lines, and the Sonnet Rédoublé is a cross between a 15-sonnet sequence and a glosa, where every line of the initial sonnet becomes the final line of one of the following 14. It has always been a serial form with all of the eponymous sonneteers—Petrarch, Spenser, Shakespeare—engaging in long sequences of more-or-less connected sonnets. Every variation, though, looks back to that 14-line norm, pays homage to it even when abusing it, repeats it as a way of breaking with it. Perhaps the point, then, is just this: the sonnet is "a little song." It's diminutive. Brevity, and it's ideal counterparts precision or density, *can* be real virtues for a poem, but they're hardly unique to sonnets.

Brevity can signify exactly the opposite of density and precision, and you could make a good historical argument that the sonnet owes its popularity to its ability to fulfill many of the functions performed by Hallmark. The explosion of the sonnets that followed the efforts of Thomas Wyatt and Henry Howard, Earl of Surrey, to bring Petrarch's sonnets into English in the 16th century are courtier's poems, moaning and sighing in verse about unrequited love in banal and endlessly-recycled metaphors. It was a game for the rich and randy, but it adapted quickly to other pedestrian functions, such as dedications and introductions. Popularity has always fed on itself; brevity can be most utilitarian. Neither contributes much substance to the sonnet, but they are everything to the sonnet's reputation. If some of the most canonical of English poets had steered clear of the trend, or if Shakespeare hadn't had time to kill when Elizabethan plays were kept off the boards by plague and official moralizing, the sonnet's history might resemble any of a hundred forms translated from another language and pinned like a specimen in a shadow box. Alternatively, they might be like other familiar "Traditional Poems of Set Length," like the villanelle or the sestina, which have their virtues but are, as Elizabeth Bishop claimed to Marianne Moore, "a sort of a stunt."[4]

Shakespeare wrote at least 154 of these "stunts"—though I'd say the sonnet's more of a trick. Phillip Sidney's *Astrophil and Stella* runs to 108 sonnets. John Donne wasn't that lunatic, though you might also argue that the first fit of sonnet-mania had started its decline by Donne's time. Sonnets didn't proliferate in what academics call "The Long 18th Century" in quite the same way, but the damage was done. Just about every canonical poet since Donne wrote at least one sonnet as though establishing their *bona fides* for considerations of membership in the canon club. For example, once you get to the 19th Century, you hit Wordsworth, with his strangely urban and political sonnets, then Keats and Shelley and those endlessly-taught sonnets "On First Looking into Chapman's Homer" and "Ozymandias." The 19th Century also gave us the most mocked sonnet—from Elizabeth Barrett Browning's *Sonnets from the Portuguese*, #43—"How do I love thee? Let me count the ways." A generation or two later, even Ezra Pound apparently wrote a sonnet a day for a few months in order to figure out the attractions and strategies of the form, but he had the good sense to throw them away. If only all well-known sonnets by canonical poets were easy to mock or, better yet, had been dismissed by their authors. But alas, they're usually good poems, and, better for them, they're usually fairly accessible poems. The former shouldn't be a surprise. These are poems by poets history has chosen not to forget, and not only for, or even substantially because of, their sonnets. Donne wasn't a hack until he dreamt up his holy sonnets; Shakespeare wouldn't have disappeared into the mists if he'd only written plays. So there they are, the honoured dead, standing in serried ranks under the sonnet's standard in the pages of every classroom anthology distributed to every university and college.

No one ever wished that Norton anthologies were bigger, but they do wish they were more inclusive, and the logistical challenge of meeting these two expectations makes short poems handy. You can squeeze "God's Grandeur" in much more easily than 280 lines (in octaves) of Hopkins "The Wreck of the Deutschland." Anyone who learns poetry through an anthology, or through contact with someone who learned through an anthology, is therefore exposed to a disproportionate number of sonnets under the Aegis of suggestive terminology such as "Major Authors." No wonder we're into the territory of the "Anxiety of Influence."[5] Faced with those sonnets by all of the "big names," how does the ambitious and susceptible student of poetry avoid the implied challenge to write her or his own 14-liner? The worst thing that could happen, and it happens regularly, is that the emerging poet writes a decent poem that happens to be a sonnet, because a side-effect of that feeling of accomplishment is the need to reaffirm that there is something especially meretricious about sonneteering. Even the impulse to experiment with the sonnet form connects to this same line of thought, though surely "experiment" isn't the best word when hewing close to English-language poetry's most tradition-bound core.

Of course, the main reason we continue to see giant, onion-skin-paged anthologies is as a service to teachers, professors, and students of literature. In this context, the sonnet's greatest virtue is that it's a grab-bag of so many of the most common elements of poetic form. The commonness of the thing makes it an irresistible choice for teachers with only a little course time to dedicate to poems, and the ubiquity of the sonnet makes for a self-defining unit across eras. The examples are many and readily available, and the lessons neatly contained: rhyme and meter; line, stanza, and enjambment; metaphor and simile; repetition, opposition, and conclusion. As a consequence, the traditional fundamentals of form are tied to the sonnet, not by the sonnet, but by how we use it in the classroom. The example becomes exemplary rather than a solid foundation; rather than a place to start but ultimately to leave behind save for the occasional visit, it becomes a marker of aesthetic achievement or of mastery of the elements of traditional poetic forms. The periodic rekindling of interest in sonnets seems to depend on a circular argument that praises sonnets for their resemblance to the textbook examples of formal achievement as defined by the sonnet. So we praise sonnets for being sonnets. It's worst when poets do the praising, because they have the facility with language to convince others something more mystical is going on here—and sometimes they praise the sonnet in sonnets.

The sonnet has become the poet's self-imposed glass ceiling. Surely we can appreciate the irony that the form whose best feature is that it encourages a poet to think through the challenges of form, rhetoric, and syntax has become the easy alternative to thinking through new ways to meet the challenges of form, rhetoric, and syntax. Surely we can see how a fervour for sonnets stunts an adaptable poetics that responds to both those old standards of sonnet tradition love, time, and death but also the alienation of digital communication, the shallowness of social networking, dystopian echoes of G20s and G8s, or science's assault on the fundamentals of the way we understand the universe—in other words, the full challenge of investigating the immediate in an art almost as old as language itself. When our response to that challenge is to take the sonnet with all its many virtues, raise it on a pedestal, and stop thinking about how else the *lessons* of the sonnet—rather than the sonnet itself—might be applied, adapted, explored, and expanded, preferring instead to churn out more fucking sonnets? Well, that is a sad and tragic decision. Me, I say fuck that. And fuck the sonnet.

Endnotes

1   I'm not counting free form, which is an entirely different animal. Haiku is certainly popular, and in some poetry communities it would easily outstrip the sonnet in terms of the number of poems produced, but that level of popularity seems restricted to certain "ghettoes" that specialize in the form and other Japanese imports. It's also rare to see haiku in literary journals except when the journal specializes. For all its charms, haiku doesn't have the same reputation as the sonnet—likely because it's a much more recent import into English and, as I discuss here, it doesn't have the backing of a long-standing tradition populated by English poetry's "Old Masters."

2   http://rpo.library.utoronto.ca/display/index.cfm

3   As Miller Williams does in Patterns of Poetry: An Encyclopedia of Forms (Baton Rouge: Louisiana State University Press, 1986).

4   "...the sestina is just a sort of stunt." (September 15, 1936; quoted in Schwartz, Lloyd and Sybil P. Estess. Elizabeth Bishop and Her Work. Ann Arbour: University of Michigan Press, 1983.)

5   The simplest definition of Harold Bloom's term is that poets learn from other poets but then struggle to escape the shadows of their models and write great, original work (see Bloom's The Anxiety of Influence: A Theory of Poetry and Agon: Towards a Theory of Revisionism).

WAGE SLAVERY, BULLSHIT, AND THE GOOD INFINITE

Mark Kingwell
Queen's Quarterly

I t has been remarked, if not often then at least poignantly, that there has not been, in the wake of 2008's economic meltdown, any sustained political critique of the system or individuals responsible for the collapse. No general strikes. No riots or mass demonstrations. No protest songs, angry novels, or outbreaks of resistant consciousness. In contrast to the Great Depression of the 1930s, the 'recession' or 'correction' or 'setback' (choose your *status quo* euphemism) has barely impinged on the popular media.[1]

Even the special class of idleness-under-duress fantasy film has disappeared without a trace: there is no contemporary equivalent of the heroes of those great 1930s and 40s freedom-from-work Hollywood comedies: Cary Grant and Katharine Hepburn in *Holiday* (d. George Cukor, 1938) or Joel McCrea in *Sullivan's Travels* (d. Preston Sturges, 1942). "I want to find out why I'm working," says the Grant character, a self-made man, in the former film. "It can't be just to pay the bills and pile up more money." His wealthy fiancée—and her blustering banker father, seeing a junior partner in his son-in-law—think it can be just that. Which is why Grant goes off with the carefree older sister, Hepburn, on what might just be a permanent holiday from work. In *Sullivan's Travels*, Hollywood honcho McCrea goes in search of the real America of afflicted life—only to conclude that mindless entertainment is a necessity in hard times. Childlike joy and freedom from drudgery is more, not less, defensible when unemployment rates rise. But there is no Preston Sturges for our own day.

The reasons are puzzling. The collapse proved every anti-capitalist critic right, though without anything much changing as a result. The system was bloated and spectral, yes, borrowing on its borrowing, insuring its insurance, and skimming profit on every transaction. The FIRE sector—finance, insurance, real estate—had created the worst market bubble since the South Sea Company's 1720 collapse and nobody should have been surprised when that latest party balloon of capital burst. And yet everybody was. It was as if a collective delusion had taken hold of the world's seven billion souls, the opposite of group paranoia: an unshakable false belief in the reality of the system. The trouble was that, in the wake of the crisis, awareness of the system's untenability changed nothing. The government bailout schemes—known as stimulus packages, a phrase that belongs easily in the pages of porn—effectively socialized some failing industries, saddling their collapse on taxpayers, even as it handed over billions of dollars to the people responsible for the bloat in the first place. Unemployment swept through vulnerable sectors in waves of layoffs and cutbacks, and 'downturn' became an inarguable excuse for all manner of cost-saving action. Not only did nothing change in the system, the system emerged stronger than ever, now just more tangled in the enforced tax burdens and desperate job-seeking of individuals. Meanwhile, the role of gainful occupation in establishing or maintaining all of (1) biological survival, (2) social position and, especially in American society, (3) personal identity was undiminished.

Capitalism is probably beyond large-scale change, but we should not waste this opportunity to interrogate its most fundamental idea: work. A curious sub-genre of writing washed up on the shore of this crisis, celebrating manual labour and tracing globalized foodstuffs and consumer products back to their origins in toil.[2] The problem with these efforts, despite their charms, is that they do not resist the idea of work in the first instance. The pleasures of craft or intricacies of production have their value; but they are no substitute for resistance. And no matter what the inevitabilists say, resistance to work is not futile. It may not overthrow capitalism, but it does highlight essential things about our predicament—philosophy's job ever.

My contention in this essay is that the values of work are still dominant in far too much of life; indeed, that these values have exercised their own kind of linguistic genius in creating a host of phrases, terms, and labels that bolster, rather than challenge, the dominance of work. Ideology is carried forward effectively by many vehicles, including narrative and language. And we see that this vocabulary of work is itself a kind of Trojan Horse within language, naturalizing and so making invisible some of the very dubious, if not evil, assumptions of the work idea. This is all the more true when economic times are bad, since work then becomes itself a scarce commodity. That makes people anxious, and the anxiety is taken up by work: *Don't fire me! I don't want to be out of work!* Work looms larger than ever, the assumed natural condition whose 'loss' makes the non-working individual by definition a loser.

CONSIDER THE NATURE OF WORK. In a 1932 essay called "In Praise of Idleness," Betrand Russell is in fact more incisive about work than he is about idleness, which he seems to view as the mere absence of work (in my terms, defended elsewhere, that is slacking rather than idling).[3] Russell defines work this way:

> Work is of two kinds: first, altering the position of matter at or near the earth's surface relatively to other such matter; second, telling other people to do so. The first kind is unpleasant and ill paid; the second is pleasant and highly paid. (p. 3)

Russell goes on to note that "The second kind is capable of indefinite extension: there are not only those who give orders, but those who give advice as to what orders should be given." (p. 3) This second-order advice is what is meant by *bureaucracy*; and if two opposite kinds of advice are given at the same time, then it is known as *politics*. The skill needed for this last kind of work "is not knowledge of the subjects as to which advice is given, but knowledge of the art of persuasive speaking and writing, i.e. of advertising." (p. 3)

Very little needs to be added to this analysis except to note something crucial which Russell appears to miss: the *greatest work of work* is to disguise its essential nature. The grim ironists of the Third Reich were exceptionally forthright when they fixed the evil, mocking maxim "Arbeit Macht Frei"—work shall make you free—over the gates at Dachau and Auschwitz. One can only conclude that this was their idea of a sick joke, and that their ideological commitments were not with work at all, but with despair and extermination.

The real ideologists of work are never so transparent, nor so wry. But they are clever, because their genius is, in effect, to fix a different maxim over the whole of the world: work is fun! Or, to push the point to its logical conclusion, *it's not work if it doesn't feel like work*. And so celebrated workaholics excuse themselves from what is in fact an addiction, and in the same stroke implicate everyone else for not working hard enough. "Work is the grand cure of all the maladies and miseries that ever beset mankind," said that barrel of fun, Thomas Carlyle.[4] "Nothing is really work unless you would rather be doing something else," added J. M. Barrie, perhaps destabilizing his position on Peter Pan. And even the apparently insouciant Noël Coward argued that "Work is much more fun than fun."[5] Really? Perhaps he meant to say, 'what most people consider fun'. But still. Claims like these just lay literary groundwork for the *Fast Company* work/play manoeuvre of the 1990s or the current, more honest compete-or-die productivity language.

Work deploys a network of techniques and effects that make it seem inevitable and, where possible, pleasurable. Central among these effects is the diffusion of responsibility for the baseline need for work: everyone accepts, because everyone knows, that everyone must have a job. Bosses as much as subordinates are slaves to the larger servo-mechanisms of work, which are spectral and nonlocalizable. In effect, work is the largest self-regulation system the universe has so far manufactured, subjecting each of us to a generalized panopticon shadow under which we dare not do anything but work, or at least seem to be working, lest we fall prey to an obscure disapproval all the more powerful for being so. The work idea functions in the same manner as a visible surveillance camera, which need not even be hooked up to anything. No, let's go further: there need not even be a camera. Like the prisoners in the perfected version of Bentham's uber-utilitarian jail, workers need no overseer *because they watch themselves*.[6] There is no need for actual guards; when we submit to work, we are guard and guarded at once.[7]

Offshoots of this system are somewhat more visible to scrutiny, and so tend to fetch the largest proportion of critical objection. A social theorist will challenge the premises of inevitability in market forces, or wonder whether economic 'laws' are anything more than self-serving generalizations. These forays are important, but they leave the larger inevitabilities of work mostly untouched. In fact, such critical debates tend to reinforce the larger ideological victory of work, because they accept the baseline assumptions of it even in their criticisms. Thus does work neutralize, or indeed annex, critical energy from within the system. The slacker is the tragic hero here, a small-scale version of a Greek protagonist. In his mild resistance—long stays in the mailroom, theft of office supplies, forgery of time cards, ostentatious toting of empty files—the slacker cannot help but sustain the system. This is resistance, but of the wrong sort; it really is futile, because the system, whatever its official stance, loves slackers. They embody the work idea in their very objection.[8]

NONE OF THAT WILL BE NEWS to anyone who has ever been within the demand-structure of a workplace. What is less clear is why we put up with it, why we don't resist more robustly. As Max Weber noted in his analysis of leadership under capitalism, any ideology must, if it is to succeed, give people reasons to act.[9] It must offer a narrative of identity to those caught within its ambit, otherwise they will not continue to perform, and renew, its reality. As with most truly successful ideologies, the work idea latches on to a very basic feature of human existence: our character as social animals jostling for position. But social critics are precipitate if they argue that all human action was motivated by tiny distinctions between winner and loser. In fact, the recipe for action is that recognition of those differences *plus* some tale of why the differences matter and, ideally, are rooted in the respective personal qualities or 'character' of winner and loser.

No tale can be too fanciful to sustain this outcome. Serbs and Croats may engage in bloody warfare over relatively trivial genetic or geographical difference, provided both sides accept the story of what the difference means. In the case of work, the evident genius lies in reifying what is actually fluid, namely social position and 'elite' status within hierarchies. The most basic material conditions of work—office size and position, number of windows, attractiveness of assistant, cut of suit—are simultaneously the rewards *and* the ongoing indicators of status within this competition. Meanwhile, the competition sustains itself backward via credentialism: that is, the accumulation of degrees and certificates from 'prestigious' schools and universities which, though often substantively unrelated to the work at hand, indicate appropriate elite grooming. These credentialist back-formations confirm the necessary feeling that a status outcome is *earned*, not merely conferred. Position without an attendant narrative of merit would not satisfy the ideological demand for action to seem meaningful.

The result is *entrenched* rather than *circulating* elites. The existence of elites is, in itself, neither easily avoidable nor obviously bad. The so-called Iron Law of Oligarchy states that "every field of human endeavor, every kind of organization, will always be led by a relatively small elite."[10] This oligarchic tendency answers demands for efficiency and direction, but more basically it is agreeable to humans on a socio-evolutionary level. We like elite presence in our undertakings, and tend to fall into line behind it. But the narrative of merit in elite status tends to thwart circulation of elite membership, and encourage the false idea that such status is married to 'intrinsic' qualities of the individual. In reality, the status is a kind of collective delusion, not unlike the one that sustains money, another key narrative of the system.

At this stage, it is possible to formulate 'laws'—actually law-like generalizations—about the structure of a work-idea company, which is any company in thrall to the work idea, including (but not limited to) bureaucracies. Parkinson's, Pournelle's, and Moore's Laws of Bureaucracy may be viewed as derivatives of the Iron Law, understood as ways in which we can articulate how the system sustains itself and its entrenched elite. While expressly about bureaucracies, these generalizations speak to the inescapable bureaucratic element in all workplaces, even those that try to eschew that element. In short, they explicate the work idea even as that idea works to keep its precise contours implicit.

Parkinson's Law is minimalist in concept but wide in application. It states: "There need be little or no relationship between the work to be done and the size of the staff to which it may be assigned."[11] This despite the lip-service often paid to the norm of efficiency. Parkinson also identified two axiomatic underlying forces responsible for the growth in company staff: (1) "An official wants to multiply subordinates, not rivals"; and (2) "Officials make work for each other." The second may be more familiar as the Time-Suck Axiom, which states that all meetings must generate further meetings. And so at a certain threshold we may observe that meetings are, for all intents and purposes, entirely self-generating, like consciousness. They do not need the humans who 'hold' them at all, except to be present during the meeting and not doing anything else.

Examining the company structure at one level higher, that is, in the motivation of the individuals, the science fiction writer Jerry Pournelle proposed a theory he referred to as Pournelle's Iron Law of Bureaucracy. It states that "In any bureaucracy, the people devoted to the benefit of the bureaucracy itself always get in control and those dedicated to the goals the bureaucracy is supposed to accomplish have less and less influence, and sometimes are eliminated entirely."[12] In other words, just as meetings become self-generating, so too does the company structure as a whole. *The company* becomes a norm of its own, conceptually distinct from whatever the company makes, does, or provides.

Once this occurs—most obvious in the notion of 'company loyalty', with the required 'team-building' weekends, ballcaps, golf shirts, and logos—there will be positive incentives for position-seekers to neglect or even ignore other values ostensibly supported by the company. More seriously, if Pournelle's Law is correct, then these position-seekers will become the dominant position-holders, such that any norms outside 'the company' will soon fade and disappear. The company is now a self-sustaining evolutionary entity, with no necessary goals beyond its own continued existence, to which end the desires of individual workers can be smoothly assimilated.

Moore's Laws take the analysis even further. If a bureaucracy is a servo-mechanism, its ability to process an error signal, and so generate corrective commands and drive the system away from error, is a function of the depth of the hierarchy. But instead of streamlining hierarchy and so making error-correction easier, bureaucracies do the opposite: they deepen the hierarchy, adding new error sensors but lessening the system's ability to respond to them. Large bureaucracies are inherently noisy systems whose very efforts to achieve goals makes them noisier. Thus, Moore concludes, (1) large bureaucracies cannot possibly achieve their goals; as a result, (2) they will thrash about, causing damage.[13]

He suggests five further laws. The power wielded by bureaucracies will tend to attach above-mean numbers of sociopaths to their ranks. Hence (3) large bureaucracies are *evil*. Because the mechanism of the system increases noise as it attempts to eliminate it, system members in contact with the rest of reality will be constrained by rigid, though self-defeating rules. Thus (4) large bureaucracies are *heartless*. They are also (5) *perverse*, subordinating stated long-term goals to the short-term ambitions of the humans within the system; (6) *immortal*, because their non-achievement of goals makes them constantly replace worn-out human functionaries with new ones; and finally (7) *boundless*, since there is no theoretical limit to the increased noise, size, and complexity of an unsuccessful system.

SO MUCH FOR ELITES LOOKING BACKWARD, justifying their place in the work idea, and finding ever novel ways of expanding without succeeding. Pournelle's and Moore's laws highlight how, looking forward, the picture is considerably more unnerving. The routine collection of credentials, promotions, and employee-of-the-month honours in exchange for company loyalty masks a deeper existential conundrum—which is precisely what it is meant to do.

Consider: It is an axiom of status anxiety that the competition for position has no end—save, temporarily, when a scapegoat is found. The scapegoat reaffirms everyone's status, however uneven, because he is beneath all. Hence many work narratives are miniature blame-quests. We come together as a company to fix guilt on one of our number, who is then publicly shamed and expelled. *Jones filed a report filled with errors! Smith placed an absurdly large order and the company is taking a bath!* This makes us all feel better, and enhances our sense of mission, even if it produces nothing other than its own spectacle.

Blame-quests work admirably on their small scale. At larger scales, the narrative task is harder. What is the company for? What does it do? Here, as when a person confronts mortality, we teeter on the abyss. The company doesn't actually do much of anything. It is not for anything important. The restless forward movement of companies—here at Compu-Global-Hyper-Mega-Net, we are always *moving on*—is work's version of the Hegelian Bad Infinite, the meaningless nothing of empty everything.[14] There is no point to what is being done, but it must be done anyway. The boredom of the average worker, especially in a large corporation, is the walking illustration of this meaninglessness. But boredom can lower productivity, so a large part of work's energy is expended in finding ways to palliate the boredom that is the necessary outcome of work in order to raise productivity: a sort of credit-default swap of the soul. Workaholism is the narcotic version of this, executed within the individual himself. The workaholic colonizes his own despair at the perceived emptiness of life—its non-productivity—by filling it in with work.[15]

It can be no surprise that the most searching critic of work, Karl Marx, perceived this Hegelian abyss at the heart of all paid employment. But Marx's theory of alienated labour, according to which our efforts and eventually our selves become commodities bought and sold for profit to others, is just one note in a sustained chorus of opposition and resistance to work.[16] "Never work," the Situationist Guy Debord commanded, articulating the baseline of opposition.[17] Another Situationist slogan, the famous graffito of May 1968, reminded us that the order and hardness of the urban infrastructure masked a playful, open-ended sense of possibility that was even more fundamental: *Sous les pavés, la plage!* Under the paving stones, the beach!

Between Marx and Debord lies the great, neglected Georges Sorel, a counter-enlightenment and even counter-cultural voice whose influence can be seen to run into the likes of Debord, Franz Fanon, and Che Guevara; but also Timothy Leary, Jack Kerouac, and Ken Kesey. Like many other radical critics, Sorel perceived the emptiness of the liberal promise of freedom once it becomes bound up with regimentation and bourgeoisification of everyday life. Sorel was a serial enthusiast, moving restlessly from cause to cause: a socialist, a Dreyfusard, an ascetic, an anti-Dreyfusard. In the first part of the twentieth century he settled on the labour movement as his home and proposed a general strike that would (in the words of Isaiah Berlin, who had tremendous respect for this against-the-grain thinker):

> call for the total overthrow of the entire abominable world of calculation, profit and loss, the treatment of human beings and their powers as commodities, as material for bureaucratic manipulation, the world of illusory consensus and social harmony, or economic and sociological experts no matter what master they serve, who treat men as subjects of statistical calculations, malleable "human material," forgetting that behind such statistics there are living human beings.[18]

In other words, late capitalism and all that it entails.

One might wonder, first, why such resistance is recurrently necessary but also, second, why it seems ever to fail. The answer lies in the evolutionary fact of *lan-*

guage upgrade. In common with all ideologies, the work idea understands that that victory is best which is achieved soonest, ideally before the processes of conscious thought are allowed to function. And so it is here that language emerges as the clear field of battle. Language acquisition is crucial to our evolutionary success because it aids highly complex coordination of action. But that same success hinges also on the misdirection, deception, control, and happy illusion carried out by language, because these too make for coordinated action. Thus the upgrade is at the same time a downgrade: language allows us to distinguish between appearance and reality, but it also allows some of us to persuade others that appearances are realities. If there were no distinction, this would not matter; indeed, it would not be possible. Deception can only work if there is such a thing as truth, as Socrates demonstrated in the first book of Plato's *Republic*.[19]

Jargon, slogans, euphemisms and terms of art are all weapons in the upgrade/downgrade tradition. We should class them together under the technical term *bullshit*, as analyzed by philosopher Harry Frankfurt. The routine refusal to speak with regard to the truth is called bullshit because evasion of normativity produces a kind of ordure, a dissemination of garbage, the scattering of shit. This is why, as Frankfurt reminds us, bullshit is far more threatening, and politically evil, than lying. The bullshitter "does not reject the authority of the truth, as the liar does, and oppose himself to it. He pays no attention to it at all. By virtue of this, bullshit is the greater enemy of the truth than lies are." (p. 61)[20]

Work language is full of bullshit, and hence so are the pages that follow. But by glossing these terms rather than using them, we hope to bring the enemy into fuller light, to expose the erasure that work's version of Newspeak forever seeks. Special vigilance is needed because the second-order victory

of work bullshit is that, in addition to having no regard for
the truth, it passes itself off as innocuous or even beneficial.
Especially in clever hands, the controlling elements of work
are repackaged as liberatory, counter-cultural, subversive:
you're a skatepunk rebel because you work seventy hours a
week beta-testing videogames. This, we might say, is meta-
bullshit. And so far from what philosophers might assert, or
wish, this meta-bullshit and not truth is the norm governing
most coordinated human activity under conditions of capital
markets. Thus does bullshit meet, and become, filthy lucre;
and of course, vice versa.

As the work idea spins itself out in language, we observe
a series of linked paradoxes in the world of work: imprisonment via inclusion; denigration via celebration; obfuscation
via explanation; conformity via distinction; failure via success; obedience via freedom; authority via breezy coolness.
The manager is positioned as an 'intellectual', a 'visionary',
even a 'genius'. 'Creatives' are warehoused and petted. Demo-
graphics are labelled, products are categorized. Catch phrases, acronyms, proverbs, clichés, and sports metaphors are
marshalled and deployed. Diffusion of sense through need-
less complexity, diffusion of responsibility through passive
constructions, and elaborate celebration of minor achievements mark the language of work.

And so: Outsourcing. Repositioning. Downsizing. Rebrand-
ing. Work the mission statement. Push the envelope. Think
outside the box. Stay in the loop. See the forest *and* the trees.
Note sagely that where there is smoke there is also fire. Casual Fridays! Smartwork! Hotdesking! The whole nine yards!
Touchdown! You-topia!

These shopworn work-idea locutions have already been
exposed, and mocked, such that we may think we know our
enemy all too well. But the upgrade/downgrade is infinitely
inventive. Even this glossary cannot be considered the final

word on wage-slave verbiage. If in *The Idler's Glossary* (2008), Joshua Glenn naively declared glossaries over, the present essay warns that the work of language-care is never over.

YOU MIGHT THINK, at this point, that a language problem naturally calls for a language solution. The very same inventiveness that marks the ideology of work can be met with a wry, subversive counterintelligence. Witness such portmanteau pun words as 'slacktivism' or 'crackberry' which mock, respectively, people who think that forwarding emails is a form of political action and those who are in thrall to text messages the way some people are addicted to crack cocaine. Or observe the high linguistic style of office-bound protagonists from Nicholson Baker's *The Mezzanine* (1988) and Douglas Coupland's *Generation X* (1991) to Joshua Ferris *Then We Came to the End* (2007) and Ed Park's *Personal Days* (2008).

These books are hilarious, and laughter is always a release. But their humour is a sign of doom, not liberation. The 'veal-fattening pen' label applied to those carpet-sided cubicles of the open-form office (Coupland) does nothing to change the facts of the office. Nor does calling office-mateyness an 'air family' (Coupland again) make the false camaraderie any less spectral. Coupland was especially inventive and dry in his generation of neologisms, but reading a bare list of them shows the hollow heart of dread beneath the humour.[21] Indeed, the laughs render the facts more palatable by mixing diversion into the scene of domination—a willing capitulation, consumed under the false sign of resistance. This applies to most of what we call slacking, a verb at least as old as 1530, when Jehan Palsgrave asked of a task-shirking friend "Whye slacke you your busynesse thus?"[22]

That was the main reason Glenn and I were at pains to distinguish idling from slacking in the previous glossary. Slacking is consistent with the work idea; it does not subvert it, merely gives in by means of evasion. As John Kenneth Galbraith pointed out a half-century ago in *The Affluent Society* (1958), such evasion is actually the pinnacle of corporate life:

> Indeed it is possible that the ancient art of evading work has been carried in our time to its highest level of sophistication, not to say elegance. One should not suppose that it is an accomplishment of any particular class, occupation, or profession. Apart from the universities where its practice has the standing of a scholarly rite, the art of genteel and elaborately concealed idleness may well reach its highest development in the upper executive reaches of the modern corporation. (p. 95)

Galbraith's 'idleness' is not to be confused with genuine idling, of course; the 'concealed' that modifies his use of the word shows why. A slacking executive is no better, and also no worse, than the lowliest clerk hiding in the mailroom to avoid a meeting. But neither is idling, which calls for openness and joy.

And so here we confront again the Bad Infinite at the heart of work. What is it for? To produce desired goods and services. But these goods and services are, increasingly, the ones needed to maintain the system itself. The product of the work system is work, and spectres such as 'profit' and 'growth' are covers for the disheartening fact that, in Galbraith's words, "[a]s a society becomes increasingly affluent, wants are increasingly created by the process by which they are satisfied." (p. 129) Which is only to echo Marcuse's and Arendt's well-known aperçus that the basic creation of capitalism is *superfluity*—with the additional insight that capitalism must then create the demand to take up such superfluity.[23] Galbraith nails the contradiction at the heart of things: "But the case cannot stand if it is the process of satisfying wants that creates the wants. For then the individual who urges the importance of production to satisfy the wants is precisely in the position of the onlooker who applauds the efforts of the squirrel to keep abreast of the wheel that is propelled by his own efforts." (p. 125)[24]

Still, all is not lost. There is a treasure buried in the excess that the world of work is constantly generating: that is, a growing awareness of a *gift economy* that always operates beneath, or beyond, the exchange economy. Any market economy is a failed attempt to distribute goods and services exactly where they are needed or desired, as and when they are needed and desired. That's all markets are, despite the pathological excrescences that lately attach to them: derivatives funds, advertising, shopping-as-leisure. If we had a perfect market, idling would be the norm, not the exception, because distribution would be frictionless. As Marcuse saw decades ago, most work is the result of inefficiency, not genuine need.[25] This is all the more true in a FIRE-storm economy. Paradoxically, idling is entirely consistent with capitalism's own internal logic, which implies, even if it never realizes, the end of capitalism. This insight turns the Bad Infinite of work into a Good Infinite, where we may begin to see things not as resources, ourselves not as consumers, and the world as a site not of work but of play.

The great Marxist and Situationist critics of work hoped that critical theory—accurate analysis of the system's pathologies—would change the system. The latest crisis in capitalism has shown that it will not. But a system is made of individuals, just as a market is composed of individual choices and transactions. Don't change the system, change your life. Debord's "Never work" did not go far enough. Truly understand the nature of work and its language, and you may never even think of work again.

Endnotes

1   There are some important exceptions. I will note just three here: Jonathan Dee's novel *The Privileges* (Random House, 2010), a sly satire of the blithe arrogance of one couple who swim through the economic collapse; Chris Lehmann's collection *Rich People Stuff* (OR Books, 2010), which lampoons the favoured tropes and preoccupations of one-percenters; and Roger D. Hodge's angry screed about the Obama Administration's complicity with minimizing the responsibility of Wall Street for the collapse, *The Mendacity of Hope* (Harper, 2010). One complicated example is the hit 2010 film *The Social Network* (d. David Fincher), which tells the story of Facebook 'inventor' Mark Zuckerberg in the unspoken context of the early-2000s bubble. But the film can't decide whether it is a revenge-of-the-nerds celebration or a moralistic slam of internet-age sharp dealing.

2   See, for example, Matthew Crawford, *Shop Class as Soulcraft* (Penguin, 2009)and Alain de Botton, *The Pleasures and Sorrows of Work* (Pantheon, 2009). Andrew Ross summarizes the political puzzle posed by these books: "It is an unfortunate comment on the generous intellects of these two authors that they do not see fit to acknowledge, in their respective surveys of working life, the nobility of those who resist" ("Love Thy Labor," *Bookforum*, Fall 2009, p. 16).

3   Bertrand Russell, *In Praise of Idleness: And Other Essays* (Routledge, 2004). I argued for a distinction between idling and slacking in "Idling Toward Heaven: The Last Defence You Will Ever Need," *Queen's Quarterly* 115:4 (Winter 2008): 569-85; later adapted as the Introduction to Kingwell and Joshua Glenn, *The Idler's Glossary* (Biblioasis/Northwestern, 2008).

4   From Carlyle's 1866 inaugural address as rector of the University of Edinburgh. Published later in *Critical and Miscellaneous Essays*, vol. 6 (London, Chapman, and Hall, 1869).

5   Quoted in *The Observer's* "Sayings of the Week" (London, June 21, 1963).

6   The working principle behind Bentham's "panopticon"—that subjects under surveillance will become their own agents of discipline—garnered much attention in the later writings of Michel Foucault, who saw the same principle at work at large across the institutions of modern capitalist society. In *Discipline and Punish* (1975, trans. 1977) he writes, "[Bentham's panopticon] set out to show how one may 'unlock' the disciplines and get them to function in a diffused, multiple, polyvalent way throughout the whole social body … It programmes, at the level of an elementary and easily transferable mechanism, the basic functioning of a society penetrated through and through with disciplinary mechanisms."

7   One could cite, in support here, the analysis of Gilles Deleuze in "Postscript on the Societies of Control," *October* 59 (Winter 1992), pp. 3-7; reprinted in Martin Joughlin, trans., *Negotiations* (Columbia, 1995). Deleuze notes three modes of social structure: sovereign states (pre-modern); discipline societies (modern); and control societies (postmodern). Whereas a discipline society moulds citizens into subjects through various carceral institutions—schools, armies, prisons, clinics—a control society can be radically decentred and apparently liberated. The difference in the world of work is between a factory and a business. A factory disciplines its subjects by treating them as a body of workers; this also affords the opportunity of organizing and resisting in the form of unionized labour. A business, by contrast, treats employees like hapless contestants on a bizarre, ever-changing game show—something like Japan's "Most Extreme Elimination Challenge," perhaps—where they are mysteriously competing with fellow workers for spectral rewards allocated according to mysterious rules. The affable boss who invites you over for dinner is a paradigm case: Is it business or pleasure? Who else is invited? Does it mean a likely promotion, or nothing at all? Thus does business invade and control the psyche of the worker, precisely because obvious mechanisms of discipline are *absent*.

8   Corinne Maier's otherwise excellent *Bonjour Laziness* (Orion, 2005; trans. Greg Mosse), especially on the language of work, is unstable on this point. She acknowledges the work system is impervious to challenge, and yet finally urges: "rather than a 'new man', be a blob, a leftover, stubbornly resisting the pressure to conform, impervious to manipulation. Become the grain of sand that seizes up the whole machine, the sore thumb" (p. 117). This confused message would seem to indicate insufficient grasp of the slacker/idler distinction.

9   In *The Protestant Ethic and the Spirit of Capitalism* (1934), Weber suggests that puritan ideals—particularly, the "Protestant work ethic" of hard labour as a sign of salvation—were highly influential in the development of capitalism.

10   Rothbard, Murray N. "Bureaucracy and the Civil Service in the United States" in *Journal of Libertarian Studies* 11:2 (Summer, 1995): 3-75, p. 4. The "Iron Law of Oligarchy" was first proposed by German sociologist Robert Michels in *Political Parties: A Sociological Study of the Oligarchical Tendencies of Modern Democracy* (1911).

11   Parkinson, C. Northcote. "Parkinson's Law" in *The Economist* (November 19, 1955).

12   From Pournelle's weblog, "Chaos Manor," (December 14, 2005) <http://www.jerrypournelle.com/archives2/archives-2mail/mail392.html#iron>

13   From Moore's weblog, "Useful Fools," (October 15, 2000) <http://www.tinyvital.com/Misc/Lawsburo.htm>

14   In his *Science of Logic* (1812–1816), Hegel characterizes the "bad infinite" as that which is "never ending" (such as an extensively infinite series of numbers—or, more appropriately, the never ending toils of Sisyphus in Camus' novel). This is contrasted against conceptions of infinity as being "end-less" (such as a closed circle) which, for Hegel, represents a *totality* insofar as it incorporates both the infinite and the finite.

15   More extreme measures can be imagined. In J. G. Ballard's novel *Super-Cannes* (2000), bored executives at a sleek French corporate park are advised by a company psychiatrist that the solution to their lowered output is not psychotherapy but psychopathology: once they begin nocturnal sorties of violence on immigrant workers and prostitutes, productivity rates soar.

16   In his *Economic and Philosophical Manuscripts* (1844), Marx characterizes four types of alienation of labour under capitalism: Alienation of the worker from (1) the product of labour, (2) from the act of labouring (3) from him/herself as a worker, and (4) from his/her fellow workers.

17   "Ne travaillez jamais" was inscribed on Rue de Seine's wall in Paris by Debord in 1953 and was later, much to Debord's disappointment, reproduced en-masse as a "humorous" postcard. <http://www.marxists.org/reference/archive/debord/1963/never-work.htm>

18   Isaiah Berlin, *Against the Current: Essays in the History of Ideas* (Hogarth Press, 1979; Viking Press, 1980), p. 320.

19   This is one implication of the celebrated exchange between Socrates and Thrasymachus at *Republic* I, 340b-344c.

20   See Harry Frankfurt, *On Bullshit* (Princeton University Press, 2005), a huge international bestseller which was in fact a repurposed version of a journal article Frankfurt had published many years earlier, included in his collection *The Importance of What We Care About: Philosophical Essays* (Cambridge, 1988).

21   See, for example, http://www.scn.org/~jonny/genx.html.

22   Jehan (John) Palgrave, *L'éclaircissement de la langue française* (Paris, 1530; Champion, 2003), p. 720.

23   Arendt famously distinguishes *work*, *labour*, and *action*—the three aspects of the *vita activa*—in her magnum opus,

The Human Condition (1958). In this schema, labour operates to maintain the necessities of life (food, shelter, clothing) and is unceasing; work fashions specific things or ends, and so is finite; and action is public display of the self in visible doings. Work as we are discussing it in the present essay is obscurely spread across these categories. As a result, Arendt could indict the emptiness of a society free from labour—the wasteland of consumer desire—but could not see how smoothly the work idea would fold itself back into that wasteland in the form of workaholism.

24   Compare a more recent version of the argument, in the nihilistic words of the Invisible Committee, a group of radical French activists who published their anti-manifesto, *The Coming Insurrection*, in 2009 (anon. English trans., Semiotext(e)): "Here lies the present paradox: work has totally triumphed over all other ways of existing, at the same time as workers have become superfluous. Gains in productivity, outsourcing, mechanization, automated and digital production have so progressed that they have almost reduced to zero the quantity of living labor necessary in the manufacture of any product. We are living the paradox of a society of workers without work, where entertainment, consumption and leisure only underscore the lack from which they are supposed to distract us" (p. 46).

It is perhaps no surprise that the authors, viewing this superfluous majority as set off against the self-colonizing desires for "advancement" in the compliant minority, suggest that the current situation "introduces the risk that, in its idleness, [the majority] will set about sabotaging the machine" (p. 48).

25   In his *One-dimensional Man* (1964), Marcuse distinguishes between "true needs" (i.e., those necessary for survival; food, clothing, shelter) and "repressive needs" (superfluous commodities; luxury items, status symbols, etc.), arguing that a worker's ability to purchase "repressive" items gives them a false sense of equality to their oppressors and, more seriously, turns them away from recognizing the true inequalities of society.

LUCKY STRIKES

Mark Mann
Maisonneuve

When I was a child I wrote a script for my life. It went like this: "Be nice and go to heaven." Then one day I saw an ad for Lucky Strike cigarettes in a magazine. It was simple: a picture of a man and a woman smoking on a fire escape. They weren't going to heaven. They were relaxing. That's when I knew that I wanted to relax too.

I had my first cigarette with my brother when I was sixteen. We smoked leaning against the trunk of my parents' Ford Taurus at a gas station in West Virginia. That was ten years ago. I love smoking. I've been told I'm good at it, a natural. It's not a technique—it's an attitude. You have to take the cigarette for granted. Treat it badly. You know you can't quit but you want to. It's got to be raw.

When I was eighteen I moved to Paris. Before I left, my dad said to me, "Whatever you do, don't come back a smoker." I smoked two packs a day the whole year I was there. I had skin like rotten curtains, but two days before I came back to Canada I quit. Then I started again two weeks later. I've quit smoking at least a dozen times since then. As an experienced smoker once said to me, it's easy to quit; it's just easier to start again.

To quit smoking is miserable. The only way to do it gracefully is to smoke for thirty years and then to stop cold turkey and never mention it again. (The "cold turkey" says it all—a sophisticated snack while out shooting foxes.) If you can't wait thirty years, keep a pack of cigarettes in your pocket when you quit. It will turn your eyes to granite. You'll wrestle buffalo. You'll eat airplanes. More likely, you will gorge yourself on junk food and hate all your friends for a week.

But no one should ever quit smoking. It makes everyone around you uneasy. I once made the mistake of quitting while I was working out west. There was a man there I respected, a foreman named Dave who looked like he was made out of mud and driftwood. When he found out I'd quit, he barked, "Either smoke or smoke, but don't not smoke." So I started again.

Nonsmokers always think they know all sorts of good reasons to quit smoking. "It makes you ugly." "It makes you smell bad." "It kills you." What they don't understand is that smoking is awesome. Nothing reasonable will contradict that fact. Honestly, the only good reason not to smoke is that teenagers smoke. Unfortunately, there's an equally good reason to keep smoking, which is to spite nonsmokers.

Sometimes when you think you're quitting you're only pretending, in which case you bum cigarettes from friends and strangers. The etiquette for bumming cigarettes is this: don't do it. You can't bum cigarettes. You think you can, and sometimes you do, but you can't. Bumming cigarettes is embarrassing for you and degrading for the real smokers who are forced to participate in the sadness and dishonesty of your life. Smoking is for smokers.

The secret of smoking is this: there are winners and losers in the world and smoking is for losers. Smoking is overtly suicidal and for that reason it is a great comfort to losers, because it is a way of keeping death on your team. If you smoke, whenever death appears it will be your old friend. Observe smoke curling in the sunlight: it is the shape of death. Cigarettes are the soothers of the afterlife.

Being a loser is important because losers are more honest. Winners enact their successes by realizing their fantasies, which is to say that they lie to themselves. Losers don't have to do anything like that. They can renounce the insanity of being pure. Smokers don't go to heaven, but they do go up on the roof.

THE PATROCLIZATION OF PAT TILLMAN

Stephen Marche
Queen's Quarterly

Pat Tillman, football star and United States Ranger, never wanted to be a hero even though he lived his life as one. Inspired by September 11, he abandoned a lucrative, promising career as a pro safety in the NFL to enlist. From the moment he signed up, the military wanted to use him for their recruitment program; he refused the offer. He had signed up to be a soldier and he wanted to be a soldier. Complicating his transformation into a great American military symbol even further was his belief that the Iraq war was illegal and a mistake. His first tour of duty was to Iraq. He only deployed to Afghanistan, the war he signed up to fight, in 2004. On April 22 of that year he was killed.

Immediately following the death of Pat Tillman, the struggle for the meaning of his death began. How was Tillman killed? And for what reason? Jon Krakauer's exhaustive study in his 2009 book "Where Men Win Glory" and the documentary film "The Pat Tillman Story" released this fall have established the existence of a conspiracy to promote a specific, narrow interpretation of Tillman's death. That interpretation insisted, against all facts, that the Taliban killed Tillman, when he was in reality killed by friendly fire. Even now the full dimensions of the conspiracy are unknown. At the very least, General Stanley MacCrystal, a three star general at the time, misled the family about the cause of Tillman's death.

The struggle over the meaning of the warrior's body is as old as war itself. *The Iliad* does not tell the story of all the major battles in the Trojan War or explain its causes or justify its outcomes. *The Iliad* concentrates on a comparatively minor incident towards the end of the conflict—a single warrior's refusal to fight. Achilles, upset at the distribution of booty imposed by the king Agamemnon, sulks in his tent, refusing to join his comrades-in-arms, and returns to the fray only after the closest of his comrades, Patroclus, has been killed. Later, after Achilles revenges himself on Patroclus killer Hector and desecrates the corpse, he returns the body of his defeated enemy to Hector's father in a moving and surprising act of grace. *The Iliad*, the greatest story of war in Western civilization, is the story of a couple of corpses.

At the heart of war is the moment when heroes are turned into inanimate objects. At the beginning of the grand interpretation of *The Iliad* by the twentieth century French Catholic philosopher Simone Weil, "The Iliad, Poem of Might," she proposes a definition of might: "It is that x that turns any-body who is subjected to it into a thing. Exercised to the limit, it turns man into a thing in the most literal sense: it makes a corpse of him. Somebody was here, and the next minute there is nobody here at all; this is a spectacle *the Iliad* never wearies of showing us." In this light, the death of Patroclus—a beautiful young man turned into nobody—inhabits the intel-lectual centre of the poem, as well as its primary plot hinge. Patrocolus final words, which amount to a lengthy oration, predict swift revenge from Achilles, but then his ability to speak is cut short by the pure effect of might, the silencing of the killed. Patroclus corpse becomes the subject of the entire next book of *The Iliad*.

At first, the struggle over the corpse may seem pointless. If Weil is correct that *The Iliad* is primarily a poem about how people become nothings, then why should these men risk their lives, indeed risk the outcome of the war, over a "noth-ing"? And yet the value of Patroclus dead body is clear to all participants:

> In the midst of the great fight
> The eye of Menelaus, dear to the wargod
> Had seen Patroclus brought down by the Trojans.
> Now he came forward in his fiery bronze
> Through clashing men to stand astride the body—
> Protective as a heifer who has dropped
> Her first-born calf: she stands above it, lowing,
> Never having known birth pangs before.

It is this struggle over the body that rouses Achilles from his sulking—not any political consequence or any sense of right or wrong or even his loyalty to his living comrades. He would not go and fight with Patroclus when alive but now that Patroclus is dead, he must fight. He must kill Patroclus killer, Hector, even though he knows that he will die shortly after Hector dies. He says as much to his mother, the nymph Thetis:

> "I must reject this life, my heart tells me,
> Reject the world of men,
> If Hector does not feel my battering spear
> Tear the life out of him, making him pay
> In his own blood for the slaughter of Patroclus!"

> Letting a tear fall, Thetis said:
>   "You'll be
> Swift to meet your end, child, as you say:
> Your doom comes close on the heels of Hector's own."

> Achilles the great runner ground his teeth
> And said:
>   "May it come quickly. As things were,
> I could not help my friend in his extremity.
> Far from his home he died; he needed me
> To shield him or to parry the death stroke.
> For me there's no return to my own country.

Achilles despises the war's leaders. He despises the war's motivation. He despises the war's indeterminacy and its foolish conduct. Only the death of Patroclus could make Achilles enter the fray.

The Iliad recognizes, and not in a peripheral way, that the fallen comrade is the single most potent motivation for combat. More than any reason, or any emotional pleading, the dead generates the blood rage necessary to war. As Patton put it three thousand years later to the troops invading Continental Europe: "When you reach into a pile of goo that used to be your best friend's face, you'll know what to do." *The Iliad* prefigures even more contemporary conflicts—the wars in Iraq and Afghanistan— and the development, in our times, of techniques of memorialization as techniques of inspiring combat.

At Pat Tillman's funeral, which was attended by various political and military dignitaries, the story was spun in the clearest terms. The traditional narrative required the fulfillment of three conventions: Tillman was killed by enemy; as a fallen soldier, he was entitled to national recognition; and he was going to a better place. No less a representative that Senator John McCain made this last point at the funeral: "You will see Pat again when a loving God reunites us all with our loved ones." Maria Shriver backed him up: "Pat, you are home. You are safe." This religious approach stung Tillman's brother, Richard, who was barely able to speak from grief and also had a beer in his hand at the podium as he spoke: "Make no mistake, [Pat]'d want me to say this. He's not with God. He's fucking dead. He's not religious. So thanks for your thoughts but he's fucking dead."

The reaction of the Tillman family to the appropriation of their son's memory has been ferocious. They have been forced to combat the idealization of their son's death. As Tillman's father began to realize that his son did not die while fighting the Taliban, his wrath overflowed. His letter to Brigadier-General Gary Jones, the lead investigator, was fuelled by a deep rage born of the hatred of lies:

> You are a general. There is no way a man like you, with your intelligence, education, military experience, responsibilities (primarily for difficult

> situations), and rank... believes the conclusions reached in the March 31, 2005 Briefing Book. But your signature is on it. I assume, therefore, that you are part of this shameless bullshit. I embarrassed myself by treating you with respect.

Tillman's mother's fury was sparked in 2007 by a comment made by a Lieutenant Colonel Ralph Kauzlarich that blamed the Tillman's inability to let go of their son's death on their atheism: "When you die, I mean, there is supposedly a better life, right?" Kauzlarich said. "Well, if you are an atheist and you don't believe in anything, if you die, what is there to go to? Nothing. You are worm dirt." The religious dimension of the traditional dead hero narrative had been violated.

What the Tillman family have been fighting all along is the Patroclization of their son. While it is true that the tip of this process, the suppression of the fact that friendly fire killed Tillman, was a conspiracy in the traditional sense of that word, the other aspects of Tillman's idealization involve a social force much more numinous and powerful than a conspiracy; a vast consonance of expectation. The expectations of a standard story of the soldier's death require clarity of conflict and the assuagements of religion. This narrative consonance has emerged from the very specific demands and failures on the wars in Iraq and Afghanistan, which have been distinct in two ways from previous wars. First, the casualties have been relatively modest. The entire death toll of the Iraq war for America and its allies did not reach the number of dead men at the Dieppe Raid during World War II. Second, the media saturation means that every single fallen soldier in either conflict has his or her picture in the newspaper. We no longer need the Tomb of the Unknown Soldier. At this point, every last soldier is known. In Canada, this personalization of the fallen has taken the form of the Highway of Heroes along the 401, where every single Canadian body is returned to the country with the adulation of crowds bearing his or her picture and name.

President Obama as well as President Bush return to this theme over and over again in their promotion of the war on terror. "Support the troops" has become synonymous with "support the war"—the dead, as sacrifices, demand more death as sacrifice. Everything else about war—its motives, its ultimate results, the quality of its leadership and so on—becomes irrelevant. An identical process, the continuation of war through a need to justify the cost of war, is the process we read in the story of how the corpse of Patroclus provokes the blood lust of Achilles. Pat Tillman and his family, through television interviews and appearances before Congress, as well as through more standard channels of protest, have offered the greatest resistance to this ancient and modern mode of memorialization, which wants to inspire other young men to war through a standardized narrative of struggle and redemption. The Tillmans have refused the Patroclization of their son.

But they are alone. Very alone. The wars in Afghanistan and Iraq are much closer to *The Iliad* than the great world wars they followed. Like Afghanistan and Iraq, the war in Troy was so long that no one could remember why he was fighting except for all those who died in the war before him.

The Iliad ends with a moment of hope, of strange respect between enemies. Priam, King of Troy, comes to beg for his son's body from Achilles. The mortal enemies find themselves weeping in each other's arms:

> Now in Achilles
> The evocation of [Hector's] father stirred
> New longing, and an ache of grief. He lifted

> The old man's hand and gently put him by.
> Then both were overborne as they remembered:
> The old king huddled at Achilles' feet
> Wept, and wept for Hector, killer of men,
> While great Achilles wept for his own father
> As for Patroclus once again; and sobbing
> Filled the room.

For the moment it is forgotten who killed whom, or why or how. All that matters, for that single moment is that they were all so young and beautiful, and they're all dead.

This ancient moment offers clues to where we are going and where we stand now. Patroclus, Hector, Achilles, their fathers, their sons—the weeping becomes confused in a great conflagration of mourning. That's how *The Iliad* ends. Only when the mourning is general, when it encompasses the whole of the brutality of the conflict outside of this or that man, can it ever come to an end.

THE PROTOCOLS OF USED BOOKSTORES: A GUIDE TO DEALING WITH CERTAIN PERILS WHICH COULD BE ENCOUNTERED IN A USED BOOKSTORE

David Mason
Descant

> *Because bookshops are among the few places where*
> *one can spend time, without spending any money, any*
> *number of practically certifiable lunatics are guaranteed*
> *to be found regularly in most of them.*
> —George Orwell

Used bookstores, in spite of their usual disorderly grunginess, still tend to give off an aura of civilization. Casual visitors may not notice much of what goes on in them. The average civilized person, who would never themselves create a problem, might be surprised, at some of the bizarre scenes and conversations which occur, some of them defying all logic—even sanity.

One of the questionable compensations which used booksellers receive in return for devoting themselves to a precarious

vocation is a constant exposure to all the varieties and ex-
tremes of human behaviour at its most eccentric. While on
a good day eccentricity can be stimulating, even exhilarat-
ing, on a bad day it can test your endurance and threaten
your ability to cope. So, the following rules and guidelines on
how to navigate a used bookshop are both to help make your
quest for a book simpler, but also to allow the proprietor and
his staff to get through another day without too much need-
less anxiety.

There will be updated versions of these guidelines from
time to time as new aberrations are brought to the editor's
notice. In the meantime you should be aware that all the
stupid questions in this piece are authentic; every single one,
no matter how ludicrous it may appear has been said to me
or one of my colleagues, often many times.

This edition repairs a few errors and adds some minor
changes, mostly to justify my referring to it in the standard
bookselling jargon as "The Best Edition, revised and aug-
mented."

The Rules

1 When you enter a used bookstore do not ask if it is a
library. A common preliminary to that question comes
from the man who stands in the entrance, looks around,
nods his head sagely and astutely observes, "Books, eh?"

A store usually exists to sell things—even a bookstore. Someone who rents a store, stocks it and hires employees, usually has
a motive: he's hoping to earn a living. On the other hand what
a used bookstore does have in common with a library—aside
from the books—is that if you misbehave and offend the proprietor, he may rescind your privileges, he may refuse to let
you buy a book. He may decide you aren't qualified to own

that book, and you will then be condemned to wallow in ignorance forever.

2 Do not ask if the proprietor has read all these books. He would have liked to, but life isn't long enough. However, many booksellers do believe that they absorb civilization by osmosis, just by being surrounded by all those books, even if they can't read them all. Many experienced booksellers, when this question is posed, respond in kind. "Yes," they reply, "of course I have. Do you think I'd sell a book I hadn't read?"

3 Do not ask the proprietor where he gets all those books, unless you have several hours to spare. If you are asking because you are thinking of opening your own store, the reply will be simple. Just go to the dump every day and put up a few flyers asking people to bring you free books. The rest is easy, then you just wait for the money to roll in.

4 Do not ask to see the oldest book in the store. Do not even ask the date of the store's oldest book. Every bookseller has had that question, some thousands of times. The owner probably won't even know, and he certainly doesn't care.

Why not ask a real question. For instance: "I really like so and so's books. Given that, can you suggest another author I might like?" You might be surprised what you discover.

5 Do not ask which is the most expensive book in the store, for the same reason. You might pick a bad day when the bookseller is looking for an excuse to strike out at anyone who gives him cause. It's not about money, it's about culture, about civilization. Money is only one way to measure importance. Booksellers, although they must put a monetary value on their books, do not much like people who demonstrate that they believe money is the only measure of value. A Shakespeare first folio might cost you $5,000,000—a recent reprint of the collected plays could be had for $5.00. What then is the value of Shakespeare?

6 Have some idea of what you are looking for, if only vaguely. Stores are usually laid out in subject order, just so you have some chance of finding something you will want to buy. You should keep in mind that the proprietor knows his stock; he has bought every book in the store and he has priced them all. And most important he wants to help you find the book you need. Even if you yourself don't know yet what that book is.

Do you remember who introduced you to your wife, or husband, or partner? Do you feel an eternal sense of warmth and gratitude to the person who did? Well, what gratitude should you feel towards a person who introduces you to a great book or a great author? Booksellers thrive on that kind of gratitude. (See Rule 36.)

7 In used bookshops the book's price will be generally penciled in on the first blank page, usually in the upper corner. The price is not the 65¢ that is printed on the flap of the dustjacket. That was its price when it was published in 1910. It is not reasonable to expect the book to be half of 65¢. A lot of things are more expensive now then they were in 1910. And just in case you think no one would be so dumb as to try that, I can assure you that every used bookseller has had that tried on him many, many times. A colleague tells me that her standard response to this affront to all intelligence is to respond, "That is a 1960 price. I'll make you a deal. I'll sell you that book at its 1960 price if you sell me your house at its 1960 value."

The first time it happened to me was forty-three years ago, in the first week I was open, and the person asking was a history professor who had just spent half an hour telling me how he was going to be my best customer. I was so shocked it took a good thirty seconds to realize I was dealing with an idiot. This also was probably my first introduction to that monster all business people call, "The Public."

8 Further to the above, do not announce loudly that the book in your hand is only the first of many, many purchases that you will be making over the next forty years or so. The owner may be skeptical since he probably will remember the previous 43,000 people who said that, who he never saw again.

The reason the bookseller doesn't gush with pleasure when you inform him of your life-long devotion to his store is because he is aware that you are about to ask him for a discount. (See Rules 9 and 10.)

9 Do not ask for a discount, unless you are well-known in that store. Certainly, do not ask for the student discount when your hair is graying and you are wearing a suit. And most crucial, never ask for a "teacher's discount." This one could be dangerous. The same with the "clergyman's discount." This one sometimes elicits interesting replies. My own favorite response to this is, "Salvation doesn't come cheap, you know." Do not bother to plead poverty; the proprietor, relative to you, is almost certainly poorer. (See Rule 10.)

10 Do not discuss discounts in used bookshops at all until you know the bookseller fairly well. You should be aware that used booksellers, unlike art or antique dealers, do not price with the notion that the price is negotiable (art) or that the asking price is 10-20% higher than what the dealer wants to get (antiques.) This is why at antique shows and such places one sees prices like $12.00 or $110.00—they have used those prices when they expect to sell at $10.00 or $100.00. You think you got a discount but you in effect paid what they intended to get. Booksellers do not do this. Their prices are what they consider fair and they expect to get that price. Therefore any discount they give is a real gift, out of their pocket into yours.

Early on, during my apprenticeship, I got a lesson on how to deal with this misconception on the high-end level. A collector, a doctor, a Métis himself I think, and a very nice man, was passionately buying everything my boss showed him on Louis Riel and his Rebellion. He spent a considerable amount of money and one day he said to my boss, "I've been spending a fair bit of money with you guys, don't you think it's time I got a discount?"

My boss replied, "Well Doctor—Riel is very popular and very saleable. First, let me ask you a question. If I have two customers for Riel and one of them, when I call him about a recent acquisition, comes in and tries to beat me down on the price and the second one comes in, thanks me for thinking of him, asks what he owes me and pulls out his cheque book, which one do you think I will call first the next time I get a rare Riel item?"

The doctor thought about this for a moment, then said, "Let's pretend we never had this conversation." And the next time my boss got another Riel item he gave our valued, and very wise client a nice discount. Establish trust first; good things will follow.

11 When coming into a shop for the first time, please try to avoid announcing loudly that you are a book lover. The proprietor understands that to mean you aren't going to buy anything. Real book lovers rarely feel the need to stress the obvious. They demonstrate their devotion by going straight to the books. No real book lover has ever left a bookstore without buying a book.

12 Just because you can get away with carrying your coffee around Chapters, setting it down on the covers of books while you browse, do not try to enter a real used bookstore with coffee or sticky food which you are eating by hand. You may find yourself humiliated in the manner such gross misbehavior would have merited in grade two.

Every used bookseller has had the experience, usually many times, of encountering an important 20th century highspot, the dustwrapper ruined by the tell-tale circular mark of the coffee cup. Maybe you wouldn't do that if you'd ever tried to sell your copy of *The Catcher in the Rye* only to be offered $500.00 instead of $15,000.00 because of that coffee stain.

13 Try to know the author and title of the book—your favorite ever—which you have been seeking since childhood. Describing the plotline or remembering the cloth colour is not helpful. There are many books about plucky dogs who rescued their master or mistress from certain death. At least try to remember the dog's name.

14 Do not pretend you are looking for a rare book and only incidentally are curious to know what it will cost you, when in fact you are speaking of the book you own and are trying to value. You have no idea how often booksellers have seen this ploy.

If you do this anyway and the bookseller replies $10.00, do not openly voice your disappointment at the price, admitting then that you actually own that book. The dealer could easily reply, "Yes, I know you do, that's why I didn't tell you the real value." Why not just tell the dealer that you own that book and ask him what its worth? Don't be shocked when he tells you the truth. Always, of course, with the inescapable caveat about condition.

15 Do not offer to leave a deposit to hold an expensive book. The dealer won't want to do this since he already knows that 19 of 20 such occasions result in you forgetting to return and him holding the book for several years. (It is only very new, inexperienced dealers who make the mistake of taking deposits.) A bookseller will be happy to hold the book for ten days or two weeks but he doesn't want a deposit. Either way, nineteen of twenty people don't come back. Readers of books are prone to enthusiasms which evaporate quickly after a few minutes, along with the recollection that they have reserved a book.

16 If you really want a book and you cannot afford to pay its price, tell the dealer that. He will know if you are telling the truth. Most dealers will respond by offering you time to pay and usually they will base their terms on your age. The younger you are the more gentle they will be. This effort to accommodate your means is not a cheap ploy to suck you in, but a sincere read of your position. Every bookseller was once young and poor too (indeed, many are now middle-aged or elderly and still poor) and has many memories of the book he lusted after but couldn't pay for and never got.

A dealer will sense how sincere you are and will do what he can to help. Almost every dealer I have ever known operates on his credit line at the bank, for which he pays interest. Which means that he is paying interest on what you are paying no interest on.

Furthermore a real bookseller will feel good by accommodating your poverty. He will see such a gesture as his justification for the pitiful living he earns. He may go home and tell his wife "I had a kid today who wanted a hundred dollar book so badly, he almost cried when I told him he could pay it off at $10.00 a month." He will feel vindicated by his generosity; not his financial generosity, but his generosity of spirit. He may think, "That kid could become a great scholar, or a famous writer and I have helped him." And I'm not kidding when I say this.

17 Do not complain loudly that the most important book published on a particular subject in recent years is not displayed prominently in the store and what kind of a bookstore is this anyway. If the proprietor happens to know that you are the author it could result in embarrassment, especially if the dealer tells you he wouldn't take that book even if it was offered to him for free. As part of that syndrome, new booksellers have many stories of authors surreptitiously attempting to move the entire pile of their book to a more prominent spot in the front of a store.

18 When you inform the proprietor that you know he won't have a certain book because it is very rare and you have searched for it everywhere for twenty-five years and the bookseller goes directly to a shelf, brings back a copy of the book and hands it to you, it is unwise to say:

   a.   "$25.00?" (in a shocked tone.) "For a book?"

   b.   "Oh! That much? I can only afford $2.00."

   c.   "Oh... I guess I'll keep looking."

   d.   "Oh, I only wanted the paperback."

   e.   "Oh thanks. I don't want it now I just wanted to

see what it looks like so I'll recognize it when I
see it again."

f.   "You're nothing but a crook."

g.   "Could you hold that? I'll give you a deposit."

h.   (Looking at watch.) "I must come back when I
have more time."

19 When the proprietor of a used bookstore asks if
he can help, he is not beginning his campaign to
sell you something you don't want or need, like a new suit
or the latest fad. He actually is interested in directing you to
the appropriate book. If you answer "Just browsing" he will
assume you are afraid of him. You should answer, "Only if I
don't find something on my own." Remember, the bookseller
wants you to buy a book, indeed he depends on it. However,
unlike many businesses, he only wants to sell you a book
that you want. The bookseller knows that he may never own
another copy of that book and he wants it to go where it will
be appreciated.

20 Do not point out that a particular book is in the wrong
section, especially in a superior fashion, in order to
show the foolish proprietor that you are truly sophisticated,
unlike him. Especially when there are so many books which
could be appropriately housed in any of several sections. *Alice in Wonderland* could be in the Children's section, or the Illustrated section, or the 19th Century English literature section, or the general literature section, or the Classics section
(not the Greek and Rome classics, that's an entirely different section) or, it could be in the *Alice in Wonderland* section
(that's beside the Omar Khayyam section).

Example: a University professor, handing me John Kenneth Galbraith's *The Scotch*, informed me, with obvious con-

descension, that it didn't belong in Ontario social history but in the Scotland section. When it is pointed out to such people that Galbraith was a Canadian and that his "Scotch" were the settlers in his particular area in Ontario, they usually leave—quickly. As with all those situations where you only think of the proper response when it's way too late to use, I regret I didn't think to say what I would now. Which would be, "Am I ever glad I didn't go fifty grand in debt to send my kid to a University which is staffed by pedantic simpletons like you."

21 It is best not to give business advice to booksellers even though it is obvious to you that they are ignoring all the basic principles of business. Many booksellers learned everything they know in the bookstore where they worked before they opened one themselves. In other words they have learned traditions which go back some five hundred years. Nobody likes to have amateurs tell him how to run his business and booksellers are no different. Similarly, lots of people seem to feel qualified to tell writers, artists, filmmakers, etc. how they should create their art. Would you tell a dentist how to fill a tooth? Or a brain surgeon how to perfect his technique? Booksellers tend to have a different take on what constitutes proper business tactics.

22 Do not question the price of that book out loud. If you are in a real bookstore the proprietor has a lot of experience and he has gone to considerable trouble to arrive at what he believes is a fair price. If his price doesn't suit you, better to just leave and go to that store you know in New York that will certainly sell it cheaper. (See Rules 29 and 30.)

23 Do not assume that the bookseller has read your favorite author and shares your devotion. "I think that's Agatha Christie's greatest novel. What do you think?" He may hurt your feelings by telling you he despises your favourite author. Booksellers handle the detritus of every literary fad. There's nothing more boring than last months bestseller to a bookseller. I could name a hundred authors, famous when they were first published, who are now forgotten and whose books abound in our stores. All of which provides us with yet another humbling example of the ephemeral nature of fame.

24 If you go into a bookstore in winter you should remember to take your gloves off before you start handling books. Tearing a dustwrapper is bad enough, but if you fumble and drop that expensive first edition on the wet floor you could be in acute danger—perhaps physical danger.

I once asked a man to remove his gloves; he became quite indignant. "I've been coming into this bookstore for twenty years and no one ever asked me to take my gloves off!" he yelled.

"I guess you must have come in on my days off—or during my holiday." I could only reply. "That's probably why I don't recognize you."

Mittens are much worse; it's even harder to turn the pages.

25 After coming in from a heavy rain, or snow storm, it is better for everybody if you don't lean against the bookshelves while you peruse a book. That sort of behavior tends to make the colour of the book cloth run, causing anxiety to the owner and perhaps pain or humiliation to you.

26 If you sit in the only chair in the store and spend two hours reading a book do not complain if the owner insults you and kicks you out when you are midway through the book. He has purposely let you get hooked so that he could have the pleasure of ruining your fun, since he was already aware that you had no intention of buying that book. And you have already been told that it's not a library. That's the reason that you almost never see a chair in a used bookshop (except the ones who call themselves "Ye Olde Booke Shoppe"). Chapters tried chairs but had to change the rules when the distributors wouldn't take back all the books and magazines ruined by grease and coffee stains.

27 Just because you have worked out a system that will save our entire civilization from the approaching apocalypse that is not a justification to harass the bookseller and his other customers by lecturing them on your philosophy. You already knew that the world was stupid and they wouldn't listen to you—so why do you think we will? Just because it's a bookstore it seems. George Orwell, who once worked in a used bookstore, said somewhere, "People go into most stores to buy something, they go into bookstores to make a nuisance of themselves."

Booksellers have an early warning system to avoid this sort of thing. It works like this; "Watch out for the ones who don't blink." This syndrome also explains why one of the first signs that a bookseller finally has his head above water is when he gets rid of the entire "Occult" section.

28 Yes, we sell Marx even though we are capitalists and yes, we can sell you a copy of *Mein Kampf* (if you can answer a few character-testing questions.) And yes, we'll even show you the racist hate literature or antiquarian pornography from the back room if you can pass the same tests. Our job is to salvage everything, both good and bad, which reflects civilization. But we will not sell you that stuff if we believe your motives are questionable. And yes—you're right—that is indeed a form of censorship. But, they're our books and we make the rules. Many booksellers seem to take a perverse pleasure in sacrificing profit because of personal principles.

29 It is not nice to lecture the proprietor on how, and why, you know that the price of his book is ludicrous. He has already concluded that you are a fool, and an obnoxious one too. The only reason he doesn't answer is because he knows that you will leave him in peace sooner if he doesn't take the bait.

Very early on, a man greatly abused me over the $15.00 price on a fat two volume history of the U.S. Civil War. He stomped out when I bravely stood my ground. Two weeks later he came in at precisely the moment I was sealing a bag containing that book for the man who had just bought it.

"Oh, all right," said the first man, in a contemptuous tone, intending to demonstrate that I was a sleazy crook, "I've decided to pay your atrocious price."

"I'm so sorry sir," I smiled. "This man here has just bought it."

This was one of the greatest put-downs I ever had the pleasure of committing. Thankfully I never saw that man again and, coincidently, in the forty years since that occurred I've never seen that book again either.

30 Be very careful, even if you think you know a bookseller well, how you suggest that his asking price is ludicrous, or criminal, or both. When you inform the bookseller that you saw the same book in New York for $5.00 and why is his $10.00, prepare yourself to hear the chopped liver story—if he is in a good mood—or to be summarily kicked out if he's having a bad day. The chopped liver story goes like this: Mrs. Lester asks the butcher, "How much is the chopped liver today?"

"It's 1.25 a pound," answers the butcher.

"That's outrageous," says Mrs. Lester. "I'll go to the butcher across the road."

Returning in a few minutes Mrs. Lester states, "So and so's liver across the road is only .95¢ a pound. Why is yours so much more?"

"Tell me," says the butcher, "If his is only 95¢ a pound why are you back here? Why didn't you buy his liver?"

"Because he doesn't have any today," says Mrs. Lester.

"Oh, of course. Well, when we don't have any liver our price is only 75¢ a pound."

But remember, that's the good-cop response. (See Rules 22 and 29.)

31 You should know that the first rule in most used bookshops is that the customer is always wrong. Before you say anything whatsoever to a bookseller it's better to be aware that the bookseller makes very little money, has never made any money and is probably by now painfully aware that he never is going to make any money. What this means is that whether you buy that book or not means very little to him and he will react accordingly. All of which should warn you that if you rile him anything could occur—you takes your chances. Better to know this. A word to the wise, as your old grandma used to say. (See all rules.)

32 If you want to look at that leather-bound book and you have never handled a leather-bound book before, it is wise to ask the proprietor how to do so (he is watching you closely anyway, ready to move in quickly—in defense of civilization—if the book is in danger.) Opening a leather-bound book improperly can be dangerous—certainly to the book, but possibly even more so to you. You should not be embarrassed that you don't know how to handle a leather-bound book correctly. Neither do 99.9% of the rest of the population—nor have they since the eighteenth century.

33 That backpack which you are so attached to (even though it makes you look like a dork) is actually considered to be a dangerous weapon by booksellers and most other shopkeepers. Especially around the new display of first editions on the shelf-top counter. The owner cannot be held responsible if another customer who you hit for the third time as you turn quickly in the aisle, reacts with violence. The only thing to be said in its defense is that, unlike a bag or a brief case, it is not seen as a danger from a theft point of view. Amongst the great mysteries of our time is what could possibly be in all those stuffed backpacks. Why is every one we ever see always bulging full?

34 Do not answer your cellphone if it rings while you are in the bookstore. Turn it off when you enter if you wish to retain the proprietor's good regard. It is not that bookstores have the "quiet, please" convention of libraries; it is that bookstores consider themselves to be havens of civilization in an increasingly vulgar and sordid world, and your puerile, loudly conducted, inane conversation, will be seen as an affront to that concept.

If you feel the need to make a call yourself, it is considered courteous to go outside in the street. For the same reason as, if you feel the need to pick your nose in public you should go to a hidden aisle to also avoid offending the sensibilities of civilized people.

35 Do not bring your bike into the bookstore with you. It is unlikely that in search of a diamond ring, or some valuable gift, to demonstrate your eternal devotion to your beloved, that you would enter a jewelry store bringing your bicycle with you and parking it against a glass case. So why do you think that's acceptable in a used bookstore? Anything in front of a shelf pretty much guarantees that no one will look there. So, in effect you're damaging his business to protect your bicycle. It is probable that the bookseller would prefer to buy you a lock rather then have your bike in his store.

36 Carry a list of the books you that currently seek. Do not be embarrassed that the mental list of books you are intent on finding evaporates from your head the instant you enter a bookstore, along with the names of your most recent favorite authors. This happens to everyone, even booksellers, when they enter other bookstores. It must be a syndrome. Perhaps it is due to natural feelings of inadequacy in the face of such an overwhelming profusion of civilization. But don't worry. The names of all those books you have sought for years will come back to you within five minutes of leaving the store.

37 When you take books for sale to a bookseller do not ask for specific offers for every book. He will not tell you. The reason for this is, that he knows if he does, you will happily sell him the ones he's offered $5.00 each for, since that is much more than you expected to get. But he also knows that you will then inform him that the one he's offering $100.00 for, you have just remembered that your mother wanted to read before you sold it. The bookseller knows that you have concluded that he's trying to cheat you on that book and you believe it's really worth $1,000. He knows that you assume he is a crook, just as he knows that if he had offered you $5.00 for that one too, you would have been delighted. But, of course he will believe your promise that you will bring it back when your mother has finished reading it, even though no one ever has before in the whole recorded history of the book trade. Booksellers love to tell stories of buying the same book later at an auction for a fraction of what they had offered in their shop.

38 It is not a good idea to bring in books you wish to sell with print-outs from AbeBooks inserted, especially when you only insert the $1,000.00 listings from internet booksellers who no one ever heard of because they are not real booksellers and neglect to insert the print-out of the same book by a real dealer whose asking price is $50.00.

It is much better to simply become a bookseller yourself on AbeBooks. Then you can ask $2,000.00. Don't worry about whether it is a first edition or not, nor about that cover which fell off. The customer won't mind. Some things to remember though; what's really important is the name you choose to call your self on AbeBooks. "Ye Olde Booke Shoppe" or "Bargain Books" are good ones, they inspire confidence. And more important is the description you choose to steal from the real bookseller who is also offering a copy on the net. It is imperative to always steal the description from a dealer who has initials after their name, which indicates that they know what they're doing. It's also a good idea to ensure that the description you steal is for a book in similar binding. If your copy is an ex-library copy better not to mention that either, a lot of people don't like ex-library copies.

When booksellers see those print-outs the smart ones will simply tell you they're not interested in your books. It's easier than attempting a three hour lesson in the economics and the psychology of the used book business.

39 Go ahead and steal that book; you have more right to it than the bookseller anyway. He's obviously rich or he wouldn't have all those books. He's also a vulgar, greedy capitalist, or he wouldn't put arbitrary prices on knowledge. All knowledge should be free and anyone like this bookseller, who doesn't believe that is obviously a fascist or a communist, or both. He deserves to lose that book, and you will be righting a wrong by taking it. Even though you have already been told that it is not a library, you know it should be and this rogue deserves to be taught a lesson.

But based on what you've already learned—that the bookseller has little to lose—you might want to consider what could occur if he catches you slipping it in your pocket. And if you are prone to philosophical speculation you might consider this, my favorite axiom on the subject; "If you want to know whether stealing is wrong, steal from a thief and see how he likes it."

40 Learn the signs that tell you that you are in the wrong sort of bookstore. Of course you should know that, as in every human activity, there are some crooks (although less than you might imagine) in the book business. But more dangerous, are the ignorant fools who run stores with no comprehension of the extent of their own ignorance.

These people constitute a greater danger to you than the rare crooks you might encounter.

Some of the cautionary signs for this type of store can be learned. Unpriced books. Beware of any store which has unpriced books, especially those who, when you are foolish enough to ask the price, start looking it up on the internet.

Or stare at your clothes trying to figure out how rich you are. Or the one where a price of $10.00, when you take it up to the pay desk, you are informed is an "old" price, years old, and it is now $25.00. And beware of any store which has prices like $4.99 or $99.95 or some such, this means they don't know if it's worth $5.00 or $100.00, indeed they don't know much of anything probably. Beware of any bookstore where they have standard purchase prices posted—i.e. $1.00 for a hardcover, 25¢ for a paperback—(especially if they are called Ye Olde Booke Shoppe.) And, unfortunately there are many more, which I don't have the space to relate. Send me two dollars and a self-addressed stamped envelope and I'll send you some more.

41 Don't expect a bookseller to be very enthusiastic about the first edition of Burns Poems that your grandfather brought from the old country when he immigrated. Every used bookseller has seen at least ten thousand copies of the first edition of Burns' Poems, That's why it's hard to understand why such a common book, that everybody's grandfather seems to have brought over here, sells for $75,000 or so today. Personally every one I've ever been offered in forty years was at least a hundred years too late.

The same with your old family bible. Even if bibles from 1890 had any value (which they don't) the missing cover and title page, and the water stains from the ship's hold on yours, would be considered in some quarters to be a crippling defect. Better to keep it—and your illusions—in the family. Re-member, if you don't show it to an expert, you can continue to believe it's a valuable treasure. In fact, you should be aware that dealers can't help wondering why, if it is such a priceless treasure to your family, you would consider selling it for mere money in the first place.

42 Try and refrain from telling the proprietor about your magnificent collection of books on budgies. He probably has his own personal interests and yours may bore him. He understands that your entire family believes you're nuts and treats your beloved collection with derision and contempt and he is aware that you are lonely and know no other collectors who you can talk to about your passion— and he sympathizes—but he actually has a lot of work to do. Also, there is something a little ludicrous, pathetic even, about a grown man boasting about his nearly complete run of "Model Railroad Monthly" or books on the Titanic.

43 Don't boast to the bookseller about the wonderful bargain you found. The bookseller doesn't really want to hear about the first edition of *Ulysses* you bought for 10¢ at the church sale, especially when you then inform him that that crooked bookseller up the street tried to cheat you out of it, by telling you it wasn't really the first edition and offering $5.00 for it. This is even more distressing to the bookseller when you show it to him and it is the Modern Library edition. And more so when the crook up the street is the bookseller's best friend, or his brother-in-law.

44 And now the final one. This is the comment which booksellers get more than any other single com-ment and certainly the one we all most despise. It is often delivered by the man in the first rule who begins by observing, "Books, eh?" It's short and simple but perhaps it will need some pondering for you to understand some of the many things it conveys to a bookseller, but let me assure you, it tells us plenty.

And so—the final rule: Don't expect the proprietor to smile with pleasure when you say, "I'll have to come back when I have more time." Many, many thousands of people have said this before you, never to be seen again.

The truth is, booksellers believe that what they sell is important to civilization and that their presence contributes to that civilization. And sometimes they don't have much more than that conviction to keep them going. Try to keep that in mind when you enter a bookshop, and try to enter in the same spirit.

THE LIZARD, THE CATACOMBS, AND THE CLOCK: THE STORY OF PARIS MOST SECRET UNDERGROUND SOCIETY

Sean Michaels
Brick

"It's a war of knowledge. Whoever knows the most is king."
—Crato

Entrances

The sun was shining on the Trocadéro, the Eiffel Tower gleamed across the Seine, and deep below ground, police came across a sign. The officers were on a training mission, exploring the 4.3 miles of catacombs that twist beneath the 16th arrondissement. The former quarries are centuries-old, illegal to enter, and the sign at the mouth of the tunnel read, "No public entry." Police are not the public; they entered. Their headlamps flashed against the limestone walls and then suddenly the officers were surrounded. Invisible dogs snarled and barked from all sides.

The men's hearts hammered. They froze in their tracks. They cooed canine comforts into the dark.

In time, the officers' lights found the PA system. They found the stereo, with guard-dog yowls burned onto a CD. They found three thousand square feet of subterranean galleries, strung with lights, wired for phones, live with pirated electricity. The officers uncovered a bar, lounge, workshop, dining corner, and small screening area. The cinema's seats had been carved into the stone itself, with room for twenty people to sit in the cool and chomp on popcorn.

On the floor of one cavern, officers discovered an ominous metal container. The object was fat, festooned with wires. The police called in the bomb squad, they evacuated the surface, they asked themselves, *What have we found?*

They had found a couscous maker.

A few days after the *couscoussière* incident, officers returned to the scene. This time they brought agents from Électricité de France. But they were too late. Already someone had undone the galleries' wiring, disappeared with the equipment, vanished with the booze. What had so recently been a private cinema, a secret hideout, was now just an empty quarry. The cinema's makers had left a note. "*Ne cherchez pas*," they wrote. Don't search.

Don't search? *For what? For whom?* While the Agence France Presse reported a possible "extreme right-wing" connection, the BBC speculated on a full-fledged "underground movement." All of Paris dreamed of its subterranean screening society.

However, the people responsible for the cinema under the Trocadéro, a place they dubbed the Arènes de Chaillot, are not quite any of these things. "We are the counterpoint to an era where everything is slow and complicated," they explain. This group also balances the aspect of today that is instant and shameless, hysterically tweeting. They are patient, serious, and they keep their secrets.

After the cinema episode, it would be two years until the city would see their work again.

Porte-parole

I AM LATE. Paris decaying public-transit system almost strands me at Gare du Nord and I arrive at Le Pantalon out of breath, panicked, terrified that Lazar Kunstmann has left. I slip past students in this noisy bar, searching for the face I have seen in a handful of photographs. I crossed the ocean to meet him and I may not get another chance.

Lazar Kunstmann is stocky, in his late thirties. He has a shaved head. He is friendly. Too friendly, almost—the eagerness in his eyes seems utterly unclandestine. This is not the mystery man I envisioned: Kunstmann is warm, cheerful, and talkative.

He first appeared in 2004, the mouthpiece for a group called La Mexicaine de Perforation (LMDP). Though it literally translates as "the Mexican of the Drilling," their moniker is best understood as something like "The Mexican Consolidated Drilling Authority." The organization was named for a bar in the 16th arrondissement's Place de Mexico. LMDP, Kunstmann revealed, was responsible for the cinema under the Trocadéro.

"Two-thousand four was the first big discovery," Kunstmann admits. "We were really caught in flagrante delicto."

I was living in Scotland at the time. The French and British press were enraptured with the underground cinema and so was I. The appeal wasn't just in the breadth of the cinema-builders' imagination but in their meticulous follow-through. "We covered our tracks," Kunstmann reassured *The Guard-*

ian. "Short of digging up every cable in the district there's no way of knowing where we took [the electricity] from."

Giddy and well spoken, Kunstmann was at the centre of every article. He had spent decades going where he wasn't supposed to: climbing onto roofs at age seven, sneaking through the subway at twelve, delving into the Paris' catacombs at fourteen. He and his co-conspirators met at school in the 1980s, when many Latin Quarter colleges still had basement access into the tunnels. Although Parisians have been sneaking into the catacombs (known as *carrières*) for centuries, Kunstmann and his friends had no taste for the usual "cataphile" hijinks. Too young to drink, not interested in drugs, they instead began to explore, map, and expand the underground network.

Eventually, Kunstmann tells me, they entered a "post-post-exploration phase." After "you go, you survey—then it's time to do something."

Five years after the discovery of the cinema, Kunstmann has written a book exposing the full scale of this "something." In *La culture en clandestins: L'UX*, published by the French imprint Hazan, Kunstmann reveals LMDP as just one wing of a larger clandestine organization called UX. UX (pronounced "oo-eex," like the French letters) has more than one hundred members, split into more than ten teams. While LMDP are dedicated to events, other branches are devoted to maps, restoration, or key-making. "[We] are determined to make these abandoned places a theater for new experiences," Kunstmann explains in his book. This means more than it seems. In French, the word *expériences* connotes both "experiences" and "experiments." UX itself, an acronym for Urban eXperiences, borrows the double meaning.

The Arènes de Chaillot were built over a period of eighteen months. Starting in 1999 and continuing every summer until the cinema's discovery, the tunnels hosted Urbex Movies. It

was a festival combining careful programming and an unusual locale to present discrete visions of urban life. Shorts
and features were grouped by unstated "intention," to allow
for each twenty- to thirty-person audience "to discover, or
merely to feel." A similar philosophy dominated LMDP's other
major film festival, the Sessión Cómoda. Whereas Urbex Movies screened films like *Eraserhead* and Dziga Vertov's *Man
With A Camera*, the Sessión Cómoda had a narrower focus
on the underground—showing *The Third Man* and Jacques
Becker's *Le Trou*. These screenings took place nearby, but
above ground—in the famous Cinémathèque of the Palais de
Chaillot. Which isn't to say that the Sessión Cómoda was part
of the Cinémathèque's official program. No—LMDP snuck in,
week after week, year after year, entering (they claim) from a
passage beneath the projectionist's chair.

For both festivals, audiences were drawn from among UX's
friends, associates, and members of the public who stumbled
across scattered fliers. "The LMDP are simply interested in
holding events in a free way," Kunstmann explains. "Clandestinity is really a detail."

It's the detail that allows them to continue what they are
doing. UX slip past the functionaries, under the cordons,
across miles of red tape. Their high-concept installations use
secrecy as a cover, but it's not their raison d'être. "We don't
seek out the forbidden," Kunstmann murmurs over radio-
pop. "We just repudiate any notion of authorization."

At the same time, UX's anonymity is a major source of
their allure. We are drawn by their gall, their pluck, but also
the burnished gleam of a mystery. The Arènes de Chaillot
would not be the same treasure if they were sanctioned, pub-
lic-funded. Kunstmann is surely aware of this, yet he balks at
being part of "something 'plugged in,' elitist, VIP." UX do not
wish to be a "secret society," he insists. "When I say secret
society, you imagine, I don't know, like, in *Eyes Wide Shut*.

But it's more basic than that. It's the patronage system. It's taking advantage of a hidden alliance."

The group's operational need for clandestinity is offset by this distaste for old boys' clubs. And so UX leave avenues for strangers to stumble across their works, they have published a book revealing certain details, and years ago they resolved to never hide what was in plain sight. This is why LMDP revealed themselves in 2004. Once the Arènes de Chaillot were discovered, with speculation mounting—"In that instant," Kunstmann says, "we had to clearly explain."

They didn't divulge everything.

D'Enfers

PARISIANS CALL IT A *GRUYÈRE*. For hundreds of years, the catacombs under the city have been a conduit, sanctuary, and birthplace for its secrets. The Phantom of the Opera and *Les Misérables*' Jean Valjean both haunted these tunnels, striking students descended in 1968, as did patriots during the Second World War. The Nazis visited too, building a bunker in the maze below the 6th arrondissement.

Honeycombed across 1,900 acres of the city, the vast majority of the tunnels are not strictly speaking "catacombs." They house no bones. Limestone (and, to the north of the city, gypsum) quarries, these are the mines that built Paris. The oldest date back two thousand years to Roman settlers, but most were excavated in the construction boom of the late Middle Ages, providing the stone that became Notre Dame Cathedral and the Louvre. Riddling the Left Bank, these tunnels were at first beyond the city's southern limits. But as Paris' population grew, so did the city—and soon whole neighbourhoods were built on this infirm ground.

The first major cave-in happened in 1774, when an entire street collapsed not far from where the Catacombs Museum stands today. After a similar incident three years later, King Louis XVI created the office of the Inspection Générale de Carrières (IGC, or General Inspection of the Quarries), designated with preventing further collapses. Officials went underground: inspecting, charting, filling chambers with concrete, digging a new labyrinth of maintenance tunnels.

Then came the dead. In the late eighteenth century, Paris overcrowded central cemeteries leaked. Fetid gases would waft into the cellars of Châtelet, marinating wheels of brie and braids of *saucisson*. Beginning in 1785 and for about a century, the government enacted its grisly solution: it transported six million skeletons to the southern quarries. Five per cent of the catacombs remain ossuaries today, and Racine, Robespierre, and Marat are among the dry, dusty residents.

Entrances to the tunnels can be found in the basements of hospitals, the cellars of bars, church crypts, subway tunnels, even at the bottom of Paris' tallest skyscraper. Many of these access points have been sealed by the IGC, who both protect the city from the catacombs, and the catacombs from the city. Circulating in the *carrières* was made illegal in 1955.

That didn't stop the catacomb craze. By the time Kunstmann and his friends were in college, almost every Latin Quarter party would end below ground. The IGC fought back, deploying a series of barrier walls that criss-crossed the passages, blocking the flow of visitors. The plan was good, but it only had so much effect: trespassers soon found ways around—and through—the concrete blockades.

By definition, Paris' hundreds of catacomb ramblers, its "cataphiles," decline to follow the rules. They are an odd gang of misfits—"urban explorers," vandals, kids who just want to hang out below ground. They chatter on online message boards, share and hoard maps; they meander, explore, drink, and drill through walls. By night they drop through manholes, or emerge from them, dusty, at dawn.

Members of UX spend time underground, but Kunstmann insists they are not cataphiles. It isn't just a matter of style. "The principle of UX is to provoke experiences using every available part of the city," he says at Le Pantalon. "Not as visitors but as *users*. Users for something other than the simple aesthetic of the places. And for something other than partying."

Their ideas are not new. It is Guy Debord's *détournement* turned loose on geography, Situationism without the politics, a no-nonsense take on Britain's art pranksters, the KLF. Yet these allusions betray UX's modest code—to do interesting things without permission. This credo allows for superficial punkery, sneaking into backyards, but considered seriously, it becomes a formula for being brave, for pursuing dreams. Which is a sappy way of saying, It grabbed me.

The first place I looked for UX was on Facebook. I typed "Lazar Kunstmann" into the search box and hit enter. There were no results. So I set my nets wider. I posted a message saying I was looking for contacts in the Paris "underground," figuratively and literally. I did the same on Twitter. I emailed friends in Paris, types who organize concerts in subway cars, asking similar questions. No one knew anything of Kunstmann, or of UX.

Next I scoured cataphile message boards, at least those that are public. Although these forums had discussed the group's works and media coverage, I found no traces of UX's authors. As Kunstmann later scoffed, these boards are full of typical internet posturing—resentful quips and knee-jerk LOLs.

I finally found Kunstmann through private correspondence with another journalist. They gave me an email address; that address told me to telephone a secret number. I asked for "Lazar," Kunstmann answered, and we met at Le Pantalon.

"Ordinary" cataphile contacts are less difficult to make. My online searchlights were glimpsed by a friend of friends, pseudonym Cavannus, who does "urban exploration" in Montreal. Cavannus put me in touch with one of his cataphile pals in Paris—a man with a fake Facebook account named for a celebrated guru. He tells me to meet him at Saint Pierre de Montrouge church, to look for a guy "on crutches." Two days after meeting Kunstmann, as I ride the subway and climb up to Alésia Square, there seem to be broken-legged people everywhere. I imagine this as cataphile ground zero, a place where everyone has limestone dust in their hair.

The cataphile who meets me looks about thirty, his dark hair pulled into a ponytail. He gestures at his crutches and says he slipped coming out of a manhole, on the rain-soaked street. He is called BHV.

"Underground, everyone has a nickname," BHV explains to me. He didn't choose his own, an acronym that refers to a famous department store. Someone else picked it about a dozen years ago, and it stuck. Other names are more esoteric, like Sork, or Crato, the man who eventually takes me into the tunnels. Some conjure deliberate images. One of the catacombs' most notorious mischief-makers is Lézard Peint, the Painted Lizard, a "devil" with alleged fascist connections, who has been known to steal fellow cataphiles' lights or to seal up their intended exits.

"What you are on the surface, you are underground," Crato later says, sucking on a cigarette. "When you are a violent person, given to fighting—you're the same below." Scoundrels like Lézard aside, the cataphile community is civil. "In general we look out for each other," BHV agrees. They share knowledge, lighters, cans of beer (never bottles, which are still heavy when empty). "People know that if they get too drunk or if they get hurt, it'll be hard to get out."

BHV and Crato's first descents were similar—they saw a hole, or heard about a hole, and they entered. Telling me, BHV begins to cough. "Sorry," he wheezes, "I still have dust in my throat." On that first journey, he and his friends ran into some unlikely mentors—off-duty police officers who offered to give them a tour—"and then I spent the whole night underground."

BHV's story is beguilingly simple. *I could go*, I realize. I could find an entrance on the internet, slip inside, wander until I find an off-duty police officer or a shy, kindly filmmaker. "It's a very supernatural setting," BHV murmurs. "You're completely autonomous. There's no light. There's no electricity. Just stones and water."

But I am here to understand UX and this is not the way that UX works. That group does not rely on word of mouth, happenstance, the kindness of strangers. UX sets goals and quietly executes them. They never get lost.

I find Crato online, just as I found BHV. Whereas BHV, becrutched, does not volunteer to play tour-guide, Crato—lanky, vaguely grumpy—makes the offer. "There are a lot of reasons to go down," he allows. "There are those who want to find a calm and pleasant spot. There are those who go down to meet a partner. There are those who go to party. There are even those who go to watch movies. Everyone has their own reasons."

We rendezvous on a bridge over train tracks. It's the middle of the afternoon, cars whizzing by, clouds meandering across a dirty blue sky. We're not far from Denfert-Rochereau, site of the official Catacombs Museum. That plain stone building offers historical displays, dioramas, entry onto a sanitized one-mile circuit of "legal" catacombs. This is not, cataphiles emphasize, the "real thing." Besides—you have to pay admission.

We look both ways and, one at a time, jump the bridge wall. It is thick, high as my shoulders. My jump is less deft than Crato's. I struggle for a moment and then I'm over, feet in the weeds, scrambling down the slope to the tracks. This is the Petite Ceinture, one of the city's abandoned railways. It is almost silent. We walk.

Crato has been visiting the catacombs for ten years. He tells me how the original quarries were built just wide enough for a man with a wheelbarrow—six feet by three feet. How they are a permanent 55° Fahrenheit, day and night, winter and summer. "I remember once it was hot in Paris, really hot, really horrible. Instead of dining in an overheated apartment, we went down into the catacombs to eat."

After a time, Crato and I come to a large train tunnel. The sunlight falls away behind us. It is easy to trip on the wooden ties of the tracks or on the irregular stones to either side. We turn on our flashlights yet I can see neither end of the tunnel. I assume the problem is fog, but Crato speaks of *fumis*, cataphile smoke-bombs, made by mixing saltpetre with sugar and flour. They are hiding something down here.

Ten minutes into the gloom, Crato swings his flashlight to the right. The darkness slips into focus. Before me, where the tunnel wall meets the earth, is a hole.

In 2009, this is the "grand entrance" to the catacombs. A craggy break in the rock, no more than two feet wide. Cataphile refuse is strewn nearby—empty beer cans, juice cartons, white paste from carbide lanterns. This is just the second "grand entrance" that Crato has known. One day the IGC will close it up, he says, fill it with concrete like the last one. But Crato hopes his fellow cataphiles do not dig a replacement straight away. Better to give the losers, the troublemakers, time to get bored and find something else to do. The committed ones already know different ways to get in. The committed ones are patient. Even Crato seems to think that secrets are best.

Deeper

FOR KUNSTMANN AND HIS ASSOCIATES, there is little appeal to wandering around underground. Their cinema aside, the catacombs are a means, not an end: a way to access UX work sites or to hide their tracks. But as a first-time visitor plunging into these grey chambers, the experience is thrilling. It is a labyrinth of branching channels and sudden openings, cool and quiet. Most of the catacombs are dry, tall enough to stand in—but from time to time we duck or crawl, or swish into ankle-high water. Still, they are not the dank, sweaty caves I imagined. Even wading into a passage called Banga, whose thigh-high water swirls like miso soup, the tunnel's soft silence recalls a theatre, a wine cellar, an attic.

In Kunstmann's book, cataphiles like Crato are called "*bodzaux*," for their wet and dirty boots, or "Ravioli," for their tendency to dine on boxed dumplings. ("I prefer wine and sausage," my guide retorts.) Ravioli seek to "consecrate" the underground, Kunstmann argues, guarding it from precisely the kind of transformation that UX enjoy. "[They] are protecting an image [of the catacombs] and they want to keep this image intact for the feelings it evokes in them."

Crato speaks of these feelings without actually speaking of them. He talks about how years ago, he and his now-wife would spend all of Saturday night in the tunnels, wandering until four in the morning. They would emerge, dust themselves off, go to sleep—and on Sunday they would walk the same route, retrace the same steps, above ground, hand in hand.

While this is a beautiful image, it is the opposite of what UX hope to accomplish. "It's a typically Parisian phenomenon," Kunstmann sighs. "Nostalgia for a period we didn't know. Areas 'flashed' in time. The work of UX is to de-flash, to thaw, to transform."

As Crato and I weave beneath the 14th arrondissement, the subway murmurs in a passage over our heads. You could walk these caves in jeans and sneakers, I think. I have read how the Painted Lizard has ordered people to do the circuit naked for his own wicked entertainment. I am in knee-high boots and a cardigan. Crato wears the basic cataphile uniform: hip aders, waterproof backpack, strong flashlight, gloves, a cap to keep off the dust. The athletics stores of Paris, he says with a grin, sell a disproportionate number of fishermen's boots and impermeable packs.

Although the catacombs are covered in graffiti tags, there are also sudden instances of art—amateur gargoyles, carved castles, life-sized sculptures of cataphiles. Crato brings me to La Plage, "the beach," a large gallery with a sand-packed floor. Our flashlights sweep across wide murals: Hokusai waves and Max Ernst-like portraits. In the Hall of Anubis we sit at a table chiselled out of stone. We light candles, drink beer, share cookies and chocolate. I am absolutely enchanted. I have no idea of the time.

For the most part, cataphiles don't dispute Kunstmann's characterization of them. BHV says his friends enjoy "taking photos, exploring a particular area, repairing things, going to spots where no one has visited for a long time." The community's holy grail, he suggests, is to clandestinely enter the Catacombs Museum. I balk at this—the same place you can visit for just eight euro, six days a week? "Yes," he agrees, "but that's the goal of tons of cataphiles. And they succeed almost every year—every year there's a hole that's drilled."

When cataphiles do stage large events, they tend to be one-off parties—not permanent "transformational" cinema installations. Crato remembers someone bringing down oysters—stupid, silly, "just as heavy on the way back as on the way down." BHV has organized two Breton-themed shindigs, where more than three hundred people joined dancers, musicians, and amateur chefs cooking subterranean crêpes. Among the largest celebrations was a farewell to Commandant Jean-Claude Saratte in 2000. Head of the catacomb police for twenty-one years, Saratte was respected for his knowledge, instincts, and moderation—pursuing the drug user, vandal, or "tibia collector" instead of the gentle catacomb geek.

Today, officers of BICS (la Brigade d'Intervention de la Compagnie Sportive) patrol the catacomb thoroughfares handing out €65 tickets. The *catacops* are regarded with resentment and disdain. But they force cataphiles to be vigilant: listening, looking out for standard-issue lights, sniffing for aftershave. It is illegal to drink on public streets, Crato proposes, but not beneath them.

"When you're caught, you have the chance to recognize or not recognize an infraction," he explains to me. "If you choose the latter, you're supposed to get an appointment with a judge." Crato has been awaiting his court date for years—and counting down the days until the automatic amnesty triggered by each presidential election.

We emerge from the maze three hours later, flashlights still shining, and again we are wreathed in smoke. It is dark as night. The opening of the railway tunnel is a circle of gold-white light in the far distance. Treading toward the open air, out and past the wild bright green of the weeds, it's as if we're passing through stained glass.

On our way back along the tracks we meet a quartet of cataphiles in black hoodies and running shoes, acquaintances of Crato's. We talk. The conversation is a mixture of bravado, feigned indifference, outbursts of earnest feeling. They talk of girls, parties, police, numbskulls with smoke bombs.

These men seem so gentle. Watching them smile, UX's rejection of this community seems unkind. No, Ravioli are not engaged in the same activities; no, their ambitions are not to the same scale. But if UX want to be something other than a secret club, at least they could be friendly with their neighbours.

Kunstmann sees it differently. UX are absolutely unrelated to these cataphiles, separate "from the start." "We were *learning* from one experience to another," he says. "We had an intention for these places." Besides, his group is not based in the catacombs. As Paris was to learn, they hide in the above ground as well.

Flying Saucer

ON DECEMBER 24, 2006, after fifty years of silence, the clock of the Paris Panthéon began to ring.

Two and a half years later, I arrive at the building for a tour. My group's guide is a man in his fifties, bird-haired, who talks in clipped and concentrated French. He doesn't mention the Panthéon's clock. Nor are there any references in the written program. After the tour ends, as the other tourists disperse, I ask him a question: "Didn't something happen with this clock?" We are standing directly beneath the three-foot minute hand.

The guide looks startled. "There are these people..." he begins to say. He does not make eye contact. "They infiltrated the Panthéon." This group had all the keys; he doesn't know how. The clock had been broken. They fixed it. They have also held plays here, and projected films. He explains everything with a weird, wry solemnity, like he both hates and relishes being asked. "Untergunther," he says finally, though he doesn't know how to spell it. "Look it up on the internet."

What the Internet will tell you is that the Untergunther are a branch of UX. Whereas the Mexican Consolidated Drilling Authority are dedicated to events, the Untergunther are the organization's restorers. In September 2005 they came here, to one of Paris' most important monuments—and they went to work.

The Panthéon was commissioned by Louis XV in 1744, as a tribute to Saint Genevieve. By the time it was finished in 1789, the French Revolution had guillotined the church idea. Instead, the domed neo-classical cathedral became a mausoleum for great French citizens. Voltaire, Rousseau, Émile Zola, and Victor Hugo are buried in its crypt; so are Marie Curie, Louis Pasteur, and Louis Braille. In the centre of the Panthéon's floor, where architect Soufflot had imagined a statue of Ste. Genevieve, Foucault's pendulum swings. Tourists like me come and gape at the way this simple experiment, commissioned by Napoleon, offers evidence of the rotation of the planet. It is such an unassuming marvel.

Another modest wonder lies at the end of the main hall, on the left, above a doorway. The Panthéon's clock is not an elaborate timepiece, like the Prague Orloj. The face is about as tall as a person, mounted on frosted glass. The clock hands and roman numerals look like they are made of cast iron. Built by the house of Wagner in 1850, it is plain, even austere. But for one year, this was the Untergunther's project.

"[The Untergunther] have compiled a huge list of slowly degrading places," Kunstmann told a *National Geographic* reporter in 2006. "The list is too big to ever be completed in our lives so each year we choose [just] one." The Untergunther have only three conditions for accepting a restoration project. First, to have the technical ability. Second, to have the means. And third, to have the desire. By 2009, they claim to have completed about twelve projects, including the Panthéon, a hundred-year-old government bunker, a twelfth-century crypt, and a First World War air-raid shelter.

"[We] are only interested in a very precise part of [French] cultural inheritance," Kunstmann writes in his book. "The part that is non-visible." These are not just places that are inaccessible or hidden to the public, like the mechanisms of a clock, but also sites that are invisible to their administrators. Since the city administration scarcely has enough money to maintain what is in plain view, UX suggest, they are doomed to ignore what is not.

This is a beautiful idea, but only compelling if acted upon. The Untergunther could be fakers, blowhards taking credit for conveniently hidden restorations. Yet as with the LMDP and their rock-hewn cinema, the endeavour at the Panthéon dismisses doubt.

The Panthéon's nineteenth-century clock had been broken since the 1960s, left to decay, but it caught the eye of a man called Jean-Baptiste Viot. Viot is a clockmaker, formerly head of restoration for the Swiss house Breguet. He is also a member of UX. Viot observed the rust caked on the Wagner's machinery and ruled that it was a "now or never" moment. If the Pantheon's clock were ever to tick again, it would need the Untergunther's help.

On September 18, 2005, the group formally adopted the project. Soon after, an eight-person "core"—including Viot and Untergunther leader Lanso—went to work. Using a copied key, they infiltrated the building after dusk, dodged security agents, and made their way up. High above the clock that had lured them there, the Untergunther arrived at a cavity along the base of the building's dome. This dusty, neglected space became their home.

They called it the *Unter und Gunther Winter Kneipe*, the Untergunther's Winter Tavern, taking their inspiration from a door marked UGWK. A similar whimsy had inspired the Untergunther's naming, back when they were just known as "the restoration wing." Unter and Gunther, Kunstmann says, were the names of the imaginary guard-dogs in the Arènes de Chaillot's security system.

For the next twelve months, the Panthéon was the Untergunther's playground. They learned every nook and cranny,
copied every key, learned the habits of every guard. It was
made easier by relatively lax security. When I visited in 2009,
there were still no real security badges, and both of my tour
guides failed to count the group with their clickers. According
to Kunstmann's stories, UX had already used the Panthéon
to stage plays and other events; the Untergunther's residency
was just a difference of scale, of persistence.

First they had to figure out what was wrong with the clock.
The UGWK became a makeshift library, stocked with books
on vintage timepieces and easy chairs that transformed into
inconspicuous wooden crates. Gradually the team concluded
that one of the clock's integral components, the escapement
wheel, had been sabotaged—likely by an employee decades
ago. The mechanism had eventually been replaced with an
electric mechanism, but this, too, had been sabotaged. Finally, they learned that fully restoring the Wagner clock would
not just mean fiddling around behind its face—the antique
mechanism had machinery located in several different parts
of the building.

The "flying-saucer-shaped" atelier of the Untergunther
became a not-quite-state-of-the-art clockmaker's workshop.
The Untergunther carried up thousands of euros in tools,
materials, and chemicals. They installed thick red curtains
along its chilly outer wall, because, Viot said, "a clockmaker
can't do anything with mittens on." They posed for photos
among the Panthéon's statues; they watched fireworks from
the roof; they made a new escapement wheel and cleaned the
clock machinery piece by piece.

Usually, Kunstmann writes, sites restored by the Untergunther remain "just as inaccessible and unknown as they
were before their repair." The Untergunther do not need to
trumpet their accomplishments: they seek only the immedi-

ate satisfaction of renewing part of their city. Often, the sites' invisibility even shields them from further damage. Alas for the Panthéon's clock, this obscurity was not to be.

Stopping Time

UX DOESN'T HAVE A BLOG. Members share a single email account. Lazar Kunstmann is not on Facebook, and the group's other members do not speak to the press. In this era of full disclosure, of never-ending networking, forwarding, and sharing, it is an organization that refuses friend requests. Members have only as many contacts as they require and they will not invite you to events.

The group's secrecy makes it hard to check their facts. Almost everything one *can* check out *does* check out. For the rest, you have to believe or disbelieve their claims. Kunstmann says the group has between one hundred and one hundred and fifty members ranging from age eleven to fifty-six. They are mostly professionals in their late thirties and early forties. UX's groups formed "by accident" in the early 1990s, gradually formalizing and adopting names. They are the product of "aggregation," the regrouping of kindred spirits within "the same, very reduced, geographic area."

Of the dozen teams that Kunstmann says exist, only three have been revealed—LMDP, the Untergunther, and a group called the Mouse House, recent inductees, allegedly an all-female "infiltration unit." All members benefit "from access to a [Paris-wide, universal, integrated] map, all the possible keys, all the possible knowledge." By sharing resources, pooling expertise, everyone is able to "work less for the same results, or to work the same amount for a better result."

Viewed a certain way, UX offers the same thing as Wikipedia or Google Earth—information for the community to do with as they please. But whereas Wikipedia relies on the wisdom of the masses to perfect its frustratingly imperfect data, while flash-mobs rally as many participants as possible, UX remains private. They reject openness, spurn crowds. The group's discretion allows them to slip below the authorities' radar, to operate with impunity, but there is more to it than that: by closing the network, they accomplish better works. There is no need to screen a film before thousands, to trumpet mysteries from the rooftops, to bring dancers and musicians and chefs making crêpes. UX quietly create wonders, carefully rescue treasures. Members are expected to be capable, informed, autonomous. "Everything is dedicated to avoiding wasted time," Kunstmann says. The doing, not the discussion, is what matters.

Because of this pragmatism, the Untergunther always knew they would have to reveal their venture to the Panthéon staff. "If you want a monumental clock to work, someone has to mount and maintain it," Kunstmann explains. Two, ten, or fifty years after the gears are set in motion, they must still be regularly tended. "The logic always being to minimize the amount of work for a given project; it's a conversation we had with the whole group. At a certain point, the administrator would need to be clued in."

Standing with my tour guide under the clock's black hands, I ask him whether the mechanism still works.

"No."

"Why not?"

"Management took a piece away."

"Why?"

I glimpse the tiniest sarcastic roll of the eyes. "Pfft. I don't know."

At the end of September 2006, the Untergunther claim they met with Bernard Jeannot, administrator of the Panthéon, and his assistant Pascal Monnet. (In the book, Monnet's name loses an *n*.) Jeannot was thrilled, delighted with the Untergunther's ingenuity, marvelling at their secret work-shop and horological handiwork. Monnet was less enthused. Still, everything seemed set for the clock to be mounted, for it to resume functioning—except that it didn't. Weeks passed. The administration, UX allege, did not want to reveal their failure to maintain the clock, or the way it had been restored.

With real sorrow in his voice, Kunstmann confesses they "misjudged the internal tensions that ruled at the CNM [the organization responsible for Paris' monuments] and the ad-ministration of the Panthéon. How different interests would exploit this affair to pursue their own agendas." Shortly after the UGWK was revealed, Bernard Jeannot left—or was forced out of—his job. Monnet ascended to the top seat. "That was the defeat," Kunstmann says. "That was the fuck-up. That we underestimated these factors."

It was an oddly naïve mistake. Most citizens of Paris—in-deed, most citizens of the world—know to never underesti-mate the hopelessness of their bureaucrats. Blinded by their own panache, UX assumed their work would be embraced by the people they shamed. Instead, two months later, the clock still had not been mounted.

The Untergunther are usually content for their restora-tions to remain hidden, but they were curious about their Panthéon handiwork. UX did not know whether their repair job had even been successful. They decided to test it on a day when the Panthéon was closed. The options were few—Christmas Eve, New Year's Day, May 1.

On December 24, the Untergunther once again slipped past security and into the building. They mounted the clock. It began to chime. The mechanism was found to lose less than one minute per day—Viot deemed it "acceptable."

But when Monnet returned from his holiday, he marched up the Panthéon's steps and gazed furiously at the tick-tick-ticking timepiece. He called a clockmaker to unmake the clock. The man who came, reportedly from the Maison Lepaute, refused to sabotage the mechanism. Instead, he removed the escapement wheel—the same piece damaged those decades before, rebuilt by Viot. At 10:51, the Wagner mechanism stopped.

Kunstmann is still livid. "The notion of conservation, the value of the objects in Monnet's care, don't concern him. He thinks only of his career, to have a good retirement."

I write to Monnet, asking for his version of events. The Panthéon administrator responds in an unmistakeable tone: "I absolutely refuse to discuss this file. It is part of an active case and the law prohibits me from commenting."

After the story of the clock repair broke, journalists swarmed—and Kunstmann once again came forward, revealing all. "Underground 'terrorists' with a mission to save city's neglected heritage," shrieked the *Times of London*'s headline. Monnet agreed with this characterization, pursuing the Untergunther in court. But there was one problem: they didn't seem to have committed a crime. Nothing was damaged during the Untergunther's stay at the Panthéon, and at the time there was no such thing as "trespassing" on public property. (This has since been rectified, with a bill passed in December 2008.) Authorities had to wait almost an entire year before finding a reason to bring UX in.

On August 14, 2007, Panthéon security claimed to find four members trying to force the building's locks. The case was heard on November 23, 2007, before the 17th Chambre du Tribunal de Grande Instance. The CNM sought a total of €51,394.76 for damage to public property. The accused: Sophie Langlade (surely Lanso, the Untergunther's leader), thirty-five, unemployed; Dorothée Hachette, thirty-nine, nurse; Christophe Melli, thirty-eight, artistic director; Eric Valleye, thirty-eight, filmmaker. Four members of Untergunther, revealed before the court.

"A real experiment never presumes its results," Kunstmann says. "If someone had asked us, 'What are the chances that one day you will appear in court to talk about the repair of the clock?' We would have said, 'Zero per cent? One per cent?' The improbable is still within the realm of the possible."

The charges were ultimately dismissed. Kunstmann says UX took back the removed escapement wheel, stealing it from Monnet's office. LMDP claim to have used the Panthéon for another full year, staging photo exhibits and a festival of police films. And the clock? "[It] is simply waiting for its chance to run again," Kunstmann told *The Architects' Journal.*

The way that Untergunther tell it, this acquittal was inevitable. UX's members are so clever, after all. They are so sophisticated. They are a world away from hoi polloi like Crato, caught in the catacombs and awaiting presidential amnesty. UX are not Ravioli. And you would certainly never see Kunstmann in the same room as the Painted Lizard.

La-zar Kunst-mann

THE PAINTED LIZARD, wrote American journalist Christopher Ketcham, is "one of the nastiest pranksters in the underworld." Cavannus, a former Parisian now living in Montreal, says something similar: "Dangerous. To avoid." Another catacomb rat goes further. "The guy's a megalomaniacal jerk and deserves no publicity of any kind," G——wrote in an email, asking that I not use his name. "He is a lesser human being."

Ketcham recalls seeing a photograph of the Lézard (and a black friend) in Nazi SS uniforms, "singing old German war songs at full throttle, stomping through the tunnels, sieg heiling, the songs echoing down the halls for a half-mile." He's a fascist, G—— tells me. "In the 1990s him and another guy going by the name of Ktu used to beat people up. They had the network shared, one 'gang' held the south, the other the north.... Idiots are in awe of him because he can break into anywhere [but] an asshole is always an asshole."

I obtain the Untergunther's court records less than a week after my visit to the catacombs. I Google the names—Sophie Langlade, Dorothée Hachette, Christophe Melli, Eric Valleye. Slim pickings, except for Valleye. He is named in Ketcham's 2002 article for *Salon*. Valleye, Ketcham writes, is the real name of the Lézard Peint.

"We dress up as Nazis, sure," the Lizard said, "but we have no politics, none whatsoever. This is all... theater. A game of transformations, masks."

I consider the Lizard, reformed, assisting the patient restorers of the Panthéon's clock. Perhaps he met them below ground. And then suddenly the darkness slips into focus. *Lazar*, after all, sounds an awful lot like *Lézard*. Kunstmann, the German word "art-man." Lazar Kunstmann—*Lézard artman*?

After that, I'm running. I dig into the Untergunther website, UGWK.org. I discover the site's files reside on a different server, and I note the URL: http://web.mac.com/peint/UGWK.

I scour cataphile forums for photographs of the Lizard, search Flickr. Most photographers lack UX's discretion. I find the Lizard, head bowed, in a series of subterranean snaps. It is the same man with whom I clinked glasses at Le Pantalon.

When I go back to speak to BHV, his ankle has healed. I ask the question whose answer he neglected to volunteer last time. Yes, the cataphile admits, "Lazar and Lézard Peint are the same single person."

I do not know how to feel. Thrilled by my discovery? Proud of my detective skills? Or utterly deflated, imagining UX as an asshole's practical joke? It is as if I am back underground.

This time I have no leader.

"Lazar always had a group of friends, but they didn't particularly have a name," BHV says. He suggests they adopted the name LMDP after the discovery of the cinema, Untergunther after the discovery of the clock, UX after the publication of his book. Whereas UX claim to have more than a hundred members, BHV and Cavannus guess that "Kunstmann's group" are no more than twenty. The Untergunther say they have completed a dozen different projects, LMDP to have hosted dozens of events, but there's scant evidence. Perhaps it is because these actions were secret. Or perhaps they didn't happen.

BHV points to another sign of obfuscation in Kunstmann's book. The volume is peppered with comic relief courtesy of Olrik and Peter, UX's goofy, incompetent jester duo. Olrik is real, well known underground. But Peter? "He is maybe Lazar," BHV supposes. "I looked into it. It might be him." *Peter*, I note, is the French word for *farting*.

At that noisy, crowded bar, as I set a pint of Leffe before him, Kunstmann had confessed that he sometimes "gives simple answers to questions that deserve complicated ones." Months later, I contemplate UX as a tall tale, an exaggeration, the invention of an arrogant catacomb trickster. And yet the truth still feels just out of reach, beyond the beam of my flashlight. It is as if I can hear the footfalls.

Misdirection

ALMOST A MONTH AFTER OUR MEETING, I confront Lazar Kunstmann (a.k.a. Lézard Peint, a.k.a. Eric Valleye) over email. Fifteen hours later, I receive a reply. Kunstmann says the Painted Lizard does not exist. He claims that this character's reputation is intentional, invented, part of a concentrated effort to muddle perceptions of UX. Stories of villainous cataphiles quickly take over the discourse, masking any other activities. I am reminded of a comment he made at the bar that night. "A secret launches any information," he said, leaning forward in his chair. "It's a very simple principle. 'I'm going to tell you something. It's a secret—above all don't tell it to anyone.' You will see two other people and say to them, 'I'm going to tell you something. It's a secret—above all don't tell it to anyone.' In four seconds, everybody knows." The greater the tale, the bigger the lizard, the faster word spreads.

Kunstmann admits that one "operation," between 1985 and 1987, "was mildly violent"—but never, he insists, "physically violent." "For a Ravioli," he writes, "anything outside of routine is psychologically violent." He does concede that one of Ktu's friends might have knocked some heads.

And then I receive a message from Lanso. This is unexpected. The head of the Untergunther does not relish the spotlight, hasn't written any books, never talks to journalists. She has not contacted me before. "I know that [catacomb adventures] are very entertaining to foreign readers," she writes, her verbiage precise. "It's the exoticism of 'subterranean Paris.' But it's not what defines [UX]. We are people who realize projects without asking permission. That's all."

From there, Lanso acknowledges that UX's cast of regulars, the nicknames most often cited, may now seem like mischievous cataphiles. But she says these are part of a "media group" led by Kunstmann—a team meant to dazzle and distract the press, mesmerizing us with catacomb talk.

"The small world of the catacombs, which is apparently your place of departure, easily amplifies the importance of Lazar's band of rascals," Lansar writes. "Lazar is a good spokesman... but all of the intox and [media] diversions that he has been able to do, he and his friends, both in the press and [among cataphiles], gets linked to *our* activities, which they have nothing to do with." Kunstmann is an important member, Lanso admits, but the Untergunther and most of the rest of UX "have nothing to do with 'cataphiles,' nor even the catacombs. Nothing to do with Ravioli forums nor the beliefs and myths of these places. Nothing to do with the dozens of confusing articles conceived by Lazar and his cohorts between 1985 and 2004. Nothing to do with the folklore of the Latin Quarter so dear to the previously-mentioned."

Kunstmann's tales, the activities he recounts, the cataphile culture he invokes—it is, Lanso suggests, a *fumis*. It is smoke. It is the smoke that fills our vision, fills newspaper pages, conceals the group's true projects and real work.

Look to the Untergunther website, available in French and English, a kind of souped-up press release, useful documents for journalists. Look to Zone Tour, maintained by Olrik and Kunstmann, ostensibly a website for Paris' cataphiles but purely in English. Look to an article in *Zurban* magazine, two years before the "restoration wing" of UX announced themselves. There are the "Untergunther," doing nothing more than run-of-the-mill culture jamming, changing George V subway station signs to George W. Fog, smoke, misdirection.

As for what this "real work" is, Lanso will not say. These projects, she underlines, are secret. "Don't think that I say this against you, or against journalists in general. It's the same for everyone. To be able to do what we do, this is how it has to work."

I have reached a dead end. Lanso's secrets are tantalizing, but I can neither confirm nor deny them. UX's deepest riddles cannot be Googled. The question I ask is, Do I believe them? And then I ask, Do I want to believe them? And then I know my answer.

Exits

DESPITE THEIR UNASSAILABLE SECRECY, UX still have something to offer the rest of us trapped on the far side of the smoke-screen. Kunstmann talked about this as we finished our beers that night. "Over time," he said, "I've noticed that the principal reason that UX completes its projects is that we dismiss past inhibitions."

The organization simply *tries* things. If one idea doesn't work, they move on to the next. And whereas doubt inhibits, precedents inspire new experiments. "If someone says tomorrow, 'Ah, I'd love to fly across the Atlantic,' no one would say, 'It's impossible! It will never work!'" Kunstmann said. "If it's already been created, it must be possible to recreate."

We cannot join UX. They will not tell us who they are, or what lies at the heart of the maze. But we can do as they did. We can make our own maps.

THE PROBLEM WITH WOMEN

Kelly Pullen
Toronto Life

Every weekday evening, when the bell rings and the markets close, dozens of suits from the financial district pour down into Ki, a Japanese restaurant smart enough to be located at King and Bay. Outstretched arms, clad in sombre Canali, eagerly pass corporate credit cards to the bartenders, who then hand back a steady stream of vodka sodas, Jäger shots and goblets of merlot. Bankers, brokers and lawyers come here to mingle and gossip with colleagues and clients. On many nights last year, the most talked-about subject at Ki was Diane LaCalamita's

$12-million gender discrimination suit against McCarthy Té-
trault, the fourth largest law firm in the country and one of
the storied Bay Street outfits known colloquially as the Seven
Sisters. LaCalamita's story is set out in a statement of claim
that stretches 66 pages. The day it became available, it was
photocopied and eagerly passed around the financial district
like the latest potboiler.

It's not just the law firms that are fixated, but other institutions, as well—the banks and brokerage houses, the
accounting and engineering firms. All have a stake in how
the case gets resolved. It's being watched—nervously or excitedly, depending on your rank and status—on both sides of
the border. Never before has a partnership of McCarthys' size
and stature come so close to having its doors blown open and
its pay scales and promotion methodology exposed for all the
world to see.

Not surprisingly, McCarthys, in its statement of defence,
denies LaCalamita's allegations, which remain unproven,
and vaunts its own efforts to promote women in the profession. The firm claims she was simply not up to the job.

On this, Bay Street is divided. For some—mainly men, but
some women, too—it's the story of a bitter, mediocre lawyer
who couldn't cut it among the top-flight litigators at an elite
firm. For others—mostly women, but some men, as well—it's
the kind of case that will finally bring to light the subtle forms
of discrimination and stereotyping that linger, like some in-
sidious mould, among the offices and boardrooms.

DIANE LACALAMITA COULD NOT HAVE KNOWN that she would one
day be at the centre of a gender war on Bay Street. She's the
daughter of a pharmacist and a photographer. Her parents
taught her not to think along traditional gender lines, and
their choice of professions would influence her own decision,
18 years ago, to pursue the burgeoning field of intellectual

property law. She attended Havergal College, the elite private school in north Toronto, before pursuing an undergrad degree in life sciences, followed by a law degree at U of T. She was called to the bar in 1992 and earned a master of laws degree from the University of London a year later. She then embarked on a career in a niche area of law.

Through the '80s and '90s, IP law was the exclusive domain of a few boutique firms in the city. The emergence of the highly litigious tech industry—including biotech, pharma and life sciences, where patent infringement can lead to lengthy multimillion-dollar lawsuits—was a boon for lawyers.

By 2000 or so, McCarthys and the other Seven Sisters firms were in a hurry to get in on the IP game. LaCalamita, then an associate with Deeth, Williams, Wall, and her fellow boutique lawyers were suddenly in high demand. Bill Richardson, a successful litigator then in his 40s, was one of the senior partners building McCarthys' IP litigation group. He first met with LaCalamita in 2001, and their personality differences must have been obvious from the start: Richardson is charming and gregarious, an outsize character at the firm; LaCalamita, while friendly and personable, is serious and sometimes quiet to the point of diffidence. Though she was intrigued by the prospect of working at McCarthys, she opted to follow Don Cameron, a former colleague and one of the premier IP practitioners in the city, to the smaller law firm Aird and Berlis. According to LaCalamita, when she declined Richardson's offer, he told her the door would always be open at McCarthys, and that she should get back in touch in six months, if only to confirm that she'd made the right choice.

A year later, the IP litigation group at McCarthys was starting to take off. It would soon become one of the most profitable departments in the firm, bringing in millions of dollars a year. The group's focus was pharmaceutical cases—the most lucrative type of litigation in the country—and it had recently landed Merck as a client. Richardson and his co-chair, Andy Reddon, had created a department very much in their likenesses. Richardson was the rainmaker; he spent most of his time out schmoozing with clients and wooing new business. The more cerebral but no less charming Reddon did the heavy lifting, overseeing files along with a junior partner named Steve Mason. The IP crew—especially the handsome duo of Reddon and Mason—were the firm's golden boys. There were jokes about Reddon's ability to charm judges during trials. The group was also extremely busy, so they decided to bring in another lawyer to help with the caseload. Through the legal recruitment firm ZSA, they were reconnected with LaCalamita.

For her, the call to join McCarthys came at the perfect time. She was in her late 30s, single, well established in her field and, after 10 years as an associate, in pursuit of a partnership position. Her friends say she was married to her work. She ran a full-service practice, covering a broad range of IP law and litigation—typical of a lawyer from a boutique firm background. LaCalamita welcomed the interest of McCarthys but had several reservations about joining the firm. At the core of her claim is a disagreement over what Richardson and Reddon did or didn't promise her during the course of negotiations.

LaCalamita claims she made it clear that she wanted to continue the full scope of her IP practice, not just litigation, and that Richardson and Reddon told her she could, though she'd be classified as a litigator in her employment contract (for budgetary reasons). She also wanted a title that was commensurate with her experience, something on par with her future colleagues, and she wanted assurance that if she were to commit to McCarthys for the long-term, she would eventually be made a partner. At the time, she had offers from other firms: Heenan Blaikie, Faskin Martineau DuMoulin, and

Ogilvy Renault, where her former IP colleagues at Aird and
Berlis had recently moved and where she had been offered
income partnership with the possibility of equity partnership
within one year. (An income partner is a junior partner—one
with the seniority of partnership but without a share in the
firm's profits.) She says she was told that, as a rule, McCarthys didn't offer equity or income partner status to new hires,
but that as a senior lateral hire, she would be given the title
of "counsel," which would not only reflect her experience but
also shorten her path to equity partnership—an eventuality
that was more or less guaranteed since the board would be
relying on their recommendations.

With her experience and expertise in the niche drug regulatory field, LaCalamita expected to play a leading role in
managing the firm's existing pharmaceutical litigation files,
as well as broaden the practice into non-pharmaceutical
work that would put McCarthys on the map in the IP world.
McCarthys offered her a starting salary of $200,000, plus
bonuses. The opportunity was too good to refuse. She signed
on as counsel on February 17, 2003, and started at the firm
on March 10.

There were red flags almost immediately. A few weeks into
the job, Richardson asked her to hand over her existing drug
regulatory files to the IP group—including patent work from
clients she'd brought with her and foreign IP associates with
whom she continued to do business—so she could focus ex-
clusively on litigation. When she objected, Richardson, she
claims, told her the IP group was short of work. If she refused, she would "not be considered a team player."

LaCalamita thought she had all the qualifications to be a
team player. She didn't have kids and was free to work late
and attend to the after-hours client commitments that are
part of any successful practice. She enjoyed sports, particularly golf, and had never had problems connecting with male

colleagues before. Still, she felt excluded from the boys' club that surrounded her.

Litigators, at least at the elite firms, are the surgeons of the law profession: they are predominantly male, and they perpetuate a cocky cowboy culture. LaCalamita's immediate colleagues, though relatively equal to her on paper (Reddon was a couple of years ahead, Mason two years behind), had less technical expertise than her in many of the specialized IP areas the firm was now covering—expertise she claims they made good use of behind the scenes. At the same time, she felt she was being sidelined by what one former employee dubbed the "Andy and Steve road show." They began excluding her from drug regulatory and biotech files, which had been her specialty. She regularly provided senior level advice on files while also carrying out junior work. She was the only litigator in the group asked to play this type of supporting role.

This did not sit well with LaCalamita, whom one former colleague describes as "quietly mulish." After a while, when she was asked to do research for her peers, she began to push back in a passive-aggressive way that further alienated her from the guys.

And yet, despite her growing uneasiness about her prospects at the firm, she continued to hold out hope for partnership. She thought an official validation of her seniority would give her some leverage within her department and things would improve. That first summer, she was asked to complete an application for admission to income partnership. LaCalamita had been expecting to skip that step and apply for equity partnership, so she went to Richardson and Reddon for an explanation. She claims they told her she should complete the income partnership application as requested, lest she be considered ungrateful.

LaCalamita submitted her application in October—the same time, she would later learn, that Steve Mason was asked to apply for equity partnership. By January 2004, she was made an income partner, while Mason was made an equity partner. Her salary increased only marginally (in line with that of a six- to nine-year associate on the firm's compensation grid) and was fixed for the year without a review. Then she saw a group of lateral hires—all men—join the firm. Four of them were admitted as either income or equity partners. It dawned on LaCalamita that her situation might have something to do with the fact that she's a woman.

LET'S RECAP, SHALL WE? It's been about 50 years since women first truly arrived on Bay Street. After those early trailblazers joined the corporate mainstream in the '60s, young women flooded the universities, got professional degrees and, over the next three decades, followed their fathers into what seemed like exciting and rewarding careers. They became traders and analysts, money managers and accountants, engineers and lawyers. They became doctors and professors and politicians. By the mid-'90s, women constituted nearly half the work force, and as they made their way up through the ranks, they earned the same as their male colleagues (sort of), and they were engaged in the same types of work. Women had finally made it, had come a long way, were doing and having it all.

And then, just when it seemed like they were on course for the corner office, they stalled. A decade or so went by and they remained stuck at the midpoint. Where were all the women executives? Where were the female CEOs and board directors? When it finally occurred to everyone that despite all the change not much had really changed, it fell to those few women sitting in management positions to organize committees and commission reports and launch task forces to try to figure out what the hell was going on.

So now the reports are all in, and the results aren't pretty. Women make up a mere 17 per cent of leadership positions in the country's 500 biggest companies. They account for only 14 per cent of corporate boards, 22 per cent of Parliament and 25 per cent of tenured positions in academia. In the legal profession, more than half of all law school graduates are women, yet only 19 per cent are firm partners. Something needed to be done.

Next thing you know, an entire industry dedicated to analyzing and promoting the advancement of women springs to life. A whole lot of meetings are held and entire forests felled in the printing of the results of those meetings. And at this very moment, in banks and investment companies, law firms and law associations and all sorts of consultancies and NGOs, well-intentioned people are working really hard to find ways for companies to "accommodate" women—women who want to have children, women who want more flexibility in their work, women who simply want a fair shot at the C-suite. But in all the talk about the various things holding women back, about maternity leaves and mentorship programs, flex time and work-life balance, there is no mention of what is actually and obviously in the most blinding way the crux of the problem: men.

A FIRM LIKE MCCARTHYS, which is extremely old (155 years) and extremely large (close to 700 lawyers), is a difficult thing to change. And, until recently, the big Bay Street firms were all so focused on nationalizing their companies in order to compete globally that they may not have seen change was a-comin'. As they grew and merged and grew some more, they faced a flood of new associates, many of whom were female and/or non-white. It suddenly seemed hasty, not to mention unprofitable, to make them partners after only five or six years. So they decided to make the path to partnership a little bit longer, say seven to 10 years. Senior associates would now spend a year or two as "income" partners or "counsel," which meant you could say you were a partner, though you didn't have a financial stake in the firm or share in the profits; you were just a salaried employee. An employee who really needed to prove herself.

By LaCalamita's second year at the firm—her first as an income partner—her relationship with Andy Reddon and Steve Mason was deteriorating. She was uncomfortable taking direction from them—especially from Mason, whom she considered her junior. She started complaining to the senior partners about her status within the department and her compensation, and about the ongoing discrepancy between what she thought she'd been hired to do and the work she was actually doing.

In October 2004, she met with Malcolm Mercer, the co-head of the litigation department. Mercer is well regarded at the firm, a fair-minded and empathetic supervisor. He's also extremely logical—the type of guy who's hard-wired to think that people will always behave rationally and not resort to backstabbing or other devious behaviour in order to get ahead, even in a hyper-competitive firm like McCarthys. At the meeting, LaCalamita told Mercer that she wanted to "get back on track." She also told him that she'd been given a commitment with respect to equity partnership, and that she wanted that commitment honoured. She then provided him with names of other lawyers in the extended IP group with whom she'd worked who could vouch for her performance. Mercer told her he would respond to her concerns at her performance review.

At the end of the year, as usual, the firm began its annual review process. LaCalamita, still an income partner, was excluded, apparently due to, among other things, discrepancies in the recording of her docketed hours—a situation she had hoped to address in her review. Though she waited through most of January, neither Mercer nor anyone else in senior management met with her. During that time, her billing rate was raised to $525 an hour—which, it turned out, was $25 less than Steve Mason's, with whom she thought she'd been in lockstep. When LaCalamita complained, the firm raised her rate to $550, without changing her compensation. Finally, on January 28, she was told she would receive a 17 per cent bonus, a signal that she had hit her billing targets for 2004. The bonus went some way toward acknowledging her contributions and led her to believe she was in good standing after all.

That February, Richardson created a new national life sciences and biotech industry group—an entity that LaCalamita, despite being one of the only lawyers with federal court experience in IP law, was not invited to join. Exasperated, she wrote Mercer to ask about the status of the issues they'd discussed. Soon after, she was called into a meeting with him and Richardson, the tone and nature of which caught her off guard. On the table before Richardson was a memo containing what LaCalamita calls "vague and impressionistic allegations" attacking her character and personality and suggesting that she wasn't cut out for equity partnership. LaCalamita says that it was the first time she had heard such complaints. She asked Richardson if she could see the memo, but, according to her version of events, he sidestepped the question. She asked if it would be placed in her personnel file, and again he was evasive. She left the meeting stunned.

By the fall of 2005, LaCalamita was feeling desperate and sent a memo to Mercer and Kirby Chown, a female senior partner with the firm. Chown was a 25-year veteran of McCarthys, having started there as an articling student before working her way up to regional managing partner for Ontario. A mother of twin boys, she was regarded as a woman who'd managed to do it all. She was chair of McCarthys' diversity task force and its women's committee, and for all appearances was dedicated to promoting women in the firm. She had recently commissioned Catalyst, a non-profit consultancy that advises companies on the retention and advancement of women, to conduct a study into gender issues at the firm. Chown was often trotted out by McCarthys—along with another senior partner, Barbara Boake—whenever the firm needed to show that women can succeed there.

LaCalamita's memo was thorough. It was part review submission, part application for equity partnership (though none had been requested) and partly an attempt to address the outstanding allegations against her. She provided supporting documents countering the claims regarding her character and performance and outlining her contributions to the fi rm. (As Mercer would later tell her, it "had the appearance of a pleading.") She was hoping to set the record straight, or at least provide her side of the story. Chown was her last resort.

They met in early November. Chown refused to talk about Mercer's report and LaCalamita's response to it. According to LaCalamita, Chown dismissed the correspondence as simply "that lawyer thing we do" and instead steered the conversation to what she called the "human side" of the matter. She told LaCalamita that her future was in the hands of Richardson and Reddon, and that she should do her best to try to win them over. She also suggested that if in her next review with Mercer she got the impression she would not be asked to apply for equity partnership before January 2007, and if by then the "human side" of her situation had not improved, then she should think seriously about her partnership and career goals lest she find herself "batting her head against a wall or door that's not going to open." And with that, Chown ended the meeting.

WOMEN LEAVE THE LEGAL PROFESSION at twice to three times the rate of men. The response of the firms has been, by and large, to empower their female employees to organize themselves into a self-supporting and self-promoting club. In many cases, the men at the company have had little or no involvement, creating a lobby of women mostly talking to themselves—in other words, more balkanization.

Many associates find the initiatives instituted by firms—women's lunches or other mentoring exercises—to be hollow or, as one woman put it, "glorified referral services" in which the senior partners dole out advice on how to outsource your life: who can tutor your kids or make your dinners or pick up your dry cleaning. One lawyer recalled sitting through one such lunch, after which her colleague turned to her and said, "Great—so who do I pay to fuck my husband?" A former Mc-Carthys lawyer told me that there are senior women at the firm who have two nannies: a day nanny who works from 7 to 5 and a night nanny who works from 5 till 11. "And people say, 'Look, she's making it work,' " she says. "In my view, the dad who leaves at 5:30 to pick up the kids from school, helps them with their homework, then does his own work from 9 to 11 is making it work far more than the mom with two nannies."

Even if the women's lunches were deemed a success as a bonding exercise, their effect on a company was next to nil. Julie Hannaford, a family lawyer who left Borden Ladner Gervais to start her own firm four years ago, says, "The committees started to look like the women's auxiliary at the church or the ladies' dining room in the old private men's clubs. And that eventually evolved into tokenism."

There are certainly token female executives, trailblazers in their field who found a way onto an otherwise all-male leadership team. But for every token female executive, there are thousands of women who have had to resort to all sorts of bizarre and unnatural behaviour in order to succeed. There are the she-males, those who clawed their way up the corporate ladder, making sacrifices along the way, and are now coaching their young female underlings on how to behave more like men. The perception among the younger generation is that these women had to work so hard to get to where they are that they've become blind to the fact that their struggle was unfair to begin with.

Other mid-level and senior women resort to pandering or other disingenuous tactics in order to get to a senior position. "You have to be perky and a cheerleader and do everything they say," one lawyer told me. "And if they suggest you should be researching down a particular line, you do it even when you know it's counterproductive." At the junior and mid-level, you'll find the handmaidens—women who, thanks to a perverse twist on male mentorship, become the perennial junior to some great man and never reach their potential. The handmaiden problem is endemic to big firms, where women are often perceived as detail oriented and not able to grasp the big picture. They're great as juniors when they're still cheap and can put in lots of hours. As they progress, they become too expensive to do the tedious work, and yet the senior guys don't want to introduce them to clients or give them big files or bring them in on important meetings. "So that's where you see all the women leaving," one senior partner tells me. "Everybody thinks they're great the first three years, then their billing rate creeps up and clients start to complain and so there's no more work for them to do because no one wants to turn them into really good corporate lawyers."

And then there are the misunderstood media darlings known as the Opt-Outs. The Opt-Outs take great pains to tell you that they left their practice or their position because they wanted to, not because they couldn't hack it. Most of them have children and are married to other professionals. You can't talk about how to keep women in big jobs without seguing into the subject of maternity leaves. The two seem intertwined. Even childless women acknowledge that the hint of a notion of a possibility that a woman may one day bear children affects the way she is perceived within a company. If she does have a baby, reaction ranges from the relatively innocent impulse to not overburden the new and obviously busy working mom, to the more damaging conclusion that she's no longer up to the job. A lot of women feel that companies are putting too much emphasis on the importance of maternity leaves, which gives employees the false impression that the lack of women in top jobs is being addressed, and has the uncomfortable side effect of positioning women as primarily reproductive and therefore less committed to their careers.

Firms are cliquey by nature, and partners will simply give work to the lawyers they like. One young associate, a refugee from a Seven Sisters firm, saw the cliquishness devolve into outright discrimination when she asked to be put on a high-profile case. She was told that the client wanted someone more senior. An hour later, she was back in her office when an associate of the same rank came in complaining that he had too much work, having just been handed the file she'd asked for. "When it came down to really high-profile work," she says, "they didn't want a female associate on it." She went to her contact in HR to talk about the incident, only to be told that she was imagining men were being favoured. So she left the firm.

Though most women will say that any attempt by their company to address gender issues is better than none, few think their firms understand the profoundly pro-male structures that govern their institutions. It's particularly challenging for women in the middle ranks, where there's a lot of politics and jockeying for position. Few managers are adept at handling and recognizing the personality issues and different work and leadership styles of their employees—all the nuances and complexities of the modern and ultracompetitive workplace. The much simpler solution, it seems, is to ask women to organize mentoring programs and networking events for themselves—as if they didn't have enough work already.

IN JANUARY 2006, LaCalamita had her long-awaited review with Mercer. To her surprise, he told her that he had no intention of discussing her October memo. Instead, he was only prepared to talk about two things that day: first, that LaCalamita had no future in pharmaceutical litigation at the firm, and second, that she should focus instead on building a drug regulatory practice. LaCalamita must have found this galling, since she'd started out with a drug regulatory practice, and rebuilding one would take another four or five years. Mercer also confirmed that he would not be considering her for equity partner that year.

And so began the long, drawn-out war of attrition that's waged when a firm refuses to fire someone it no longer wants and that some one refuses to leave. LaCalamita hovered in a kind of limbo, haunting the office despite not having much in the way of work. No one would speak to her, and none of her colleagues outside the small litigation team knew what was going on.

Finally, on April 25, the standoff was broken when McCarthys handed her a letter stating that her employment would be terminated at the end of June.

But it wasn't over yet. Summer stretched into fall and fall into winter as LaCalamita tried to negotiate a better settlement package. The two sides eventually hired a mediator, to no avail. Finally, she decided to sue.

This isn't the first time McCarthys has been accused of sidelining its female lawyers.

The Catalyst report prepared for Kirby Chown and McCarthys back in 2004 evaluated firm data from 1999 to 2003 and spoke with lawyers there at all levels. The report stated that, among other things, women voluntarily exited the firm at twice the rate of men; that male income partners were admitted to equity partnership at twice the rate of their female counterparts; and that over those four years, only male lateral hires were admitted directly into equity partnership. Qualitatively, the report found that while many lawyers believed the firm environment was characterized by great people and great work, a majority of women felt marginalized by subtle stereotypes, that they perceived "male" and "female" types of work, and that they felt excluded by "boys' clubs." More generally, it revealed that employees found the criteria for admission to partnership unclear. The report concluded by commending McCarthy Tétrault for being among the first elite law firms to recognize gender diversity as a business issue, something that could help the firm gain a competitive advantage. It advised that change would come only from a steady, measured approach—a common refrain among advocates for women's advancement.

A couple of years later, McCarthys' women's task force, headed by Chown, completed an internal study following the assessments in the Catalyst report. It found that in 2006, although women made up 51 per cent of the senior associates at the firm, they comprised only 29 per cent of income partners, 18 per cent of equity partners and 15 per cent of the leadership roles.

In McCarthys' statement of defence in the LaCalamita case, the firm insists there is no culture of discrimination. McCarthys says it only ever offered her a position as a litigator, that it has strict selection criteria for partnership admission, and that LaCalamita simply failed to meet them. She was unable to meet deadlines and the minimum expectation for billable hours, the company maintains, and she showed poor judgment as a litigator, to the point that her colleagues "didn't trust her instincts." When McCarthys attempted to help her by offering her professional coaching for performance issues, she declined. The statement of defence also notes that LaCalamita never complained of discrimination of any kind while she was employed there, "despite being aware of the formal complaints process in place to address such allegations."

It says that LaCalamita was one of the highest paid income partners at the firm, and yet her billable contributions were among the lowest. The retention of women in senior positions is a profession-wide challenge, McCarthys insists, and it points to the Catalyst report as evidence of the firm's efforts to promote talented female lawyers.

JOY CASEY KNOWS FIRST-HAND what Diane LaCalamita is going through. She sued her former employer, Blake Cassels and Graydon, in 1998 for $1.1 million. Hers was the first gender discrimination lawsuit brought against a Seven Sisters firm. The case was settled in 2003, and although the terms of the settlement are confidential, the claim was essentially the same as LaCalamita's: it was based on denial of partnership and an alleged misrepresentation of partnership prospects. She acted for herself in the suit and has since represented another female plaintiff who was denied partnership at one of the major firms—a suit that was settled quickly and quietly. "Everyone tells you not to sue, that it will affect your reputation and that you'll never get hired by a big firm again," she says. "But litigation makes people sit up and take notice." Casey now runs her own commercial litigation and employment law practice, and recently launched an organization called A Call to Action Canada, which encourages corporate in-house counsel to push for more diversity in their supplier law firms.

Groups like Casey's walk a fine line: they must court the male execs at the big firms, encourage participation and gently nudge them toward a new way of doing things. For their part, the execs have to be prepared to admit to real systemic problems. The irony for McCarthys is that in its attempt to address gender issues through the Catalyst study, the firm left itself vulnerable to the type of lawsuit it's now fighting.

LaCalamita is being represented by Malcolm MacKillop, an employment lawyer at a boutique labour firm, and Mary Eberts, a well-known equality lawyer who started the women and law course at U of T. McCarthys is represented by a 60-something commercial litigator named Terrence O'Sullivan. The two sides expect to go to trial in the next year. That is, of course, unless they reach a settlement. They have to be working hard at it. No one at the firm wants the confidential compensation and billing information they were recently forced to produce to be exposed at trial. Then again, LaCalamita may decide to hold out, roll the dice and see what the court has to say.

At the moment, she's also trying to get a job. According to friends, she's living with her parents and recently wrote the British bar exams in the hope that she might find work overseas. She figures she'll never be hired in this town again.

THE ARMS OF MY INHERITANCE

Barbara Stewart
Event

Kenneth Stewart should have run away from home. He should have joined the fledgling Greenpeace in 1971, claimed a berth on the *Phyllis Cormack* to protest the nuclear testing on Amchitka Island. They would have loved him. In the sixties, he could have joined the Sons of Freedom fighters in Nelson, B.C., or later in the seventies, if not the Greenpeace adventure, opted for a dodge south to serve Nixon in Vietnam. Instead, 1971 was just another year of 41 years employed as a kiln operator for Canada Lafarge Cement. My father should have left us all behind.

A life of compromise torques the personality. We never knew for sure how many guns he had—some hidden and loaded, he said—or dared to question his fascination with knives. He had navigational maps of the British Columbia coastline, dozens of them, tender paper telescopes rolled up in a basement closet. He drove a four-wheel-drive Ford Explorer, with a winch mounted on the front, from the bungalow in Surrey to the cement plant in Richmond. At home, he regularly commandeered the kitchen table for rituals of preparation, scouring gun barrels and sharpening knife blades until the oil on the whetstone was hot. Every year for 40 years, he took two weeks off work and went moose hunting. He let his thick black hair grow and didn't shave. Even his dark blue eyes changed, enlivened by the wilderness north of Fort St. John. Why did he come back? At any time he could have quit his job, built a cabin for himself, and joyfully lived off a fishing rod, a shovel and a shotgun.

Yet his will to stay and support his wife and three children was equally steel, to rule by fist as the head of a household he both protected and punished. The hours of his employment measured our lives like the recipe for concrete: dayshift, afternoon shift, graveyard shift. Normal household rhythms wrenched against the natural clock of daylight, season, tide and moon. We ate when he ate, we slept when he slept. All the while he suffered the Lafarge lime dust that pitted the Explorer's paint and his sinuses. When he came home, the kiln came home with him, molten in his gut.

He hated the cost of feeding us. Piece by piece, he would examine our household garbage for evidence of waste. He routinely shut off the hot water and heat to the house. Yes, my father drank, raged, punched my mother and threw her into the walls. He spanked us, lifted us, dangled us, dropped us and broke a wooden pole across my little sister's legs, and later I counted his hand-shaped welts like red paint on her white back, indelible to my memory. We crouched on the car floor when he raced down Marine Drive and held our breath when he dragged us into water over our heads. He laughed and called us crybabies when we were afraid for our lives.

In 1971 I graduated from high school. The New Westminster Credit Bureau hired me as a file clerk, and soon after I rented my first apartment. My father was eating his supper at the kitchen table as I went out the back door with a pillow under my arm. When I said goodbye, he flicked his hand at me without looking up from his plate. I was 17 years old and I wished my father dead.

"I PEED IN THE SNOW LAST WINTER AND IT WAS PINK," my father said one spring day in 1997. After the usual tests, his doctor cancelled a scheduled angioplasty to open up those clogged heart arteries. Within six months, the cancer spread from his kidneys to his spine. Kenneth Stewart died of a heart attack on September 1, Labour Day, 1997, five months short of his 65th birthday and retirement. He had just begun to clear a spot in the Comox acreage for the log house he was going to build.

"I know it's crazy, but I'm afraid your father's going to come back any minute, furious because I gave away his things." My mother looked out the kitchen window toward the garage my sister and I had plundered a week after the funeral. "I have nightmares," she said, twisting her wedding bands. On the table between us, his wallet, gutted. Suddenly I wanted to put everything back, to empty my hands of his things. The edge of inheritance was an open blade.

A YEAR AFTER MY FATHER'S DEATH, I was flying from Victoria to Calgary for a convention. I had shown my boarding pass and placed my purse and camera bag on the conveyor for inspection. It was the usual walk through and pick up. I found the camera bag and looked for my purse. It wasn't there. A Victoria airport official had his arm buried in my purse up to his pudgy elbow.

"Oh, it must be my cell phone," I said.

"No, I don't think so," he said. He pulled out the cell phone. Then my wallet. Then a mirror. This was ridiculous. And then a knife. Oh. The man did not speak, but held the knife like a candle in the air between us. For a moment, we both gaped.

"Oh that," I laughed, my face hot. "I forgot all about it—it's just my dad's knife." The man had not said a word. Slowly he moved his thumb—*thwack*—a six-inch blade shot up from inside the handle. His eyes popped.

"It belonged to my dad," I repeated. Other passengers, held up, now stared.

"Come and see this," he called to a co-worker.

"Wow."

"This is an illegal weapon," he pronounced. "I have to impound this."

"Fine," I said, "just so long as I get it back. Like I said, the knife belonged to my father. How will I get it back?" I imagined him pocketing the knife to show off to his friends.

He reassured me the knife would be in safekeeping. I collected myself and walked into the preboarding lounge, by then almost full. Moments later, two RCMP officers entered with the airport official. "That's her over there," he said loudly, and pointed across the room at me.

The female officer escorted me to a small room. I laughed and explained how the day after my father's funeral my sister and I divided up his knives and I took this one and dropped it into my good purse, the one that I don't use very often, but today I changed purses at the last minute and forgot the knife was rattling around in the bottom, you know how purses are, you know how funerals are, I wanted to have something of my father's close to me... until an inner voice interrupted: *If you don't stop laughing and shut up, you're going to go for a car ride.* Then the officer arrested me for attempting to board an aircraft with an illegal weapon.

Matters of inheritance generally circle around money, possessions and family disease. *What will I get?* Practical advice is everywhere. Books by the truckload. Typically, websites advertise tax shelters or discuss how to preserve artefacts like sable coats. One site called apartmenttherapy.com has an entire page dedicated to "Inherited Clutter." It offers upbeat suggestions: Grandma's teacups make a nice lamp stand; sixties furniture is cool; and hey, *repurpose* those vintage tea towels into wall hangings. One writer reflects how grateful she is that her grandparents were burglarized five times before they died. Still others refer to eBay, craigslist and grief counsellors to "let go" of the unwanted, yet emotionally charged, knick-knacks.

It isn't all teacups and linen. What about the secret bottom-drawer hordes of outright weirdness? Just scroll the bizarre collections on the website Neatorama.com: banana labels and navel fluff? Consider your own hidden indulgences. Or the shameful. When an elderly man died in a care facility where once I worked, I pulled the smutty paperback from his cold hands and with the coroner's permission hid it before his family arrived. Why should the last memory of their father include *that?* The coroner laughed: "He's probably got a trunkful of smut at home." So what about the heartbreaking act of pawing through your father's unmentionables, of finding things you never dreamed he owned, and now cannot unsee, untouch, unknow? Read the unlocked diaries of the deceased with care. Some inheritances you have to bury in a closet or drown with drink.

EVENTUALLY I CONVINCED THE RCMP OFFICER that I was merely stupid, incapable of crime at knifepoint. I was just a middle-aged woman, a mother and a homeowner, practically Anglican, on her way to a photographer's convention in Calgary. The officer was an unsmiling younger woman in her 30s, black hair pulled back tight, abrupt in her questions. She searched my camera bag and found another knife, a Swiss Army with attachments to open bottles, sever limbs or sew them back on. The bear spray turned out to be illegal too—a handy palm-size no longer sold in Canada.

"Where did you get these things?" She motioned to empty my pockets. "What are you doing with these knives?"

"I do nature photography… I hike in the wilderness, sometimes alone. These belonged to my father. He died last year and I took them."

"What were you going to do with these knives?" she repeated, louder.

I didn't know how to answer her question. I thought I *had* answered it. How could I explain how normal it felt to hold a knife? "Nothing. I wasn't going to do anything. I just have them, you know, just in case." Knives were just ordinary hardware.

"Just in case of what?" she shot back.

"I don't know." Then I started to cry. "They were my father's knives." It might have been the crying. Whatever it was, she seemed satisfied. I dared a stupid question: "Am I going to miss my flight?"

The officer looked me hard in the face and for a few moments did not speak. Then she said, "No. Give me your contact number in Calgary and your return flight information.

You can go." After I fumbled and scribbled, she handed me the camera bag. "You'll be notified when to appear in court."

I put the bag on my shoulder, picked up my purse and straightened my jacket. She pointed to the door—dismissed. The lounge was empty. I was last to board the aircraft, my face ready to burst into flame when I found my seat.

All the way to Calgary, I worried. Would the RCMP search my home? I had skinning knives, filleting knives, pocket knives, homemade knives with antler handles, strange knives my father bought in Kuwait and Germany, knives in fancy cases and knives for fun. There were guns in the attic, wedged between insulation and rafters: a pellet gun, a shotgun, a .22 and a 30.6 rifle. All those boxes of bullets. They would find all that easily and then, in the back of my bedroom closet, wrapped in a black plastic bag, out would roll my great-grandmother's double bedspread, hand-crocheted by her arthritic fingers, featuring a huge swastika in ecru cotton. My grandmother had given to my mother. My mother had given it to me with the same explanation given to her: "She made it before the Germans took it over—when the swastika was a symbol for good luck—it's such a shame." And I was hiding it for my daughter.

When I returned from Calgary, I wrote the Crown Counsel and promised never to attempt air travel with a stiletto again. "I have no knowledge of how my deceased father came to possess such a knife," I wrote and further confessed, "and it was extremely foolish to carry the knife as an inherited object of comfort." In October 1998, the Crown replied they were "exercising discretion to direct that proceedings not be taken in Criminal Court," but if any other offences occurred, "you may expect formal proceedings."

WE INHERIT. My father gave me meaty calf muscles and the tools to kill and skin a moose. "Cut out the middleman," he

always said, except he was the one snared between a bucca-
neer's heart and the bonds of domesticity. Who needed survival skills in the well-stocked aisles of Hi-Low Foods? What
good was a compass during evening rush hour on the Pattullo
Bridge? The passion of the hunter came home to a turquoise
living room, a wife and three kids. When the neighbourhood
car lot raised helium balloons to advertise their location, my
father took aim from the bedroom window and shot them all
down. He tried to forge a truce between the life he was born
to live and the life that gave him birth. Yet he could not deny
his inheritance any more than I could mine.

On February 17, 1933, he was born Kenneth Richard Nelson to a young woman named Betty Greenland. Months earlier, the father of her child had left her, literally, waiting at
the altar. My grandfather, a man named Menzel, was never
seen again. Unwilling to face the grim prospects of an unwed mother, Betty answered two immediate questions: What
should she name the baby, and who was going to raise him?
She decided to give the baby to her parents and surname him
after the Richmond road they lived on: Nelson.

   For the first six years of his life, Kenneth Nelson knew
his grandparents as parents and spoke only Finnish. His
aunts and uncles were his older brothers and sisters. The
open fields around the large family farm cradled Kenneth
with duck and heron, bulrush and frogs. He slept and woke
to the practical lullaby of seed and belly. Then one day Betty returned with Orton Stewart, her new husband, and two
more children in tow. My old aunties told me how little Kenny
hid under his bed from the cries of his heartbroken mother
and the screams of the stranger who had come to take him
away. Betty took Kenneth to live with his new family in a
crowded Dundas Street apartment in Vancouver. Orton was

a tall, narrow-faced man who favoured the willow switch to discipline his offspring. While one more child increased the meagre dole, it brought another mouth to the table, a foreign child who couldn't have resembled the family less. It was a good thing Kenneth didn't speak English, the aunties said, because he might have thought his new name was "bastard."

Was shame the legacy Kenneth refused to leave his own children? If it was, then he sacrificed in an order of mystery I find myself unfit, unable, to judge. He never spoke of his German father. My mother kept the secret. She said she would have never known at all if my father had not needed a copy of his birth certificate to apply for their marriage license. He never spoke about his grandparents. All the time I lived with him, I never heard a word in Finnish—only English words I thought he pronounced wrong on purpose.

How can we know what force will speak through one generation to another? In 1956, my father was lucky enough to get a good union job at a newly constructed cement plant in Richmond. For the next 41 years, on his coffee breaks and lunch hours, he looked over those same bulrush ponds, the fields of his childhood, from the high platform of Lafarge Cement, located at the end of Nelson Road. It is unlikely he could have heard the mallard's call over the immense slow-turning kiln.

IT IS EMBARRASSING TO CONFESS how long I pondered the officer's question: *What are you doing with all these knives?* I should have recognized the inheritance of compromise was in my blood and that, in some contradictory ways, it has always been 1971 inside of me. This liminality, the 17-year-old girl on her father's threshold, had misinformed my understanding of daily life and ordinary streets. Three years after my arrest and pardon, I phoned the Saanich RCMP and asked them to come and take away my father's guns. The decision was not easy. I could hear his outrage at the violation of trust: I was supposed to take care of the guns, eventually pass them on to my own son. Besides, the guns were valuable—*You're not even going to sell them?*

The argument continued until the police car turned into the driveway. I had the guns ready at the front door, all the bullets in a grocery bag. It was a simple transaction, no questions asked. The female officer held out her arms. One by one, I gave her the guns. Then she turned and walked down the sidewalk with the long barrels swaddled across her forearms like a rigid child I had finally released. Sunlight fell equally on her blonde hair, the blue uniform and the black steel. Over the Quadra Street traffic, I heard *shhhhh* through the oak leaves.

For most of my adult life, I have lived alone. The knife is an unambiguous companion, certain in function, balm to my fears, a comfort in my loneliness. More than a decade has passed since my father's death on the kitchen floor of the childhood home I hated and tried to escape. Only now do I consider the life he loved and never lived, and allow myself to believe that cancer ended his hope and grief stopped his heart. Yes, a fine blade calms the ambivalent soul. Even now I can hear my father's deliberate circles, the rhythmic pitch of steel on the oiled stone.

TOURISTS OF CONSCIOUSNESS

Jeff Warren
Maisonneuve

"If you get into any trouble, try concentrating on your breath. Sometimes the breath is all you have."

Brian looked concerned, though he also looked weirdly elongated, so it was hard to tell what was actually happening. I was on drugs, you see, and not just any drug. Thirty minutes earlier I had gulped back a cupful of ayahuasca, a plant-based hallucinogen that William Burroughs—no slouch when it came to chemical experimentation—once described as the most powerful he had ever experienced. This was my third trip in six days, and I'd taken half again as much as anyone else in the group. Now nobody would look me in the eye.

This was several years ago, during a perspective-altering ten-day workshop in South America. Today, most armchair adventurers will have heard of ayahuasca, which first escaped from the Amazon jungle in the 1930s and has recently leapt from underground curiosity to zeitgeist sensation. Following in the footsteps of celebrities such as Sting and Oliver Stone, every year thousands of people fly to countries like Peru, Brazil and Ecuador, where ayahuasca can be sampled in the company of professional shamans—some respectable, some not. Having had their fill of physical travel, Westerners now want to sail right out of their minds.

Others quaff more locally. British Columbia's Pender Island, Toronto's beaches and Montreal's suburbs host gatherings of the curious (supervised by imported boutique shamans) and congregations of the two fastest-growing syncretic churches that use ayahuasca as a sacrament: the Santo Daime and the União do Vegetal. Both churches—part animist, part Christian—have outposts across Latin America, Europe and North America; none other than Jeffrey Bronfman, third-generation member of the famous Montreal whisky family, heads the Santa Fe chapter of the União do Vegetal. Ayahuasca's precise legal status in the US and Canada is ambiguous. But, if you're determined, getting your hands on the stuff isn't hard.

Ayahuasca owes its popularity to its alleged psycho-spiritual benefits. As one retreat centre's website puts it: "the equivalent of ten years of therapy in one night, ayahuasca can promote healing and transformation in areas of relationships, self esteem and creative potential, to name a few." Claims like this (circulated in online forums and, increasingly, in feature-length documentaries and mainstream news outlets) are part of a larger renaissance in the world of psychedelic-drug research; clinical trials are now exploring the potential of drugs like LSD and ecstasy to treat everything from post-traumatic stress disorder to addiction to cluster headaches. Yet of all these drugs, it's ayahuasca that has generated the most interest outside the world of test subjects and clinicians. Call it hippie Prozac: the must-have miracle cure for the new New Age.

This is startling enough. But ayahuasca may be at the nexus of an even deeper revolution, one that explores how indigenous forms of knowledge—long discounted in the West— could contribute to our understanding of consciousness and reality. That's because, according to devotees, ayahuasca is a direct channel to nature's interior aspect, to a whole pantheon of extrasensory intelligences: other human psyches, alien beings, the spirits of plants and animals. To update Aldous Huxley's famous quip about mescaline, ayahusaca blows the doors of perception right off their hinges. It disables what Huxley called the "cerebral reducing valve" and plunges the stunned psychonaut into a seething ecology of other minds.

Of course, for every investigator who holds this rather unscientific point of view, there is another who points out that such testimonials are, after all, generated by people *on drugs*. Although sympathetic to some of the therapeutic claims made on behalf of ayahuasca, I wasn't sure the plant mixture could support the West's collective expectation of spiritual-satori-slash-psychological-analysis. I was even more skeptical about the metaphysical assertions. We don't believe dreams are "real"—why should an ayahuasca vision be any different? Nevertheless, the rich history of ayahuasca usage has undeniable authority; in the end, the only way to really answer these questions was to launch into the psychedelic troposphere and find out for myself.

THE NAME OF MY DESTINATION, as well as its location, is secret. All I can say is that it was a family-run compound at the edge of a dark forest. Though ayahuasca is legal in this tropical country, there are politics surrounding its use, and the owner of the compound—I'll call him Alejandro—prefers to keep a low profile. I learned about the workshop through word of mouth, though similar opportunities can be found online. Where once ayahuasca-seekers had to ford piranha-infested rivers and barter with locals, now, for a few thousand dollars, tour operators will pick you up in air-conditioned coaches, cook you delicious vegetarian meals and ensure your linen is changed daily.

My host was waiting in the parking lot when I stepped out of the taxi. Alejandro, brown-eyed and courteous, shook my hand, and in the fading light ushered me inside. Alejandro began studying with traditional Amazonian shamans—*ayahuasqueros*—in the seventies. The men showed him how the plant mixture can be used for healing and revelation, and he began to think that ayahuasca might also facilitate a kind of secular enlightenment.

Two hours after I'd arrived, our group gathered in a large room with hardwood walls. We were invited to explain why we had come. There were about a dozen of us, and perhaps a third were there for therapeutic reasons: therapists looking to incorporate ayahuasca into their practices, or patients seeking treatment. One forty-year-old woman had been abused as a child and wanted to make peace with her history. Another, a Finnish professor, sought insight into his embittered relationship with his wife. There was even an RCMP officer on a private mission to bring law and order to his own mind.

The rest were an eclectic collection of anthropologists, research psychologists and students. This group—the deep-cave spelunkers of consciousness—had more profound goals. They believed that ayahuasca didn't simply lift users to new levels of perception, but also brought them into direct contact with a spirit realm inhabited by nonhuman intelligences. They dubbed it "DMT-space," after one of the drug's compounds. Most ayahuasca brews are made from two ingredients. The first is a leafy plant called *Psychotria viridis*, which contains the powerful psychoactive alkaloid dimethyltryptamine, or DMT. If eaten alone, the digestive system neutralizes DMT's effect. But, when it's combined with the *Banisteriopsis caapi* vine—which inhibits the enzymes that suppress DMT—the real trip begins. While other psychedelics might hint at this spirit realm, some claim that ayahuasca is unique in teleporting you directly inside it, providing multi-sensory initiations into landscapes of great beauty and complexity.

I felt conspicuously skeptical in my corner of the room. "Journalisto de consciousness," I joked, pointing to my head, when it was my turn to explain my intent. I said that I had just finished writing a book on the waking and sleeping mind, and believed that what happened on ayahuasca could be explained by the neurological mechanics of Rapid Eye Movement sleep, recursive sensory feedback loops and the human brain's amazing ability to build immersive models of the world during dreams. "With the careful application of reason," I wrapped up, "we can shed some much-needed light on the phenomenology of this curious plant mixture."

The room, I noticed, was mostly empty. Somehow I had not heard the dinner bell.

That night I had a dream. I stood in a dark room next to a flickering fire. Someone handed me a cup of muddy liquid. As I brought it to my lips I heard Alejandro repeat what he told us that day: "You will look different once you leave here. You will not recognize yourself in the mirror." I woke with a start. I could hear sounds coming from the jungle outside, soft trills and staccatos. My belly was tight with expectation.

THE NEXT DAY WE EACH SIGNED A WAIVER, assuming all risks. Ayahuasca is in no way a recreational drug. Though I had never heard of it killing anyone, compounds in the plants react very badly with common antidepressants. It can also cause severe headaches and even cardiac arrhythmia if combined with beer, cheese, wine, coffee and a number of other foods. Two weeks before arriving, we had begun a salt- and sugar-free diet, and for the duration of our stay we ate no meat or spicy foods.

It was winter in South America; the sun set early. At 8:30 pm we met in the main room under soft yellow lamps. Along each wall was a row of evenly spaced mattresses, which fanned out toward the centre of the room like the spokes of a square wheel. Next to each mattress sat a plastic bucket. On a shelf at the front was a clear bottle filled with dark fluid.

We sat in a circle and discussed our intentions: who we were grateful to, what we hoped to accomplish. I felt reassured. One of the abiding lessons of sixties psychedelic experimentation—and something indigenous shamans have long appreciated—is that both your mindset and environment matter enormously when you ingest plant medicines. Positive outlook, controlled surroundings, supportive company: good trip. Terrified outlook, chaotic surroundings, hostile strangers: bad trip. The former is a recipe for profound insight retrieval. The latter is a recipe for ending up naked and raving in the back of a paddy wagon after a Grateful Dead concert.

Alejandro handed out plastic glasses and we gathered round to receive our portions. Everyone would start with around eighty millilitres, though we had the option of taking boosters later on in the night. I reached out my cup and watched as Alejandro filled it with purple liquid.

We raised our glasses—"Salud!"—and gulped the drug back, Alejandro included. Disgusting, but not as bad as I had expected; it tasted like rancid grapefruit juice. Each of us chose a mattress and settled down, sitting cross-legged to stave off the nausea. Vomiting and diarrhea—*la purga*, they called it—was part of the experience, and according to some a necessary catalyst. But first the drug had to snake its way down into our systems, a process that could take up to an hour. I looked around the dimly-lit room. Hunched, people looked as though they were meditating. I closed my eyes and waited.

After about forty minutes, Alejandro picked up a rattle and sang a short, haunting *icaro*—a shamanic chant. In *Singing to the Plants*, scholar Steve Beyer calls *icaro* "the language of the plant." Natural spirits give the shaman these *icaros*, which become the voice of the shaman in ceremony.

Alejandro, defiantly modern, put down the rattle and selected an *icaros* playlist from his laptop. I felt something shift in the room. The jungle sounds were louder. I heard a faraway hiss. One indigenous group calls ayahuasca "the airplane" because the trip arrives from high overhead with a low buzzing. When I opened my eyes the room had a fuzzy, vibrating quality. The halo of colour around each lamp deepened. I realized I was holding my breath. As I exhaled I felt something pour into me, an upwelling of alertness. It felt vaguely sexual, as if I were being seduced from the inside. I knew my mouth was hanging open but I couldn't close it. My body was heavy all over, my lips thick. There were no ideas and no visions, only a powerful physicality, a high not unlike what I'd experienced from ecstasy.

With his white robe and screen-lit features, Alejandro looked iconic, the eternally-presiding cosmic DJ. From the speakers, a low drumming began to build, a woman's voice crying eerily overtop. Suddenly everyone was standing up. I was unsure how much time had passed, but saw that the group had clustered around Alejandro to receive boosters. I staggered across the room with my glass extended and shot back another forty millilitres of liquid. It was a mistake. The rush that followed flattened me to my mattress.

Someone was on the floor by my feet. I squinted and recognized Susan, a retired schoolteacher. A composed, white-haired woman in her sixties, she was now moaning and squirming like a lizard, hands pressed to her pelvis and breasts. Another woman, Masha, leapt up and began a slithery Medusa dance, her voice raised to a high-pitched keening, accompanied now by Alejandro's furious bongo-playing, which echoed off the walls with percussive force.

As if on cue, the Estonian psychologist, Alar, vomited into his bucket, setting off a domino effect of throaty purges around the room. Susan began humping the air. The Mountie groaned and raised his arm, as if to ward off an assailant. Someone else started barking. The Finnish professor—also in his sixties—came spinning in from the sidelines, hair shocked upwards in an Elvis-style pompadour, and pranced around Susan's undulating body.

It was all too much. I struggled to my feet, teetered, and fell sideways over a chair. On my hands and knees I managed to crawl to the bathroom, where I was noisily ill. I spent the next two hours slumped next to the toilet, disappointed by my lack of visions, but also giggling at the whole bizarre circus. Behavioural reality, at least, was beginning to shift.

IN THE MORNING, the group reported generally satisfactory experiences. As is customary with ayahuasca, many people saw snakes when they closed their eyes, and Masha matter-of-factly described transforming into a reptile.

The snake motif puzzles consciousness theorists. How is it possible that almost everyone seems to see serpents, regardless of cultural background or personal expectations? There are other recurring elements, too: jaguars, ancient cities, ornamentation. The first written description of an ayahuasca trip comes from an Ecuadorian geographer named Manuel Villavicencio, who, in 1858, perceived "the most gorgeous views, great cities, lofty towers, beautiful parks, and other extremely attractive objects." Believers use accounts like this as proof of a coherent alternative reality.

The late psychedelic trickster and author Terence McKenna popularized what is perhaps the strangest meme associated with DMT: under its influence, people come into contact with alien beings he called "machine elves," or more colourfully, "self-dribbling bejewelled basketballs." By turns courteous, cruel or indifferent, these enigmatic characters beep and trill and execute various mind-boggling stunts in the drinker's DMT space. They are not to be confused with the plant spirits, who have their own particular proclivities and personalities.

Are these entities ambassadors from other levels of reality, as shamans believe? Or are they dramatizations of our own interior processes, as is the standard Western judgment? James Kent makes a strong case for the latter. The battle-hardened psychonaut, editor of DoseNation.com and author of *Psychedelic Information Theory* argues that hallucinogens interfere with receptors in the visual cortex, provoking a cascade of phosphenes we then anthropomorphize into grinning human features. Psychologists call this "gap-filling."

This, of course, is the rationalist perspective. But some Westerners closest to indigenous societies—the actual anthropologists who live and drink with them—have come to disagree with that view. Steve Beyer lists in his book at least four anthropologists who, in their own ways, argue that the spirit world is ontologically real. Even the respected Israeli cognitive psychologist Benny Shanon, who describes his own ayahuasca experiences in *The Antipodes of the Mind*, grudgingly admits his visions may "reflect patterns exhibited on another, extra-human realm."

Beyer himself takes a slightly different tack. Yes, he says, after many encounters he has come to accept the spirit world as real. But reality itself cannot be confined to a single point or plane. We may actually live, he said recently, on a "spectrum of reality."

AFTER A DAY OF REST, I took a second trip across the spectrum of reality. It unfolded in much the same manner, beginning with awe, a great sense of mystery, something stirring in the room. I felt as if I were strapped inside an enormous vibrating didgeridoo. Behind my closed lids, purple blobs of colour receded into a distant grid. When I opened my eyes, everything was bordered by concentric Aztec squares, recursive and symmetrical. They were similar to the geometric distortions I had perceived on magic mushrooms and LSD. Occasionally I thought I saw figures and shapes coalesce on the periphery of my gaze, straining toward some kind of incarnation. But no machine elves came.

And yet, near the end of my trip, as the music tapered into more reflective hymns, something did happen: I had a wave of insights about my relationship, my family, my friends. I saw my actions as if from far above and watched as they rippled out into other people's lives. There was nothing recriminatory about the experience—rather, it had a gentle, matter-of-fact character that slipped through my usual psychological defenses. It was easy to see how this could be therapeutic. The supercharged circumstances of the ceremony only reinforced my realizations; it was like having my thoughts underlined with a psychic highlighter.

The next day, as before, we described our experiences. Brian had catapulted to a place where "language and syntax don't exist." Later, coming down, he had a vision of a tree heavy with fruit. Each piece, he knew, represented a different relationship in his life—his mother, his girlfriend, his peers. As he pulled each fruit from its stem he looked past the flesh to the pit and saw, systematically, how to manage each relationship with more love and compassion. He was grateful, he said, to the plant teacher.

We began to discuss the origin of our visions. I suggested the most prudent explanation lay with the brain's chemistry and the intersection of the drug's two active agents. One plant boosts the amount of serotonin in the body, creating a hyper-alert ecstatic feeling, while the other boosts the amount of DMT, a naturally-occurring brain chemical thought to play a role in REM sleep. "Thus," I said, "the serotonin circle overlaps with the DMT circle, and we sit in the middle, submerged in a waking dream."

Ayahuasca is a catalyst for therapeutic insight, I continued, because "normal" thinking—all our dependable assumptions about the world and the self—cannot proceed. We're forced to make new connections. What's more, this happens within a larger climate of what psychiatrist Daniel X. Freedman called, in a classic 1968 paper on LSD, "portentousness," or "the capacity of the mind to see more than it can tell, to experience more than it can explicate, to believe in and be impressed with more than it can rationally justify."

"Psychotropics like ayahuasca," I concluded, "allow us to both see the world anew, and overlay that world with an abiding sense of its irreducible complexity and mystery. Isn't that enough?"

Michael, a well-known anthropologist and author, shared his own theory. Psychedelics, he explained, acted as "psycho-integrators," linking up three evolutionary layers of the brain: the ancient reptilian brain stem, the middle-aged mammalian limbic system and the relatively modern frontal cortex. Ayahuasca, he told the group, rerouted habitual ways of thinking down through the primitive brain stem. "That's why you can't put so many of these experiences into words," he said. "The reptile brain stem can't make words. It's pre-verbal."

Matt from San Francisco was shaking his head. "You guys have no idea. You can talk about the brain all you want, but it says nothing about the experience and the reality of these encounters."

Brian joined him. "Ayahuasca shows that what we think of as boundaries are really borders. This reality here," he said, gesturing around the room, "is just a container for one kind of order. There are others. The truth of this isn't something you can 'figure out.' It works on you from the inside, until you arrive at a different way of seeing. It only seems strange because we don't understand it."

I wanted to believe them, of course. Who wouldn't? The alternative was imprisonment in my own head—the crisis of the lab technician, cut off from a nourishing world of spirit and connection. I envied people like Brian and Matt. They were smart and informed, yet they also believed. Perhaps they had the best of science and spirituality. Could I arrive at this place too, without becoming some disorderly mystic? I didn't know, but after our discussion I was hell-bent on finding out.

AT THE BEGINNING OF THE THIRD TRIP, I asked for 160 millilitres—double what I'd started with the first time. Alejandro, hesitating, said I would need a straightjacket if I wasn't careful. I laughed and told him to pour my rations. He obliged, shaking his head.

Within half an hour I knew I was in trouble. Shadows cast by a flickering candle crowded in on me. When I closed my eyes, the shadows were still there, moving closer, bent into impossible angles. My last coherent emotion was shame. "I am a fool," I said out loud.

Brian told me to concentrate on my breath, but it was too late: I had no breath, or hands for that matter—both arms had dissolved into green and yellow pixels. A moving front of particulate matter surged up my neck and into my throat, my whole yapping head apparatus suddenly flipped inside out. Every category immediately became meaningless. There was no "up" or "down," no "real" or "hallucinated." My thoughts were no different from physical objects. Everything—mind and matter—was composed of the same omnipresent material, pressing and twisting against me.

Was I breathing? I couldn't tell—that idea was inconsequential, too. So was the concept of my death, which felt imminent. I tried to summon an image of my mother, but her disappointment had too many dimensions. I began to laugh, hunched on my mattress, hands gripping my head as I peeled over sideways like a Picasso abstract. I recognized, even in my terror, the situation's dark comedy, the spectacle of my rational mind scurrying through the maelstrom with its pathetic building materials. I wanted to ask for help but couldn't formulate the words.

Finally, after what seemed like a very long time, it passed. My forehead was clammy with sweat. Alejandro squatted by my side and asked if I was all right. I was, but also not. I lay on my mattress, feeling very alone, as if I had been to the dark sub-basement of the mind, where all the big, clunky turbines operated. There was no intelligence there, just the hardware, the machinery, constructing a seamless hidden world, overtop of which glided our everyday minds, confident and oblivious. Once again, I had not seen the nurturing plant spirits. I felt forsaken.

I wasn't alone. "This is my fiftieth ayahuasca session," said Susan the next day, her voice cracking. "I can't remember the last time I had a visit from the Mother. I keep drinking, but nothing helps." She looked around the room for help, but no one knew what to say. This wasn't in the brochure.

I was afraid to take ayahuasca again, but later that night I forced myself to drink. The brew tasted much worse now, foul beyond belief. Two hours in, something unexpected happened. Watching the others—Brian staring calmly into the room, Susan mumbling softly to herself, the professor on his back, turning his hands in front of his face—I felt a very present and immediate tenderness. I closed my eyes. I could sense them all, moving in their private worlds, but also brushing up against my own. It was an odd feeling. My skin tingled as if each person were right up against me, but when I opened my eyes everyone was still on their mattresses. Was this the feeling of unity they were talking about? Brian told me that in a session he had done the previous year, he "crashed" into the mind of a woman sitting next to him. Both of them could sense the other's freaked-out thoughts, an event the two later discussed, even though, he said, "we didn't need to."

My heightened sensitivity persisted through the night. Toward dawn, after everyone else had gone to sleep, I went outside and stood at the edge of the forest next to the compound. Everything was very still, yet the trees had an uncommon expressiveness. They reached upward to the brightening sky, but remained protective of their many shadows. I strained my ears, trying to pick up the solemn vibes of some fibrous tree spirit. I wrapped my arms around what looked like a sympathetic araucaria. It had happened: tree-hugger. I whispered endearments into the smooth bark.

The following day we said our goodbyes, and I returned home feeling unusually calm and lucid. It was a sensation similar to what I had experienced after a meditation retreat, a state of composure I have heard described by other long-term consumers of psychedelics, the ones who hadn't come unhinged. Many forms of intense introspection, it seems, lead to clearings. So what had become clear to me? What kind of knowledge do psychedelics like ayahuasca impart?

THE POET DALE PENDELL has a term for the practice of sacred plant use: "the poison path." The poison's first victim is certainty; it weakens pre-existing worldviews and self-conceits. This can be terrifying, and liberating, and desolating, sometimes in that order. Especially if—as in my case—the plant continues to confound our hopes and expectations. In the end, the psychedelic seeker must depend on her own capacity to discriminate, to artfully integrate the lessons and visions—and, sometimes, lack of visions—into her life. If you have a good shaman you don't have to do this alone. Part of the shaman's craft is to work creatively with plant energies as they interface with our own. Though the shaman keeps the energy moving, so much depends on individual context. It is not a case of taking your medicine and being handed the truth. This may be what Westerners seek, but it is not what the shaman—or the medicine—offers.

Ayahuasca, however, does leave one certainty intact: our kinship with nature. Like other psychedelic thinkers, Alejandro believes that ayahuasca and other organic psychotropics act as nature's corrective. They bring us back into alignment with ecological reality, with the tangled web of biological dependencies—human and extra-human—through which we move so carelessly. This is why, Alejandro told me, so many of those who try ayahuasca end up changing careers, becoming environmental lawyers or field biologists or organic farmers. They see with new clarity how abusing the planet—dumping pollution into the air and sea, eliminating entire species, hacking down jungles—is a kind of self-harm. The reverberations of this truth depend on how far along the spectrum of reality you are willing to go. For some, the fact of ecological connection is enough. Others go further.

Ayahuasca has been called "one of the most sophisticated and complex drug-delivery systems in existence." One oft-mentioned mystery is how indigenous people knew to combine the elements of the drug, since they grow in separate ecological niches and are just two of over eighty thousand plant species that exist in the Amazon basin. Shamans say the plants told them. When you delve into the anthropological literature on indigenous views of nature, from the Cherokee to the Iroquois to the Shipibo, shamans say the same thing: via visions and dreams and waking intuitions, the plants tell them things, things they have no way of knowing otherwise. They are not speaking metaphorically. Rather, they are literally saying that all things are alive and talking to one another. It may not even be necessary to ingest a plant to partake in this dialogue. The simple act of walking through the woods, if done with the correct attitude and sensitivity, can be a learning experience. It is a matter of bringing to the forest the same empathy and openness we should bring to human society. In this sense, all of nature is very subtly psychoactive.

This kind of knowledge relies heavily on one's internal state, which drives hardcore skeptics batty—accessing it depends in part on one's openness to the situation. But that's the mind for you. You can't escape it or even properly assess its influence. It's like the eye trying to see itself. Amateur psychonauts, too, would do well to consider this: no matter how many perspective-expanding substances you take, no matter how many insights you generate and genuine multi-dimensional perceptions you entertain, you will never expand past the incontrovertible fact of your own subjective filter. This may be the central insight of psychedelic philosophy.

So where does all this leave the shaman's anomalous spirits? I didn't encounter any elves or vegetal entities. But ayahuasca did leave me with the sense that the world is humming with organizing patterns that affect our minds in ways we've hardly begun to appreciate. Our psychology and neurobiology, of course, shape how we receive and interpret these patterns. But my feeling is that we do not create them any more than we create the songbird's call or the movement of wind in the trees. What seems like nature mysticism now could be the next generation's environmental science: both an intimation of the biosphere's complex information exchange and a glimpse into nature's vast interiority, intelligence—maybe even agency.

These are grand claims, especially given the case I've just made for the mind's fundamental indeterminacy. I recognize my own existential neediness; I'm not unbiased. No one is. The mind's shaping power, however, is actually good news. It suggests that, when it comes to some aspects of consciousness and reality, you get to choose the kind of world you want to live in. I know what it's like to follow a mechanistic outlook through to its logical conclusion: it's lonely and scary and it made me want to roll up in a fetal position next to a bucket of my own barf. But in my tiny moment of connectivity with all things—my immersion in a shared world of living presence—I felt a consolation and a wonder I will not forget.

BLOOD MEMORY

Lisa Wilson
Geist

Every pregnant woman dreams of what her baby will be like. But babies shouldn't have to dream their mothers. It's been more than thirty years and I still struggle to quell the haunting voice at the back of my mind that urges *find her find her*. Instead I invent her.

I want to start at the beginning but beginnings are slippery to pin down. What would hers look like? Was it the moment she realized her period was late? I can imagine the instant of understanding that her actions, up to now carefree and light, came with real consequences. Or maybe the beginning was the conception itself, when she and my father pushed the limits behind the big barn that housed the cattle in winter, the small heated calf-shack tucked into its shadow. What made her think she was immune to it all, to the fecundity of the land and animals that every day plugged her nose with pungent odours, filled her ears with bawling bleating madness?

More likely, the beginning had something to do with the day the gnarly, squashed fetus (she made herself call it a fetus, to avoid thinking of it as a b-a-b-y) squalled its way into her world and she made her way out of its world—a double beginning. Each a newly released hostage, not quite believing she had survived, fleetingly grateful before moving on as though nothing of import had occurred. There's got to be a reason why babies and mothers forget the pain of birth.

I picture what she went through something like this. At the height of the ninth month, swollen like an overstuffed olive, lungs and other internal organs squeezed so tight she felt out of breath on the wide staircase of the antiseptic "home for unwed mothers" (read "institution for misfits and fuck-ups"), she tried to understand, but she could not find a reason for the mythical underwater creature swirling beneath skin stretched so thin and taut that in her dreams she popped herself with a shiny dinner fork. All the while, inside, the fetus (repeat: *fetus, fetus*) sank and swam in murky depths of blood memory bonding secret-identity-mother to child. And a word bobbed about in the depths, tickling the tadpole, the word waiting to be picked up and held in the palms of two hands, examined then crushed to the chest rubbed into arms, over shoulders, across the belly, the word more than a word, to be inhaled then expelled bit by bit with every breath—the word *Métis*.

I DON'T KNOW ABOUT THE HOME AND THE WIDE STAIRCASE; she could have been kept like an animal in a barn for all I know. But going off to a home seems the kind of thing that would have happened, back in the day. I imagine them saying she'd been sent away to live with a sick aunt after her father made an angry visit to the neighbouring farm and scared the hell out of the farmhand, who was really just a boy, while her mother got on the phone with the priest. Sent away for five months before returning deflated, with large leaky breasts, eyes swollen from lying in the back of the family station wagon and bawling all the way home.

"Growing nicely," Dr. Dubious pronounces as he measures my belly from pubic bone to top of fundus—some of the new words I've been learning. What about the words she learned? Not the words of a fantastic and beautiful anatomy to be revealed during the rite of passage through pregnancy and birth toward motherhood. Instead the words she learned— truly learned in their deep and hurtful meaning, maybe for the first time—those words may have been *shame, wrong, bad, disgrace*, words that make her cover her head and stop her ears to deflect their blows.

I also learned, on my visit to Dr. Dubious, that it's awkward to have a baby when you don't know your medical history. *Any history of heart disease?*

No.

What about in your family?

Nana died when I was nineteen, and my mother dug into herself to find the words to tell me her mother was dead. That is when I understood that my mother had been a daughter

first. But Nana's stroke doesn't count for Dubious question—
he is looking for hereditary conditions. I have nothing to offer,
only a great yawning blank. I give him the only thing hereditary I know: *Métis*.

Not a baby, not a baby. She must have willed herself to
remain blank and distant from what was right below the sternum. No picturing startled fingers, tiny heels that would fit in
her palm, a dark silken bloom of hair, down-covered shoulders. Instead, a fishy eyeless globe, a silent sea monster in
the well of her incubator body, gnawing at the base of the
cord that attached them, one to the other, trying desperately
to escape as a muskrat will chew its own leg off to get out of
a trap. She once saw her father open a ripe sturgeon, full of
black eggs, and saw him lament the lost potential of those
eggs, as though somehow he'd been a careless steward. But
her insides only harbour a single shimmery orb shadowed
by a thin stretch of tail. She imagines this thing contained,
herself a container. She is filled with blue-green water, soft
seaweed tendrils undulating in time with her movements, a
secret underwater world like a dark aquarium. There must be
a reason we're grown in the dark, submerged in water, her-
metically sealed—what is it we're trying to keep out?

She dreams of gigantic garden shears sharpened to a ra-
zor's edge, oiled and free of catches, her hands holding the
rubber-coated grips and cutting the briny cord, setting herself afloat as the fetus *fetus fetus* drifts lazily away like Huck
on his raft, and she is laughing.

In one of her dreams she finds a small blue jewellery
box bobbing in the toilet. She scoops it out and holds it in
her palm, wet and messy, leaking onto her bare toes. She's
afraid to open it because she thinks it is ticking. She pan-
ics and tries to hide the thing before it explodes. She blurts

out mock-Latin words, *cul cum id esto*, grievous, faulty, in a solemn voice, flicking her fingers over the box, a magician's black-magic flourish, *léger de main*, before flushing it down.

I tell Dubious that I'll have my baby at home with midwives, that my baby must remain with me at all times, particularly during those few first lucid hours when the most intense bonding is said to occur. I mention my anxieties about "attachment capabilities" and "emotional glue." But I don't tell him that I'm teetering on the edge of an insurmountable regret, a loss so large it threatens to smother me—the loss of what was mine by birth, a deficit that I wear like a scar.

When I was a child I had two best friends—both adopted, both Native. It was as if we each recognized each other's wounds, as though we saw the pieces that hadn't formed, the missing parts that would have made each of us whole. Instead we were left inhibited, less attached, without much capacity for love and intimacy. I turned into an angry teenager, hungry for an unnameable, unknowable presence. I tell Dubious that I want the best for my baby. "All expectant mothers say that," he laughs. I don't tell him he's wrong.

DURING THE LAST MONTHS OF MY PREGNANCY, my mind becomes watered down with the weight and change in my body. I sit for hours dreamily staring into space while the radio plays softly in another room. I relish the quiet, the peace, the opportunity to do nothing that those with experience tell me will soon end. I imagine what these months were like for her, in that home, day after day, a prisoner serving a sentence, waiting to be let free.

At the home there's a girl she's taken to calling Mary K. Mary K is lithe and sexy, even at nine months, while she herself is

puffy, toxic with high blood pressure and nauseating headaches. She can envision Mary K sitting on an older man's
lap and fiddling with his pants, toying with the idea of being
taken advantage of, a spunky, sway-back, streetwise Lolita,
her slippery seal's body a horny turn-on. If she'd had something other than sex to peddle she'd be the queen of snake-oil
sales. If life had dealt her a different hand she'd be driving
a big pink Cadillac with vanity plates that read Mary K. As
they smoke in the alley behind the home one girl dares to
confess she misses her boyfriend. The rest of them drag on
their smokes and say nothing.

The days are long and bleed one into the next. The girls are
not allowed out of the nuns' sight; many resent not being free
to walk and shop and pretend to live a different story than
the one they do; many are from remote rural places and being on the edge of the city, only to be forbidden a trip downtown, vexes them to the point of tears. Only Mary K, looking
like a malnourished, pot-bellied orphan, manages to slither
out under the cloak of night to secure cigarettes. She brings
back small flat bottles of lemon gin and the girls, with their
skewed centres of gravity, tumble one atop the other with
shrill delighted screams. The Mother Superior threatens to
put them out, to call their parents.

One evening at the home, as she makes toast, she looks
at her bloated reflection in the chrome and dreams of being
thin again. The girls can talk of nothing else. As she reaches
into the toaster with the point of a knife she knows that it's a
stupid thing to do. Would the shock throw her back onto her
ass? She thinks about the pond of dew she might have been
standing in were it not enclosed inside her body and how
water and electricity make bad company, and what might
happen to the cloudy lagoon sloshing about in her distended

belly with its fragments and bits, if it were touched the way she once saw a loose live wire send a blue-white spark to skip over puddles in the barn like stones over water. I don't know what happened, but my own mother, the one who raised me, told me what the social worker had said. There was an accident and I could have been lost. She's told me this story as confirmation of how much I was wanted, even before they knew who I was, even before I was born. I want to be grateful, I *am* grateful. But still I know she wouldn't understand my feeling that I've always been lost.

As she completes her sentence at the home, waiting for me to be born, shameful words creep up on her. In Cree one word is spoken over and again in her head—*macitwawiskwesis*, a bad girl. Perhaps she had a note from her mother on her birthday, expressing hope for a better year, yet between the lines she reads her mother's desire for a good daughter, not such a bad *nitanis*. My heart twists, half with empathy and half with jealousy, for at least she got to know these words, difficult as they are. At least she was *nitanis*, no matter how *bad*. When my husband returns home from work I chalk up my tears to hormones and he holds me until I sleep.

I IMAGINE THAT ALL HER DREAMS OCCUR UNDER WATER. The night she goes into labour, she floats peacefully, hair swaying about her face, hands gripping her garden shears, only to be tossed on shore by the insistent tides of her body. She gasps, lying in a puddle. Has she breached the thin membrane between dream and wakefulness, somehow exposing the netherworld to this one? She cries out with her first conscious contraction and the girl in the next bed tells her *shuddup, fer fucksake*.

A sentimental girl might name the baby. It never occurs to her, before, during or after the birth, that it is anything other than the black-penny-eyed tadpole of her imagination. She fills in the blanks as best she can—there are rules about these things—but no one can make her open her heart and no one can force her to leave anything behind, not even a name.

I sit in my bathtub at home, riding waves of contractions, soothed by the warm water, two midwives amiably attending, prepared for the long haul that most first births are. I can't shake the dream-world mother I've created. *Nitanis*, she whispers, as I let my head flop wearily between contractions; one midwife mops my brow with a cool cloth while the other perches on a chair and sips tea. Someone's put soft music on, my husband warms towels in the dryer, and I can hear the excited voices of our families downstairs in the living room.

My mother, real or dreamed, never had any of these things. No one whispered *nitanis* in her ear, mopped her brow, made the tea, warmed the towels, waited in the wings, treated my birth like a celebration. Instead, I imagine harsh words, harsh towels. Maybe a younger nun secretly attempted to mitigate the punishing experience of most births at the home. I am confused and angry over the loss of what I needed: identity, blood inheritance, to be Métis, to know where I've come from, something to pass on to my own child, who will be blinded when she sees all the things she lost as well.

HOURS LATER MY DAUGHTER IS BORN amid scurry and scuffle, worry and joy. I hold her next to my skin and she looks at me–looks and looks–her eyes wide and serious. And I think, *This is the first and only blood relation I have.* Together we will invent ourselves, she and I. She is beautiful and real.

contributor biographies

CAROLINE ADDERSON is the author of three novels (*A History of Forgetting*, *Sitting Practice*, *The Sky Is Falling*), two collections of short stories (*Bad Imaginings*, *Pleased to Meet You*), as well as several books for young readers. Her work has received numerous prize nominations including the Scotiabank Giller Prize longlist, the Governor General's Literary Award, the Rogers' Trust Fiction Prize, and two Commonwealth Writers' Prize nominations. A two-time Ethel Wilson Fiction Prize and three-time CBC Literary Award winner, Caroline was also the recipient of the 2006 Marian Engel Award for mid-career achievement.
http://www.carolineadderson.com/

DANIEL BAIRD lived and worked in New York City from 1989, where he was a founder of *The Brooklyn Rail*, a magazine for which he worked as an art editor, feature writer, and monthly columnist. Since moving to Toronto in 2000, he has written on the arts for numerous Canadian publications, including *Canadian Art* and *Border Crossings*. He has been an editor at *The Walrus* since 2005 and remains a regular contributor on topics as diverse as contemporary art and history, political theory, and religion.

KERRY CLARE reads and writes in Toronto where she lives with her husband and daughter. Her essays, short fiction and criticism have appeared in magazines including *The New Quarterly*, *The Globe & Mail*, *Quill & Quire*, *Canadian Notes & Queries*, and *Reader's Digest*, and she writes about books and reading on her blog, *Pickle Me This*. "Love is a Let-Down" was featured by the *Utne Reader* and shortlisted for a 2011 National Magazine Award.

DAVID CRANE is an award-winning Canadian writer on economic, political and environmental issues. His writings appear in publications across Canada. He has written several books, including *The Next Canadian Century*, *The Canadian Dictionary of Business and Economics*, and *Controlling Interest*. A graduate of the University of Toronto, he holds honourary doctorates from Wilfrid Laurier University and Victoria University. He was awarded the Queen's Jubilee Medal for his contribution to Canadian life.

JOHN DUNCAN is the director of the Ethics, Society, and Law

program at the University of Trinity College in the University of Toronto. He is the founder of the international bilingual society for the study of Existential and Phenomenological Theory and Culture, and the co-founder and academic director of the Humanities for Humanity outreach program at Trinity and Victoria University in the University of Toronto. He writes on philosophy, the humanities, and politics.
http://utoronto.academia.edu/JohnDuncan

RANDY FREEMAN is a Yellowknife-based heritage consultant, writer and broadcaster. In 1985, after completing his Master's degree in Historical Geography, he moved "down north" to work for the Government of the Northwest Tertritories. It was through his extensive research into the origins of northern place names that he uncovered hundreds of exciting, unusual and often unbelievable stories from northern Canada's past.

Over the past 15 years, he researched and wrote more than 500 northern history scripts and columns for both CBC North Radio and *Up Here* Magazine (2010 "Magazine of the Year" 33rd National Magazine Awards).

C.E. GATCHALIAN is a playwright, fiction writer, poet, editor, and teacher based in Vancouver. He is the author of three books: *Motifs & Repetitions & Other Plays* (2003), which was a finalist for the Lambda Literary Award; a chapbook of poetry, *tor/sion* (2005); and *Broken*, a suite of one-act plays. His work has been produced on stages in Vancouver, Toronto, Winnipeg and New Zealand, as well as radio (CBC) and television (the Bravo! Channel). He is currently a resident playwright at the Vancouver Playhouse.

"Notes Towards An Essay About Maria Callas" is part of a book-in-progress about literature, art, popular culture and gay male sensibility.

NICHOLAS HUNE-BROWN is a Toronto-based writer whose work has appeared in *Toronto Life*, *The Walrus*, *Reader's Digest*, and other publications.

CHRIS JENNINGS' writing on literature has appeared in a number of magazines and journals. He taught writing and literature at the University of Toronto and the University of Ottawa and was an editor for *University of Toronto Quarterly*, *filling station*, and *Representative Poetry On-Line*. He lives in Ottawa where he is on the board of *Arc Poetry* and edits the on-line column "How Poems Work."

MARK KINGWELL is a Professor of Philosophy at the University of Toronto and a contributing editor of Harper's magazine. He is the author of fifteen books of political, cultural and aesthetic theory, including the national bestsellers, *Better Living* (1998), *The World We Want* (2000), *Concrete Reveries* (2008), and *Glenn Gould* (2009). His articles on politics, architecture, and art have appeared in, among others, *Harper's*, *The New York Times*, *New York Post*, *Utne Reader*, *BookForum*, *The Toronto Star*, and *Queen's Quarterly*. He is also a former columnist for *Adbusters*, *National Post*, and *The Globe & Mail*.

MARK MANN is a writer and musician living in Toronto. He is a member of L'Arche and the Rectory Collective, a community project focused on arts and spirituality. Currently he works as a toy stuffer.

STEPHEN MARCHE is the author, most recently, of How Shakespeare Changed Everything.

DAVID MASON was born in Toronto and has been an Antiquarian bookseller in that city since 1967, after serving an apprenticeship with Joseph Patrick Books. He has, during that period, had five different locations and continues to insist on having an open shop in downtown Toronto in spite of the huge costs, general indifference, and the disappearance of most of his colleagues.

SEAN MICHAELS lives in Montreal, where he is completing his first novel. "The Lizard, the Catacombs and the Clock" was written with the support of the Banff Centre's literary journalism program. It first appeared in Brick and won a 2011 National Magazine Award. Sean's work has appeared in The Observer, The Believer, and Maisonneuve. He founded the unusual music blog, Said the Gramophone in 2003.

KELLY PULLEN is a senior editor at *Toronto Life* magazine. She lives in Toronto with her husband and two daughters.

BARBARA STEWART grew up in Surrey, BC. She has worked as a banker, homemaker, housecleaner, nail girl, and furniture salesperson. In 2010, she graduated with a Bachelor of Arts (With Distinction) from the University of Victoria's Writing Program. While Barbara completed her degree, she served on the editorial board for *The Malahat Review*. She has been published in various newspapers and magazines, including *Event*, *Grain* and *The Walrus*. Barbara was shortlisted in the CBC Literary Awards for non-fiction (2008) and the Event Creative Non-fiction Contest (2009). Heritage Publishers in Victoria will release her first book, *Campie*, August 2011.

JEFF WARREN is an award-winning writer, broadcaster, public speaker and all-purpose enthusiast. He has written for *The New Scientist*, *Discover*, *The Walrus*, *Maisonneuve*, and *The Globe & Mail*, among others, and is a freelance producer for CBC Radio's *Ideas* and *The Current*. He is author of *The Head Trip* (Random House, 2007), an acclaimed travel guide through sleeping, dreaming and waking consciousness. Jeff is currently working on a book about animal consciousness and mind in nature, a seemingly endless project, perhaps on account of how ever since he drank ayahuasca all these trees keep interrupting him with ludicrous unsolicited suggestions. He lives in Toronto's Kensington Market.
http://www.jeffwarren.org/

LISA WILSON is a Saskatchewan Métis writer whose fiction has appeared in magazines like *Grain*, *Geist*, *The Dalhousie Review*, and *Prairie Fire*, as well as in an anthology of Aboriginal love stories. Lisa's book, *Just Pretending*, is slated for publication by Coteau Books for the spring of 2013. She is currently at work on a young adult book that centres on Métis culture and the folklore of Rougarou. Lisa lives in Saskatoon with her husband Declan and their seven children.

permission acknowledgements

editor biographies

IBI KASLIK is an internationally published novelist, freelance writer, and teacher. Her most recent novel, *The Angel Riots*, is a rock'n'roll comic-tragedy and was nominated for Ontario's Trillium award in 2009. Her first novel, *Skinny*, was a *New York Times* Bestseller and has been published in numerous countries. A native of Toronto, Ibi teaches creative writing at the University of Toronto's School of Continuing Studies and works as an art educator for youth.

CHRISTOPHER DODA is an award-winning critic, editor, and poet. He is the author of two collections of poetry, *Among Ruins* (2001) and *Aesthetics Lesson* (2007). His poems and reviews have appeared in journals and magazines across Canada and he was an editor at *Exile: The Literary Quarterly* for five years. He is currently the review editor for the online journal *Studio*.